Miskawayh

The Refinement
of Character
(Tahdhīb al-akhlāq)

TRANSLATED BY
CONSTANTINE K. ZURAYK

SERIES EDITOR
SEYYED HOSSEIN NASR

GREAT BOOKS OF THE ISLAMIC WORLD

Library of Congress Cataloging-in-Publication Data

Abū ᶜAlī Aḥmad ibn Muḥammad ibn Yaᶜqūb Miskawayh 932 AD (320 AH), *The Refinement of Character* (*Tahdhīb al-akhlāq*).

1. Islamic psychology. 2. Ethics. 3. Islamic philosophy—Early works to 1800. 4. Miskawayh b. 932 AD. I. Title.

ISBN: 1-57644-716-3 pbk

Cover design: Liaquat Ali
Cornerstones are Allah and Muhammad connected by *Bismillāh al-Raḥmān al-Raḥīm* (In the Name of God, the Merciful, the Compassionate).

Logo design by Mani Ardalan Farhadi
The cypress tree bending with the wind, the source for the paisley design, is a symbol of the perfect Muslim, who, as the tree, bends with the wind of God's Will.

This publication was made possible
by a generous donation from the
Malik Usman Hassan Family

Published by
Great Books of the Islamic World, Inc.
Distributed by
KAZI Publications, Inc.
3023 W. Belmont Avenue
Chicago IL 60618
Tel: 773-267-7001; FAX: 773-267-7002
email: info@kazi.org /www.kazi.org

To

NABIH AMIN FARIS

Lifelong colleague and friend

IN MEMORIAM

CONTENTS

PREFACE

The object of this volume is to present to scholars who are not familiar with Arabic a translation into English of an important— in many ways the most important—treatise on philosophical ethics in medieval Islam, *Tahdhīb al-Akhlāq* of Aḥmad ibn-Muḥammad Miskawayh. This work has long been known and has been studied by scholars in the East and in the West. Although it has appeared in many editions,[1] the only critical one was issued in 1966 and was prepared by the writer.[2] The present translation, the first to a Western language, is based on this edition and was announced in its introduction.[3]

The purpose of this preface is to introduce briefly the author and his work, and to indicate the method I have followed in the translation. It has not been my intention to undertake a detailed study of Miskawayh's life, work, and influence, or a critical analysis of the *Tahdhīb*. In the appended bibliography, the reader is referred to studies which have appeared on this subject. Although I have annotated the text, and tried to show in particular Miskawayh's debt to the *Nicomachean Ethics*, the *Tahdhīb* still awaits a comprehensive analysis embracing its sources, contents, and influence.[4] It is hoped, however, that the

---

(1)   India, 1271 A.H.; Cairo, 1298, 1299, (on the margin of al-Ṭabarsi's *Makā-rim al-Akhlāq*) 1303, 1306, 1317, (on the margin of al-Māwardi's *Adab al-Dunya wa-al-Dīn*) 1318 and 1320, 1322, 1323, 1911, 1959; Stambul, 1298, 1299; Teheran, 1314; Beirut, 1327, 1961. See Dār al-Kutub al-Miṣrīyah, *Fihris al-Kutub al-'Arabīyah al-Mawjūdah bi-al-Dār* ... (9 vols., Cairo, 1924–59), I, 282 and its appendix, 30; Yūsuf Ilyān Sarkīs, *Mu'jam al-Maṭbū'āt al-'Arabīyah wa-al-Mu'arrabah* (11 parts in 4 vols., Cairo, 1928-30), I, 238; and C. Brockelmann, *Geschichte der arabischen Litteratur* (2nd ed., 2 vols., Leiden, 1943-49), I, 342–43, *Supp.* (3 vols., Leiden, 1937–42), I, 582–84.
(2)   American University of Beirut Centennial Publications (Beirut, 1966).
(3)   *Ibid.*, p. 1.
(4)   Both Mohammed Arkoun and M.S. Khan have announced that they are preparing studies on Miskawayh and his works. See M. Arkoun, "Deux épîtres de Miskawayh," *Bulletin d'Etudes Orientales* (Publications de l'Institut Français de Damas), XVII (1961–62), 10, and "Textes inédits de Miskawayh," *Annales Islamologiques* (Publications de l'Institut Français d'Archéologie Orientale du Caire), V (1963), 181, n. 2; and M.S. Khan, *An Unpublished Treatise of Miskawaih on Justice* (Leiden, 1964), 1, n. 1.

translation as such will be of service in furthering studies on Miskawayh and Muslim philosophical ethics in general, and in making this important treatise available to the wider circle of historians of philosophy or of medievalists who are not acquainted with Arabic.

The main facts of our author's life can be stated briefly. Abu-'Ali Ahmad ibn-Muhammad ibn-Ya'qūb Miskawayh[5] belonged to the class of cultivated officials and intellectuals who flourished under the patronage of the Buwayhids (4th to 5th c. A.H., 10th to 11th c. A.D.) and who contributed to the rich intellectual and cultural life of the period. He was born probably around 320 A.H. (932 A.D.) in al-Rayy, whose ruins lie near modern Teheran. He began early to study the sciences and letters which formed the main elements of the culture of his times, and remained, until his death, an assiduous scholar and writer. As a young man, he became attached to the service of al-Muhallabi, the vizier of the Buwayhid prince Mu'izz al-Dawlah in Baghdād. After al-Muhallabi's death in 352 A.H. (963 A.D.), he sought and obtained the favor of ibn-al-'Amīd, the vizier of Mu'izz al-Dawlah's brother Rukn al-Dawlah whose seat was in al-Rayy. Ibn-al-'Amīd was himself a broadly cultivated man and a prominent literary figure. During Miskawayh's seven-year service as ibn-al-'Amīd's librarian, he was able to pursue his studies, to benefit from his association with this prince, and to enjoy an influential position in that provincial Buwayhid capital.

After ibn-al-'Amīd's death in 360 A.H. (970 A.D.), Miskawayh was kept in the service of his son abu-al-Fath who succeeded to the vizierate of Rukn al-Dawlah and who was also known for his literary ability. Our author remained in this position until the imprisonment and death of abu-al-Fath in 366 A.H. (976 A.D.) and his replacement by his bitter enemy, the celebrated vizier and man of letters, al-Sāhib ibn-'Abbād. He then left al-Rayy to Baghdād and became attached to the court of the Buwayhid prince 'Adud al-Dawlah, whom he served as treasurer and in other capacities. Following this prince's death in 372 A.H. (983 A.D.), he remained attached to his successors

---

(5)   This title (laqab) is his own and not that of his father or grandfather, as is erroneously implied in the designation: "ibn-Miskawayh" which was current for some time. Another title, "al-khāzin," usually adjoined to his name is due to his long service as librarian or treasurer to several Buwayhid princes or viziers.

Ṣamṣām al-Dawlah (+388 A.H., 998 A.D.) and Bahā' al-Dawlah (+403 A.H., 1012 A.D.) and rose, during the period of the latter, to a position of great prestige and influence. He spent the last years of his life in the pursuit of his studies and writing and died at an old age in 421 A.H. (1030 A.D.).

Miskawayh was an active scholar in many fields of knowledge. His own writings and the accounts about him in the sources bear witness to his great learning and to the broad culture of his times. But his main contribution lay in two fields: History and Ethics. In the former, he wrote a significant work *Tajārib al-Umam* [*The Experiences of the Nations*],[6] a universal history extending to 369 A.H (979–80 A.D.) which is specially important for the period following al-Ṭabari, and in which, according to its editor and translator D.S. Margoliouth, Miskawayh showed a marked superiority to that earlier eminent historian.[7]

In Ethics, his most important and influential work is the *Tahdhīb*, the subject of this translation. His other ethical works, as reported in the sources, include: *al-Fawz al-Akbar, al-Fawz al-Asghar,*[8] *Tartīb al-Sa'ādāt,*[9] *Kitāb Ādāb al-'Arab wa-al-Furs,*[10] and short epistles for the

---

(6) Parts of this history were reproduced in facsimile from the Âyâ Ṣûfiyya Ms. under the editorship of L. Caetani: *The Tajârib al-Umam or History of Ibn-Miskawayh* (Gibb Memorial Series VII, 3 vols., Leyden and London, 1909-17: Vol. I [to 37 A.H.], Vol. V [284–326 A.H.], and Vol. VI [326–369 A.H.]. H.F. Amedroz and D.S. Margoliouth edited and translated the concluding portion of the *Tajārib* in *The Eclipse of the 'Abbasid Caliphate*: Arabic text, Cairo, 1914–15, Vol. I [295–329 A.H.], Vol. II [329–369 A.H.]; English translation, Oxford, 1921, Vol. IV, V, and VII.

(7) *The Eclipse of the 'Abbasid Caliphate*, VII, vii.

(8) Beirut, 1319; Cairo, 1325.

(9) We believe it is the same work as that erroneously cited by Yāqūt as *Tartīb al-'Ādāt, Irshād al-Arīb* (ed. D.S. Margoliouth, Gibb Memorial Series VI, 7 vols., Cairo, 1907–1926), II, 91, and also as that which was published under the title *al-Sa'ādah*, Cairo, 1917, 1928. See *infra*, p. 197, First Discourse, n. 4.

(10) A collection of ethical sayings, maxims, and epistles derived from Persian, Indian, Arab, and Greek sources; edited under the title *al-Ḥikmah al-Khālidah, Jāwīdan Khirad* by 'Abd-al-Raḥmān Badawi, Cairo, 1952. The sub-title *Jāwīdan Khirad* is the name of the Persian original on which the Persian part of the text was based, and the Greek part contains, among other material, *Laghz Qābis Ṣāḥib Aflāṭūn* which has been edited separately, notably by R. Basset, *Le Tableau de Cébès*, Algiers, 1898.

THE REFINEMENT OF CHARACTER

edition of all but one of which we are indebted to Mohammed Arkoun: *Fi al-Ladhdhāt wa-al-Ālām*, *Fi al-Nafs wa-al-'Aql*,[11] a number
of other philosophical texts as well as his own "testament," [12] and
Risalāh fi al-'Adl.[13] To this category should be added certain works
which are described in the sources[14] as ethical or poetical anthologies:
Uns al-Farīd, *al-Mustawfi*, and *al-Siyar*.

Apart from the two fields of History and Ethics, Miskawayh
had other interests and contributions: He is described as having at
a certain period of his life actively pursued alchemy; the biographer
of philosophers and wise men, al-Qifṭi (+ 646 A.H., 1248 A.D.),[15]
and the biographer of physicians ibn-abi-Uṣaybi'ah (+ 668 A.H.,
1270 A.D.),[16] ascribe to him medical treatises; he himself in the
Tahdhīb mentions that he wrote a compendium on the science of
arithmetic,[17] and, finally, the literary historian al-Tha'ālibi (+ 429
A.H., 1038 A.D.) speaks of him as being "in the acme of excellence,
of literature, rhetoric, and poetry" and records some of Miskawayh's
poems in his anthology.[18]

But the best evidence of his encylopedic knowledge and interests
and his rationalistic attitude, as well as of the rich and extensive culture
of his times, is in the accounts that we have of the discussions and
controversies, which used to take place among cultivated officials
and intellectuals in cultural circles *(majālis)*, usually around a prince,
vizier, or other patron, and in which Miskawayh was a frequent

---

(11) Both of these were edited with an introduction in "Deux épîtres de Miskawayh," *Bulletin d'Etudes Orientales* (Publications de l'Institut Français de
Damas), XVII (1961–62), 7–74.

(12) See M. Arkoun, "Textes inédits de Miskawayh," *Annales Islamologiques* (Publications de l'Institut Français d'Archaéologie Orientale du Caire), V (1963),
181–205, and "Notes et documents. Miskawayh: de l'intellect et de l'intelligible," *Arabica*, XI (1964), 80–87.

(13) Edited and tranlated by M.S. Khan, *An Unpublished Treatise of Miskawaih
on Justice* (Leiden, 1964).

(14) Particularly Yāqūt in *Irshād al-Arīb* (ed. D.S. Margoliouth, Gibb Memorial
Series VI, 7 Vols, Cairo, 1907–26), II, 91.

(15) *Ta'rīkh al-Ḥukamā'* (ed. Lippert, Leipzig, 1903), p. 332.

(16) *Ṭabaqāt al-Aṭṭibā'* (2 vols., Cairo, 1300), I, 245.

(17) *Infra*, p. 101, ll. 32–33.

(18) *Tatimmat al-Yatīmah* (2 vols., Teheran, 1353), I, 96–100.

participant. These discussions covered a wide scope and afforded an opportunity to the participants to exhibit, and to vie in, their command of knowledge and their mastery of expression. Special mention should be made in this connection of the works of the eminent intellectual abu-Ḥayyān al-Tawḥīdi (+ca., 413 A.H., 1023 A.D.),[19] and of the record of questions which abu-Ḥayyān addressed to Miskawayh and of Miskawayh's answers to them embodied in *al-Hawāmil wa-al-Shawāmil*,[20] a most interesting work and an attractive and meaningful reflection of the culture of the period.[21]

Turning now from the man to his work *Tahdhīb al-Akhlāq*, we note that it occupies a prominent place in a particular branch of Muslim ethical literature. This literature is abundant and varied: some of it belongs to the specifically religious and legal tradition and is based on the Qur'ān and the Prophet Muḥammad's precepts; some is of a literary nature and is embodied in poems, sayings, and fables, derived from the various traditions of the Muslim world and aiming at the cultivation of *adab* in the sense of both breadth of culture and refinement of character; some is aimed particularly at the education and guidance of princes and other men of authority; some is a product of the mystical attitude and experience and is most eminently represented in the works of the great theologian al-Ghazzāli (+ 505 A.H., 1111 A.D.); and some, of which the *Tahdhīb* is the most notable example, is philosophical in character and relates primarily to the Greek philosophico-ethical tradition. It is this last form which was specifically called: " '*Ilm al-Akhlāq*" (*The Science of Ethics*) and reckoned as a part of "*al-Ḥikmah al-'Amalīyah*" (*Practical Philosophy*).

This body of ethical literature owed its concepts and methods of treatment to the Greek ethical works which were known to the Muslim scholars. First among them came the works of Plato and Aristotle, but there were also other writings available to these schol-

---

(19) Notably *al-Muqābasāt* (ed. Ḥasan al-Sandūbi, Cairo, 1929) and *al-Imtā' wa-al-Mu'ānasah* (ed. A. Amīn and A. al-Zayn, 3 vols., Cairo, 1939–44).

(20) Ed. A. Amīn and A. Ṣaqr, Cairo, 1951. The book includes 175 questions and their answers. They range over a wide variety of subjects: philological, scientific, philosophical, legal, theological, etc., but are not systematically presented.

(21) See M. Arkoun, "L'Humanisme arabe au IVe/Xe siècle...", *Studia Islamica*, XIV (1961), 73–108 and XV (1962), 63–87.

lars, as is evidenced, in the case of the *Tahdhīb*, by the specific references to, or borrowings from, 'Bryson', Galen, Porphyry, Themistius,[22] the Naturalists, the Stoics,[23] or, in general, "the commentators of his [Aristotle's] works and the followers of his philosophy."[24] The writings of these commentators and followers were particularly important, because it was through them, and with their help, that the Muslim authors knew the works of the two masters, particularly Aristotle: *"al-ḥakīm" (the philosopher)*,[25] and *"al-muʿallim al-awwal" (the first teacher)*.[26] These representatives or heirs of later Greek thought were also responsible for the pseudo-Aristotelian writings, which the Muslims took as genuine works of Aristotle. The ideas embodied in the works of these Greek thinkers were readily accepted by the Muslim thinkers, as the latter, like the former, were eclectic in their approach and attitude. No wonder, therefore, that we see, in the *Tahdhīb* for instance, Aristotelian ideas with the deep impress of the Neoplatonic, the Neopythagorean, the Stoic, and other late Greek schools. Of these, the influence of the Neoplatonists was undoubtedly the strongest, and the result was a harmonizing Neoplatonized system of ethics. Naturally, the Muslim ethicists tried also to harmonize this system with their fundamental Muslim beliefs,[27] but the original content is unmistakable and prominent.

Practically every Muslim *faylasūf*[28] dealt with ethics, since this science formed a part of philosophy, according to the Aristotelian scheme of classification which the Muslim philosophers adopted. Miskawayh, for example, quotes from al-Kindi,[29] the first Muslim

---

(22) Miskawayh wrongly attributed to Socrates a quotation derived from a philosophical treatise by this commentator. See *infra*, p. 206, Fifth Discourse, n. 21.

(23) For these references or borrowings, see "Index."

(24) See *infra*, p. 65, ll. 14–15.

(25) See *infra*, p. 77, 1. 33; p. 82, 1. 18; p. 135, 1. 28; p. 153, 1. 9.

(26) *The second teacher* was al-Fārābi. Al-Sayyid Muḥsin al-Amīn (+1371 A.H., 1952 A.D.) in his biographical work on eminent Shīʿite personalities cites among Miskawayh's titles: *"al-muʿallim al-thālith" (the third teacher)*: *Aʿyān al-Shīʿah* (48 vols., Damascus and Beirut, 1936–60), X, 139.

(27) See *infra*, p. 202, Third Discourse, n. 10, and p. 204, Fourth Discourse, n. 16.

(28) "Philosopher" in the sense used at that time, namely, one belonging to the school which followed the Greek philosophical tradition.

(29) See "Index."

philosopher (+ ca., 260 A.H., 873 A.D.). Ethical works by this and other Muslim philosophers are cited in the biographical and bibliographical sources. But the principal early writer on ethics in Arabic was a Jacobite Christian, Yaḥya ibn-'Adi (+ 364 A.H., 974 A.D.), a famous translator and logician,[30] the author of an ethical work bearing the same title as that of Miskawayh, *Tahdhīb al-Akhlāq*,[31] which is "based entirely on a lost Greek treatise,"[32] and which could very well have been known to our author, though there is no reference to it in his text.

Miskawayh seems to occupy a central place in the Muslim tradition of philosophical ethics. On the one hand, he summed up and expounded in a remarkable manner the basic elements of this part of "practical philosophy" as it was known to the Muslim world up to his time, and, on the other, he exerted a significant influence on the Muslim ethicists who came after him, whether they followed the philosophical tradition, or belonged to other schools. Among the former, the most evident influence is seen in the later Persian philosophico-ethical literature, notably in the *Akhlāq-i Nāṣiri* of Naṣir al-Dīn al-Ṭusi (+ 672 A.H., 1274 A.D.), whose ethical portions were in the main taken from the *Tahdhīb*,[33] and in *Akhlāq-i Jalāli* of Jalāl al-Dīn al-Dawwāni (+ 908 A.H., 1502 A.D.)[34] which in its turn was dependent on al-Ṭusi's. Among the latter, the outstanding example is the influence on the ethical works of abu-Ḥāmid al-Ghazzāli (+ 505 A.H., 1111 A.D.), particularly on his *Iḥyā' 'Ulūm al-Dīn (The Revification of the Sciences of Religion)*,[35] as it was through al-Ghazzāli, the greatest theologian of Islam, that this philosophico-ethical element became

---

(30) Ibn-al-Nadīm, *al-Fihrist* (ed. Flügel, 2 vols., Leipzig, 1871-2), I, 264, speaks of him as "the leader of his school in our time."

(31) Cairo, 2nd ed., 1913; and in *The Journal of Semitic Languages and Literatures*, XLV (1928-29), 1–34 and 94–129. See A. Périer, *Yaḥyâ Ben 'Adî, un philosophe arabe chrétien du Xe siècle* (Paris, 1920).

(32) R. Walzer, *Greek into Arabic* (Oxford, 1962), p. 165, n. 1.

(33) G.M. Wickens, tr., *The Nasirean Ethics* by Naṣir ad-Dīn al-Ṭūsi (London, 1964).

(34) W.F. Thompson, tr., *Practical Philosophy of the Muhammedan People* (London, 1839).

(35) Cairo, 4 vols., 1352 A.H., III, 42–68 (Third Quarter, Second Book). See *infra*, p. 207, Sixth Discourse, n. 2.

incorporated in the religious tradition which dominated later Muslim Sunnite thought.

Even aside from this influence, a careful reading of the *Tahdhīb* and a comparison of it with other Muslim ethical writings will tend to support the judgment of T.J. De Boer: "... and in any case we ought not only to praise in general terms his attempt to give a system of Ethics which should be free from the casuistry of the Moralists and the asceticism of the Sufis, but also to recognize in the execution of his design the good sense of a man of wide culture." [36]

In this translation, and in my edition of the text, I have adopted the common title by which the work was called, *Tahdhīb al-Akhlāq*, although there is much confusion in the Mss. and among later authors regarding this title. The only indication in the text itself is the statement by Miskawayh: "And this is why I have *also* (the italics are mine) called this work *The Book on Purification*." [37] The titles given on the title-pages of the Mss. and at the beginning and the end of the discourses may have come from the pens of the copyists. [38] The two names: *Ṭahārah* or *Ṭahārat al-Nafs (Purification, or Purification of the Soul)*, and *Tahdhīb al-Akhlāq*, may have formed either parts of the same title or alternative titles, but, in view of the confusion, I have preferred to adopt the more common of the two titles and the one which corresponds most to the subject of the work. [39] It is to be noted also that the title *Tahdhīb al-Akhlāq* is sometimes followed by: *wa-Taṭhīr al-Aʿrāq* [40] *(and the Purification of the Dispositions)*, but this is found only in later and related Mss. and seems to be an addition by a copyist.

Another innovation in the same late Mss. is the division of the sixth discourse into two; hence most of the editions of the text, which are based on these Mss., have the book in seven discourses.

---

(36) *The History of Philosophy in Islam*, tr. by E.R. Jones (London, 1903, reprinted 1965), p. 131.

(37) *Infra*, p. 82, ll. 1–2.

(38) The reading I adopted at the end of the Third Discourse (*infra*, p. 91, last line) is "*The Refinement of Character* and also *The Purification of the Soul*," and that at the end of the book (*infra*, p. 196, ll. 15–16) *The Book of Purification Concerning the Refinement of the Soul*."

(39) This confusion in the titles led C. Brockelmann to cite *Ṭaharat an-Nafs* separately from *Tahdhīb al-Akhlāq*. See *GAL*, Vol. I, *Supp.*, 584, no. 3 and no. 9.

(40) Brockelmann, *loc. cit.*

I should now state briefly the method I have followed in the translation of the text and in its presentation. I have based the translation on the text of my edition. I have tried to meet, at the same time, the two requirements of faithfulness to the original Arabic and concern for the correctness and clarity of the English style. This has often been difficult, particularly in the long and involved sentences of the original. In many cases, I have given more weight to the first requirement than to the second in order to maintain accuracy and to preserve the original spirit and form. I have endeavored, in so far as the context permits, to use the same rendering for the same technical term, and I hope that the glossary at the end of the volume will be useful to the reader familiar with Arabic.

Except in rare instances, I have followed the divisions into paragraphs adopted in my edition. All the titles of the discourses and of their sections are my own, except in the few instances where they appear in the original: these have been indicated in the notes. Any additions on my part to clarify the text are placed within brackets. With regard to Miskawayh's borrowings from Aristotle or other sources, I have put quotation marks only when Miskawayh states specifically that he is using the words of his source,[41] or when he quotes literally from the Qur'ān, traditions, or poems. Wherever I have referred in the notes to the *Nicomachean Ethics*, these notes do not necessarily imply that Miskawayh knew this work of Aristotle at first hand or quoted directly from it. On the left-hand margin, I have indicated the pages of the original and their lines, in multiples of five, to facilitate comparison with it. Finally, I have annotated the text, but I do not claim that my notes embrace all the problems which it raises—particularly in regard to its sources and its influence on later works—or form a comprehensive commentary on it.

Finally, it is my pleasant duty to acknowledge the various forms of help which I have received in the course of this project. My interest in the *Tahdhīb* was first aroused, many years ago, by the late Professor Martin Sprengling when I was one of his graduate students at the Oriental Institute of the University of Chicago. I then began a study of this work and immediately afterwards embarked on a translation

---

(41) See *infra*, p. 49, ll. 8–10; p. 77, l. 36 – p. 81, l. 10; p. 108, ll. 18–39; p. 169, l. 26 – p. 170, l. 25.

of it, which I completed under the supervision of Professor Philip K. Hitti of Princeton University and which was included as a part of my doctoral dissertation submitted to that University. I am happy to take this occasion to record my indebtedness to these two eminent scholars. Two years ago, I returned to the *Tahdhīb*, undertook the preparation of a critical edition, and thoroughly revised the first translation. In the course of this project, I have derived great benefit from the knowledge and judgment of my colleagues in the Departments of History, Arabic, and Philosophy at the American University of Beirut—a benefit which I am happy to acknowledge with gratitude. My thanks go also to Dr. Fûad Sarrûf, General Editor of the Centennial Publications of this University, for his cordial attention and constant support; to Dr. Robert Sample for his thorough reading of the translation and for valuable stylistic and editorial emendations; to Mrs. Suha Tamim Tuqan for assistance in the reading of the proofs and in the supervision of the printing; and to my secretary, Miss Samia Ghobriel, for the burdensome tasks of typing, checking, indexing, and various other forms of help.

C. K. ZURAYK

Beirut

March, 1968

BIBLIOGRAPHY

The following bibliography, compiled for the users of this translation, is necessarily restricted to studies in the Western languages, and does not include primary sources in Arabic. Of the items listed, only two are in Arabic, those of Badawi and 'Izzat. The reader will find additional information in other studies cited in the notes.

Ansari, M.A.   "Miskawayh's Conception of God, the Universe and Man," *Islamic Culture*, XXXVII (1963), 131–144.

Amedroz, H.F.   "Note on the Historian," in *The Tajârib al-Umam or History of Ibn-Miskawayh* reproduced in facsimile from the Âyâ Ṣûfiyya Ms. in Constantinople under the editorship of L. Caetani (Gibb Memorial Series VII, 3 vols., Leyden and London, 1909–1917), I, xvii-xxvii.

Arkoun, M.   "Deux épîtres de Miskawayh," *Bulletin d'Etudes Orientales* (Publications de l'Institut Français de Damas), XVII (1961-62), 7–74.

————.   "L'Humanisme arabe au IVe/Xe siècle, d'après le *Kitâb al-Hawâmil wal-Šawâmil*," *Studia Islamica*, XIV (1961), 73–108; XV (1962), 63–87.

————.   "A propos d'une édition récente du *Kitâb Tahḏib Al-'Akhlâq*," *Arabica*, IX (1962), 61–73.

————.   "Textes inédits de Miskawayh (m. 421)," *Annales Islamologiques* (Publications de l'Institut Français d'Archéologie Orientale du Caire), V (1963), 181–205.

————.   "Notes et documents. Miskawayh: de l'intellect et de l'intelligible," *Arabica*, XI (1964), 80–87.

Badawi, 'Abd-al-Raḥmān (ed.)   *al-Risālah al-Khālidah, Jāwidān Khirad*, Cairo, 1952, "Introduction," pp. 7–64.

De Boer, T.J.   "Ethics and Morality (Muslim)," *Encyclopaedia of Religion and Ethics*, V, 507b–508a.

————.   *The History of Philosophy in Islam*, translated by E.R. Jones, London, 1903, reprinted 1965, pp. 128–131.

Brockelmann, Carl.   *Geschichte der arabischen Litteratur*, 2nd ed., 2 vols., Leiden, 1943–49, I, 342–43; *Supp.*, 3 vols., 1937–42, I, 582–84.

Donaldson, D.M.   *Studies in Muslim Ethics*, London, 1953, pp. 121–33.

'Izzat, Abd-al-'Azīz.   *"Ibn" Miskawayh, Falsafatuhu al-Akhlāqīyah wa-Maṣādiruha*, Cairo, 1946.

Khan, M.S. *An Unpublished Treatise of Miskawaih on Justice*, Leiden, 1964, "Introduction," pp. 1–11.

Margoliouth, D.S.   "Ibn Miskawaih," *Encyclopaedia of Islam*, old series, II 404a–b.

_____. *The Eclipse of the 'Abbasid Caliphate*, edited by H.F. Amedroz and D.S. Margoliouth, 7 vols., Cairo and Oxford, 1914–1921, "Preface," VII, i–xi.

Walzer, R.   "Some Aspects of Miskawaih's *Tahdhīb al-Akhlāq*," in *Studi Orientalistici in onore di Giorgio Levi della Vida*, Roma, 1956, II, 603–21; reprinted in *Greek into Arabic*, Oxford, 1962, pp. 220–235.

_____. "Akhlāḳ" (ii, Philosophical Ethics), *Encyclopaedia of Islam*, new series, I, 327a–329a.

The Refinement
of Character

PREAMBLE

[1]   / In the name of God, the Compassionate, the Merciful :

O God, we turn to Thee, and strive towards Thee; we exert ourselves in Thy obedience, and follow the straight path, which Thou hast set before us, to Thy satisfaction. Help us, then, with Thy strength, and guide us with Thy might; protect us with Thy power, and cause us to attain the highest rank by Thy mercy and the supreme happiness by Thy generosity and Thy compassion.
5   Verily, Thou art powerful over all Thou willest!

The object of this book

Aḥmad ibn Muḥammad Miskawayh says: Our object in this book is to acquire for ourselves such a character that all our actions issuing therefrom may be good and, at the same time, may be performed by us easily, without any constraint or difficulty. This object we intend to achieve according to an art, and in a didactic order. The way to this end is to understand,
10 first of all, our souls: what they are, what kind of thing they are, and for what purpose they have been brought into existence within us – I mean: their perfection and their end; what their faculties and aptitudes are, which, if properly used by us, would lead us to that high rank; what the causes are which hinder us from that rank; and what it is that keeps our souls pure so that they prosper, as well as what it is that corrupts them so that they fail. For God (mighty and exalted is He!) has said: "By a soul and That which shaped it, and breathed into it its wicked-
15 ness and its piety; he who keeps it pure prospers, and he who corrupts it fails!" [1]

1

FIRST DISCOURSE

THE PRINCIPLES OF ETHICS: THE SOUL AND ITS FACULTIES;
THE GOOD AND HAPPINESS; VIRTUES AND VICES

./ FIRST DISCOURSE [1]

THE PRINCIPLES OF ETHICS: THE SOUL AND ITS FACULTIES;
THE GOOD AND HAPPINESS; VIRTUES AND VICES

Since every art has principles on which it is built and by
which it is formed, and since these principles are derived from
another art—so that it does not fall within the scope of any art
to set forth its own principles—we are clearly justified in indicating
in a general, concise way, the principles of the art with which
5 we are dealing, although this is not our primary object. We will
then proceed to our goal, which is the acquisition of a noble character, i.e., a character which imparts to us a nobility that is
essential and real, not one that is accidental, unstable, and unreal.
By the latter nobility, I mean that which is acquired through
wealth and competition in its accumulation, or through power
and contest, or through agreement and compromise.

The soul is not a body, nor part of a body, nor an accident

10 Thus we proceed—our success depending upon God—to
a discussion in which we show that there is within us something
which is not a body, nor a part of a body, nor an accident;
something which does not need any bodily power for its existence,
but which is, on the contrary, a simple substance not preceivable
by any of the senses. We will then go on to demonstrate the aim
we should seek with regard to this substance, [the aim] for
which we are created and to which we are summoned. So we say:–
[4] / Having found within man something which, by its definition
and properties, is opposite to bodies and parts of bodies and,
by its actions, is opposite to the actions and properties of the body
to such an extent that it has nothing in common with it under

any condition; and having found also that this thing within man is
5   totally different from accidents and opposite to them, and that this
opposition to, and difference from, bodies and accidents is precisely
in their being bodies and accidents—having found all of this, we
judge that this thing is neither a body, nor a part of a body, nor
an accident, since it does not transform or change.

Furthermore, it conceives all things equally and is not subject
10   to any lassitude, weariness, or diminution. This can be demonstrated as follows: Each body which has a certain form does not
assume another form of the same type until it has abandoned
the first one completely. For instance: When a body takes on
a certain form or shape such as, for example, that of the triangle, it
does not assume another shape such as that of the square, or the
15   circle, or anything else until it has lost the first one. In the same
way, if it takes on the form of a certain engraving, or inscription,
or any other form, it does not receive another form of the same
type before the first one has disappeared and become absolutely
nil. Should any impression of the first form remain, the body
would not take on the next one entirely, but both forms would
become mixed in it and neither would be its own purely and
20   fully. For example: After wax has assumed the form of an
engraving on a ring, it does not receive the form of any other
engraving until the impression of the first one has disappeared.
The same is true when silver is given the form of a ring. This is
a persistent characteristic of all bodies. [On the other hand,] we
find that our souls receive completely and entirely the forms of
[5]   all things, / in all their diversity, whether they be sensible or intelligible, without any separation from earlier forms, or any
alternation, or the loss of any impression. The first impression
remains complete and entire, and the one which follows is also
received completely and entirely. Forever and always our souls
continue to receive one form after another without weakening
5   or failing at any time to receive whatever forms appear and come
forth. On the contrary, the first form makes our souls more capable
of receiving the second form which follows. This property is opposite to the properties of bodies; and it is for this reason that man
gains in understanding as he acquires training and education in
the sciences and letters. The soul, therefore, is not a body.
10   That it is not an accident is evident from the fact that an

accident cannot support another accident as attribute, since it is itself always attributed, i.e., existent in something else, and it is not self-subsistent. But this substance [the soul], whose character we have been describing, is always receiving and supporting attributes, in a manner more complete and perfect than that in which a body supports accidents. Thus, the soul is neither a body, nor a part of a body, nor an accident.

Other proofs that the soul is different from the body and superior to it

15 Furthermore, the length, breadth, and depth by which a body becomes what it is occur in the soul and in its imaginative faculty, without the soul becoming thereby long, broad, or deep. These attributes accrue in it constantly and infinitely, but the soul does not thereby necessarily become longer, broader, or deeper, nor does it ever become a body. Nor does the soul assume bodily

20 qualities when it conceives them. I mean that when it conceives colors, or flavors, or odors, it does not assume their forms as bodies assume them. Again, none of these qualities prevents the

[6] soul from receiving / any of its opposites, as is the case with the body. On the contrary, the soul receives them all in the same condition and equally. The same is also true with intelligibles. Every intelligible it acquires gives it greater power to continue to receive other intelligibles constantly and infinitely. This is a condition which is opposite to the conditions of bodies, and a

5 property extremely far from their properties.

Moreover, the body and its faculties cannot apprehend the sciences except through the senses, and are inclined towards them only. The body longs for them through contact and intercourse, as in bodily pleasures, the desire for revenge and victory, and, generally, all that can be perceived by, and reached through, the senses. These things add to the strength of the body and

10 impart to it fullness and perfection, for they are its substance and the causes of its existence. The body delights in them and longs for them because they complete its existence, and increase and sustain it. As for this other entity which we have called soul, the farther it keeps from these bodily things which we have enumerated and the more it becomes self-contained and freed from the

senses, the greater is its capacity, its completeness, and its perfection,
15   and the abler it is to perceive sound judgments and the simple intelligibles. This is the clearest proof that the nature and substance
of this entity are different from the nature of the body, and that
it is of a nobler substance and higher nature than all the bodily
things in this world.

Furthermore, the fact that the soul longs for that which is
20   not bodily, is concerned to know the realities of the divine,
[7]   desires and prefers what is superior to the bodily, / and turns
away from the pleasures of the body to seek those of the intellect—
all this demonstrates to us clearly that its substance is much
higher and nobler than that of bodily things, for it is impossible
for anything to desire what does not pertain to its nature or to
turn away from what perfects its essence and sustains its substance.
5   If, then, the actions of the soul, when it turns to itself and
forsakes the senses, are different from the actions of the body and
are opposed to them in their attempts and intents, there is no
doubt that its substance is distinct from the substance of the body
and different from it in nature.

Again, though the soul derives many of the principles of the
sciences from the senses, it has from itself other principles and
10   actions which it does not, in any way, derive from the senses.
These are the noble, high principles on which sound deductions
are based. Thus, if it judges that there is no mean between the
two extremes of a contradiction, it does not derive this judgment
from something else, because it is a first [principle] and would
not have been so had it been derived.

Moreover, the senses perceive the sensibles only, whereas
15   the soul perceives the causes of harmonies and the causes of differences which exist among the sensibles. These causes are its
intelligibles, which it apprehends without the help of any part or
trace of the body. Similarly, when it judges that the sense is either
correct or wrong, it does not derive this judgment from the
sense itself, for the sense does not contradict itself in the judgment
20   which it makes. Thus, we find that our rational soul rectifies many
of the errors of the senses which lie at the origin of their actions
and rejects their judgments. For instance: Our vision errs in
[8]   what it sees / from a near distance or from afar. An illustration of
the latter error is its perception of the sun as small, one foot in

diameter, while it is more than one hundred and sixty times as large as the earth, as attested by rational proof. The soul accepts this attestation and rejects the testimony of the senses, which it does not accept. As an illustration of the error in our vision of
5   what is near, we may mention the case of the light of the sun when it comes to us through small square holes such as, for instance, those of mats and their like which are used for protection from the sun. The sense of vision perceives the light infiltrating to us as circular in shape, but the rational soul rejects this perception, shows its error, and realizes that the light is not as the sense sees it. The sense of vision errs also in its perception of the movement of the moon and the clouds, and of the ship and the
10   coast, as well as in the case of striped columns, palm trees, and their like, which appear to it differently from what they are. It errs also with rotating objects, seeing them as if they had the shape of a ring or a circle, and with objects plunged in water, making some appear larger than they are, some broken when they are whole, and some twisted when they are straight
15   or inverted when they are upright. But reason deduces the causes of all these [errors] from rational principles and arrives at sound judgments with respect to them. The same is true of the senses of hearing, taste, smell, and touch. I mean that the sense of taste errs when it judges the sweet to be bitter, and the sense of hearing when it misjudges the echo and similar phenomena in places surrounded by polished spherical surfaces and their like. The
20   sense of smell often errs in putrid objects, and especially when it passes from one odor to another. Reason rejects all these
[9]   sensations, questions them, / and then deduces their causes and makes sound judgments in their regard. And the judge of a certain matter, showing its falseness and rectifying it, is superior to the judged and higher in rank.

To sum up: When the soul knows that the senses are wrong or right, it does not derive this knowledge from the senses themselves. Furthermore, when it knows that it has apprehended its own
5   intelligibles, it does not derive this knowledge from another source, for, if this were the case, the knowledge of this source would have to be derived from still another source, and so on *ad infinitum*. Therefore, its consciousness of its knowledge is not by any means derived from another source, but comes from its

own essence and substance, i.e., reason. Also, in apprehending
itself, it does not need anything other than itself. This is why
10 it is said at the end of this science that the intellect, the intelligent,
and the intelligible are one and the same thing, and there is no
otherness therein. This statement will become clear in its proper
place. We shall also explain that the senses do not perceive themselves or what conforms to them completely.

The virtue of the soul and hindrances to its achievement

Now that it has become clear from the above discussion that
the soul is neither a body, nor a part of a body, nor a state in it,
15 but something else distinct from the body in substance, judgments,
properties, and actions, we proceed to say:–

The soul's desire for its own actions—I mean for the sciences
and the forms of knowledge—as well as its flight away from the
actions proper to the body, constitute its virtue. A person's
excellence is measured by the extent to which he seeks this virtue
20 and cares for it. It is enhanced as he pays greater attention to
his soul and strives in all his power and capacity to renounce the
things which hinder him from achieving this attribute. The
[10] previous discussion has elucidated / what those things are which
hinder us from the virtues, i. e., the bodily things, the senses,
and all that relates to them. As for the virtues themselves, they
are not achieved by us until we have cleansed our souls of the
vices which are their opposites—by which I mean the souls' wicked
bodily passions and their vile beastly lusts. When a person realizes
5 that these things are not virtues but vices, he will avoid them and
be loath to be known for them. But if he believes that they
are virtues, he will pursue them and become accustomed to
them; and to the extent to which he is involved in them and
polluted by them, he gets away from the acquisition of the virtues.
Sometimes it may dawn upon a person that, if he looks among
the other animals for these things which the body desires through
the senses and which the common people pursue—I mean food,
10 drink, and sexual intercourse, which are vices and not virtues—
he will find many of these animals more capable of obtaining
them abundantly, and more strongly attached to them than is

man. For instance, the pig, the dog, and many species of aquatic
animals, wild beasts, and birds are all more strongly attached
to such things than is man and abler to bear them; yet, they
do not become thereby superior to man. Moreover, when man
15 has satisfied his want of food, drink, and other bodily desires, if he
is offered to continue to seek them—as one continues to seek the
virtues—he will refuse and shun such a course. He will realize
the vileness of those who pursue them, especially when they can
do without them or be satisfied [with some measure] of them,
and will go further to dislike and reproach such people and even
to try to reform and educate them.

Goods and evils

20   Now, as a prelude to our pursuit of the happiness and
of the virtues of the soul, we proceed to a discussion which
will facilitate the understanding of our aim. So we say:–
          Every existent, be it animal, plant, or inanimate object, as well
[11] as their simple elements, / namely: water, fire, earth, and air, and
also the celestial bodies—every one of these has certain faculties,
aptitudes, and actions which make it what it is and distinguish
it from everything else, and other faculties, aptitudes, and actions
5 which it shares with the rest. As man is the only existent whose
desired end is a praiseworthy character and satisfactory actions,
it is necessary that we do not consider at this time those of his
faculties, aptitudes, and actions which he shares with the other
existents, for this falls within the scope of another art and another
science called "Natural Science." As for the actions, faculties,
and aptitudes which characterize him as man and by which his
10 humanity and virtues are realized, they are the voluntary matters
which are related to the faculty of reflection and discernment.
Their study is called "Practical Philosophy."
          The voluntary matters which pertain to man are divided into
goods and evils. For it is by virtue of the end for which man is
created that he who keeps directing his efforts towards it until he
15 attains it is the one that should thereby be called good or happy,
while he who allows himself to be hindered from it is indeed
wicked and miserable. Consequently, goods are those things
which man gains by the exercise of his will and his endeavor

and which pertain to the ends for which he was made and created; while evils are those which hinder him from goods, whether this hindrance is through his will and endeavor or through laziness and neglect.

20   The ancients divided goods into many categories, for some
[12] goods are noble, some are laudable, others are useful, / and still others are goods in potency. By potency, I mean disposition and aptitude. God willing, we shall enumerate all of them later on. [2]

Man's good is in discernment and reflection

We said previously that every existent has, in virtue of what it is, a perfection proper to it and a certain activity which it does
5 not share with the rest. In other words, it is not possible that some other existent be better suited than it for this activity. This is an invariable law governing all things, both heavenly and earthly, such as the sun and the other planets, all the different kinds of animals— as, for example, the horse and the falcon—the plants, the minerals, and the simple elements. If you examine the conditions of all of them, you will see clearly the truth of what we have said and
10 of the judgment we have made. It follows, therefore, that man is distinguished from all other existents by a certain activity which is proper to him and is not shared by any other. This activity is the one that proceeds from his discerning, reflective faculty. Thus, he whose discernment is truer, whose reflection is sounder, and whose choice is better has achieved greater perfection in his humanity.

Although the sword and the saw may each carry out the act
15 which is characteristic of its own form and for which it was made, the best sword is the one which is sharpest and most piercing and which needs little manipulation to attain the end for which it was prepared. The same is true of the horse, the falcon, and
[13] the other / animals; the best horse is the most agile and the most alert to the will of the rider in submitting to the reins and in being responsive in movement, speed, and sprightliness. Such also is the case with man. The best of men is he who is most capable of performing the actions proper to him [as man] and
5 most strongly attached to the requirements of his substance

which distinguishes him from the other existents. Consequently, our unquestionable duty is to seek the goods which represent our perfection and for which we were created, to endeavor to attain them, and to avoid the evils which hinder us from them and diminish our share of them. For if the horse fails to achieve its perfection and to perform its own distinctive actions in the best possible manner, it is degraded from the rank of the horse and is used with a pack-saddle as donkeys are used. The same is true of the sword and all other instruments. When they become inadequate and deficient, they are degraded from their ranks and are used in the ways of their inferiors. Similarly, when a man's actions are less than, or fall short of, the object for which he was created—I mean when his reflection is imperfect and the actions which issue from him and from his reflection are imperfect —he deserves to be degraded from the human rank to the beastly. So much if his human actions are deficient and incomplete. But if he performs actions which are contrary to the object for which he was created—in other words, if he performs evils through deficient reflection and its misuse under the influence of lust which he shares with the beasts, or through delusion by sensual desires distracting him from the opportunity to achieve his soul's perfection which leads him to the lofty kingdom and the real pleasure and to the delight of which God (exalted is He!) has said: "No soul knoweth what delight of the eyes is hidden in reserve for them," [3] and brings him near to the Lord of the worlds in the everlasting bliss and to the pleasures / which no eye has ever seen, of which no ear has ever heard, and which never occurred to any man's heart—if he is lured away from this noble and heavenly gift by such base and unstable evils, then, indeed, he deserves to be despised by his Creator (mighty and exalted is He!) and to suffer a speedy punishment which will deliver the people and the land from him.

It has now become clear that the happiness of every existent consists in the complete and perfect performance of the actions which are distinctive of its own particular form, and that the happiness of man consists in the performance of his properly human actions in accordance with discernment and reflection. It has also become evident that this human happiness is of different grades depending upon the kind of reflection and of what

is reflected upon. Thus, it has been said: "The best reflection is reflection upon what is best." Then reflection declines from one grade
10 to another until it reaches the level of the consideration of possible
things in the realm of sense. He who considers these things uses
his power of reflection and his own distinctive form, through
which he may attain happiness and be worthy of the everlasting
kingdom and the eternal bliss, in the pursuit of base things
which have no real existence. From this discussion, we can see
clearly the different kinds of happiness, in general, and the op-
15 posite kinds of misery, and [recognize] that goods and evils in
voluntary actions consist, respectively, in choosing the best and
living up to it or in choosing the lowest and tending towards it.

Necessity of association and cooperation

Since these human goods and the corresponding aptitudes
in the soul are many in number, and since it is not within the
power of any one man to achieve them all, it is necessary that a
20 large group associate in this total achievement. That is why the
number of individual human beings should be large, and they
[15] should get together at the same time / for the achievement of
these common kinds of happiness, so that each one among them
may attain his perfection through the cooperation of the others.
[In such a situation,] goods would be common to them all, and
happiness would be diffused among them. They [the people] would
distribute these goods among themselves, so that each one might
achieve some of them and all might gain, through common cooper-
5 ation, human perfection and the three kinds of happiness which we
discussed in the book, *al-Tartīb* [*The Order*].⁴ To this end people
must love one another, for each one finds his own perfection in
someone else, and the latter's happiness is incomplete without
the former. Each one thus becomes like an organ of the same
body; and man's constitution depends upon the totality of the
organs forming his body.

The three faculties of the soul ⁵

10   He who examines the nature of this soul and of its faculties
finds that it is made up of three parts: the faculty which has to do

with reflection, discernment, and the consideration of the realities
of things; the faculty which finds expression in anger, intrepidity,
the risking of dangers, and the desire for dominance, self-esteem,
and the different kinds of honor; and the faculty by which we have
15 passion, the quest for food, and the desire for the pleasures derived
from food, drink, sexual intercourse, and the various sensual
enjoyments. These three faculties are distinct one from another.
This is known from the fact that the overdevelopment of one
impairs the others, and that one of them may nullify the action
of another. Sometimes they are considered as three souls, and
sometimes as three faculties of the same soul. This is not the
place to discuss this subject, and it is sufficient for you, in the
20 study of ethics, [to know] that they are three distinct faculties,
[16] each of which may be strong / or weak depending upon temperament, habit, or discipline.

The rational faculty is the one called the kingly, and the
organ of the body which it uses is the brain. The concupiscent
faculty is the one called the beastly, and the organ of the body
which it uses is the liver. The irascible faculty is the one called
5 the leonine, and the organ of the body which it uses is the heart.

The four cardinal virtues and the opposite vices

It is logical, therefore, that the number of virtues accords
with the number of these faculties, and that the same also applies
to their opposites which are vices. When the activity of the rational
soul is moderate and not extraneous to itself, and when this soul
seeks true knowledge, not what is presumed to be knowledge but
10 is in reality ignorance, it achieves the virtue of knowledge[6]
followed by that of wisdom. Similarly, when the activity of the
beastly soul is moderate, when it yields to the rational soul and
does not reject what the latter allots to it, and when it does not
indulge in the pursuit of its own desires, it achieves the virtue of
temperance followed by that of liberality. When the activity
of the irascible soul is moderate, when it obeys the rational soul
15 in what it allots to it and is not aroused at the wrong time nor
becomes unduly excited, it achieves the virtue of magnanimity
followed by that of courage. Then, when all these three virtues
are moderate and have the proper relation one to another, a

virtue is produced, which represents their perfection and completeness, namely, the virtue of justice. Thus, the philosophers[7]
agree that the virtues are of four genera: wisdom, temperance,
20 courage, and justice. Consequently, no one should take pride or
[17] glory in anything but these virtues, and if one / takes pride in his
ancestors or predecessors, it should be on account of their possession of some or all of them.

Furthermore, a person is said to possess one of these virtues
and is praised for it only when it goes beyond him to others. If he
5 confines it to himself alone, it cannot be attributed to him and
its name will then be changed. Thus, generosity, when it
does not extend beyond its possessor, is called prodigality, and
[similarly] courage is termed arrogance and zeal, while knowledge
becomes [merely] the seeking of discernment. Also, when the
person who is both generous and courageous reaches out to
others with his two virtues, and does not confine them to himself
alone, people seek him because of the former virtue, and respect
10 and fear him because of the latter. But this is true in this world
only, for both of these virtues are animal virtues, whereas, when
knowledge spreads beyond its possessor, he is sought and re-
spected in this world as well as in the next because it is a human,
kingly virtue.

The opposites of these four virtues are also four in number:
ignorance, intemperance, cowardice, and injustice. Under each
15 of these genera, there are numerous species, of which we shall
mention as many as is possible for us. As for the individuals under
each species, they are innumerable. They are diseases of the soul
and generate many pains. As examples, we mention fear, grief,
anger, the types of love and desire, and varieties of bad character.
God (exalted is He!) willing, we shall mention them as well as
their remedies later on.[8]
20 Our task at this moment is to define these things [which we
have mentioned], namely, the four genera which comprise the
sum of all virtues. So we say:–
[18] / Wisdom is the virtue of the rational and discerning soul.
It consists in the knowledge of all existents *qua* existing, or, if we
wish to say so, the knowledge of things divine and human. This
knowledge bears the fruit of understanding which of the possible
actions should be performed and which should not be. Temper-

5 ance is the virtue of the concupiscent part. This virtue becomes manifest in man when he directs his passions in accordance with his [good] judgment; when, in other words, he conforms to sound discernment so that he is not led by his passions, and thus becomes free and not enslaved by any of them. Courage is the virtue of the irascible soul and appears in man to the extent to which this soul submits to the rational and applies what [good]
10 judgment prescribes in confronting dangerous things, namely, that one should not fear alarming things if to perform them is good or to withstand them is commendable. As for justice, it is a virtue of the soul which it gets from the union of the three above-named virtues, when the three faculties act in harmony one with another and submit to the discerning faculty so that they do not combat
15 among themselves or follow their desires according to the dictates of their natures. The fruit of this virtue is the acquisition of an attitude which induces a person to choose always to be fair to himself in the first place, and, then, to be fair to others and to demand fairness from them. We shall speak more fully of each of these virtues when we discuss the virtues which are subsumed under each of these four genera, for our purpose at this moment
20 is to allude to them in brief terms in order that the learner may have an idea about them.

The divisions of the virtues [9]

We should now proceed from what we have said to enumerate the species that come under each of these genera. So we say:–

[19] / The divisions of wisdom

The divisions which come under wisdom are the following: Intelligence, retention, rationality, quickness and soundness of understanding, clarity of mind, and capacity for learning easily. The possession of these virtues constitutes a good prepara-
5 tion for [the acquisition of] wisdom. In order to grasp the essences of these divisions, we must have recourse to their definitions, for it is by the knowledge of definitions that we understand the es- sences of things sought, which are always constant. This is demon-

strative knowledge which never changes and is not impaired by doubt in any way, for just as the virtues which are in essence virtues do not become, under any condition, other than virtues, so also is the knowledge of them [always the same and never changing].

10   Intelligence is the quick flaring of conclusions, and the soul's easy understanding of them.

Retention is the persistence of the image of what is derived by the mind or the imagination.

Rationality is the conformity of the soul's investigation of objects to what they are.

15   Clarity of mind is the readiness of the soul to deduce what is required.

Excellence and strength of understanding consist in the soul's contemplation of what follows from the antecedent.

Capacity for learning easily is a strength of the mind and a sharpnesss of understanding, by which theoretical matters are apprehended.

[20] /*The divisions of temperance* [10]

Modesty, sedateness, self-control, liberality, integrity,[11] sobriety, benignity, self-discipline, good disposition, mildness, staidness, and piety.

Modesty is self-restraint of the soul for fear of committing bad deeds, and carefulness to avoid blame and justified insult.

5   Sedateness is tranquility of the soul during the agitation of passions.

Self-control is the resistance of the soul to its desires lest it be led to vile pleasures.

Liberality is keeping the mean in giving and taking, i.e., it is spending money for what is right, in the right amount, and

10 in the right manner. This virtue in particular comprises a number of species which we shall mention later because they are greatly needed.

Integrity [11] is a virtue of the soul which makes a person acquire money in the right way, give it in the right way, and abstain from acquiring it in any other way.

15   Sobriety is moderation in food, drink, and adornment.

Benignity is the disposition of the soul to what is praiseworthy, and its zeal to accomplish the good.

Self-discipline is a state of the soul which leads it to judge things rightly and to arrange them in the proper way.

[21]   / Good disposition is the desire to complement the soul with beautiful adornment.

Mildness is a meekness which comes to the soul from an innate aptitude that is free from perturbation.

5   Staidness is tranquility and stability of the soul during the agitations which accompany the pursuit of desires.

Piety is the constant performance of good deeds which lead to the perfection of the soul.

The divisions of courage [12]

Greatness of spirit, intrepidity, composure, fortitude, magnanimity, self-possession, manliness, and endurance.

10   Greatness of spirit is the disdain for what is insignificant, and the ability to bear honor or abasement. He who possesses this virtue is always preparing himself for great deeds and is deserving of them.

Intrepidity is confidence of the soul in the face of the dreadful, which keeps it from being troubled by fear.

15   Composure is a virtue of the soul which causes it to endure calmly both the happiness of good fortune and its opposite, even the distresses which accompany death.

Fortitude is a virtue of the soul which gives it strength to bear pains and to resist them, especially in dangerous situations.

[22]   / Magnanimity is a virtue of the soul which imparts to it tranquility and keeps it from becoming turbulent and from being moved easily and quickly by anger.

Calmness, by which we mean self-possession, is shown either in disputes, or in wars when one is defending one's women or

5   the Law.[13] It consists in a power of the soul which restrains its movement on such occasions because of their seriousness.

Manliness is the aspiration to perform great deeds in expectation of a good reputation.

Endurance is a power of the soul which uses the organs of the body for what is good through practice and proper habits.

The divisions of liberality [14]

10   Generosity, altruism, nobility, charity, open-handedness, and remission.

Generosity is the ready spending, in the right way, of much money for the things of high merit and great usefulness. It also conforms to the other conditions of liberality which we have mentioned.

Altruism is a virtue of the soul which causes one to abstain
15   from some of his own needs for the sake of giving what he would have spent for them to those who deserve it.

Nobility is the rejoicing of the soul in great deeds and its delight in constant attachment to such a conduct.

Charity is the assistance of friends and deserving persons, and the sharing with them of money and food.

[23]   / Open-handedness is the spending of part of what should not be [spent].

Remission is the cancellation of part of what is due [to one]. All of this should be the result of volition and choice.

The divisions of justice [15]

Friendship, concord, family fellowship, recompense, fair
5   play, honest dealing, amiability, and piety. [a]

(a)   In two of the six Mss. on which my edition was based (Mss. ‍ꝫ and l, of which the latter seems to be a copy of the former), there is an addition, which comes probably from the pen of a later writer with religious tendencies. The text of this addition, which continues to enumerate and explain the virtues embraced by justice, is as follows:

"Abstinence from hatred, return of good for evil, courtesy, practice of manliness under all conditions, renouncement of enmity, abstention from reporting the sayings of those who are not trustworthy or acceptable, and the search for the conduct of those who are deemed to be trustworthy. [Among these virtues there are also:] avoidance of the use of one single word about a Muslim, even if it does not cause him any harm, to say nothing of any tale which may bring punishment, defamation, murder, or mutilation; distrust of what is said by people who are mean or base; and neglect of the reports of those who go around begging either openly or secretly, or are importune in their requests or insistent in their pleas. For these people are pleased if they get a little and repay it with good words, but are angered when they are refused a little and retaliate with bad words. [It is also part of justice] not to be greedy in

[24]   / Friendship is a sincere love which causes one to take an interest in all that concerns his friend and to choose to do all the good he can for him.

Concord is the agreement of opinions and beliefs brought about by close contact and leading to cooperation in the management of livelihood.

5   Family fellowship is the sharing of the goods of this world with one's relatives.

Recompense is the repayment of a beneficence with its equivalent or more.

Fair play is to give and take in business with fairness and according to the interests of all concerned.

10   Honest dealing is to recompense without regret or reminding others of favors done to them.

Amiability is the desire to win the affections of the deserving and the virtuous with a pleasing disposition, and the performance of deeds which inspire such affections.

Piety consists in honoring, glorifying, and obeying God (mighty and exalted is He!), in revering His favorites: the

---

lawful earning; not to be mean in one's pursuit of earning for the sake of one's family; to have recourse to God, to His promise, and to His covenant at the utterance of every word, at every glance of the eye, and at every thought which occurs to one concerning one's enemies and one's friends; and to refrain from swearing directly by God, or by any of His names or attributes.

Again, he is not just who does not honor his wife, her relatives who are connected with her, and those who know him intimately. The best of men is he who conducts himself best towards his relatives, his kinsmen, and those who are connected with him such as a brother, or child, or one connected with a brother or child, or a relative, a kinsman, a partner, a neighbor, a friend, or a loved one. Finally, he is not worthy of this rank [—that of the just man—] who has an excessive love of money, for his eagerness to acquire money prevents him from being kind, from observing what is right and from giving what he should, and leads him to treason, lying, fabrication [?], false testimony, standing in the way of duty and assiduous search, and the pursuit of the small coin, the grain, and the trifle, for which he sacrifices his religion and his honor. He may spend large amounts of money because of his desire for praise and good reputation and not for the sake of God and what He holds. Rather, he uses this as a trap and a means for gain, and does not realize that such conduct brings him evil and abuse."[16]

angels, prophets, and *imāms*, and in following the commands
15 of the Law. The fear of God (mighty and exalted is He!) is the
culmination and perfection of all these things.

Virtues are means between extremes and the extremes are vices [17]

Now that we have investigated the cardinal virtues and
their divisions, and have mentioned their species and their parts,
you are in a position to know the vices which are the opposites
of the virtues. For, from each one of those virtues, one can derive
[25] all its opposites—the knowledge / of things opposite being one and
the same. Since these virtues are means between extremes, and
since these extremes are the vices, the latter ought to be under-
standable from the former. If the space at our disposal permits,
we shall mention them, for we cannot give their names at this
time.

5   From our statement that every virtue is a mean between
vices, one should understand the following: The earth, being at the
extreme distance from [all of] the heavens, is called a mean.
Putting it in general terms: The center of a circle is at the extreme
distance from the circumference, and if a thing is at the extreme
distance from something else, then it should, from this point of
view, fall on the diameter. In this way, we should understand
10 the meaning of virtue as a mean, for it lies between vices and
at the extreme distance from them. For this reason, when a
virtue deviates the least bit from its particular location, it comes
near to another vice and becomes defective in proportion to its
nearness to that vice towards which it tends. Thus, it is very
hard to achieve this mean, and to keep it once it is achieved is
15 harder. It is in this sense that the philosophers have said: To hit the
target point is more difficult than to miss it, and to keep hitting
it afterwards without missing it is still harder and more difficult. [18]
The reason is that the extremes which are called vices, viewed
in terms of actions, or states, or time, or in any other way, are
very numerous, and, consequently, the causes of evil are more
numerous than the causes of good.

The means of these extremes should be sought separately for
20 each individual person. Our own task here is to note the general
means and the laws governing them according to the requirements

of our art, and not for each individual person, for this would be impossible. The carpenter, the jeweler, and all the artisans acquire in their minds laws and principles only, for the carpenter knows the form of the door and that of the bed and the jeweler the [26] form of the ring / and that of the crown, in the absolute. Then each of them derives by these laws the individual things which he has in mind, but he cannot master all the individual things because they are infinite in number. For every door or ring is made in a certain required size and in accordance with the need and the material 5 at hand. The art ensures the knowledge of principles only.

The cardinal virtues and the vices which are their extremes

Having stated the meaning of the mean in ethics and what should be understood by it, let us proceed to enumerate these means so that their extremes, which are vices and evils, may be deduced from them. So we say: –

Wisdom is a mean between impudence and stupidity. By impu-
10 dence, I mean here the use of the rational faculty for wrong ends and in the wrong ways. Some people have called it slyness. By stupidity, I mean the suppression and disregard of the rational faculty. We should not understand by stupidity here a natural deficiency, but the deliberate suppression of this faculty. Intelligence is a mean between slyness and dullness, for one of the extremes of every mean is an excess while the other is a deficiency.
15 In other words, the one extreme is going beyond the mean, while the other is falling short of it. Thus, slyness, craftiness, and bad tricks are all on the side of excess beyond what intelligence should be, while dullness, stupidity, and the inability to apprehend knowledge are all on the side of deficiency in that virtue. Retention is a mean between forgetfulness, which consists in neglecting what should be remembered, and attentiveness to what
20 should not be remembered. Rationality, which is sound concep-
[27] tion, is a mean between going / too far in the consideration of the object until one is led beyond what it is, and the failure to consider it sufficiently for what it is. Quickness of understanding represents a mean between the quick snatching of the image of a thing without grasping it thoroughly, and being too slow to grasp its reality. Clarity of mind is a mean between a darkness in the soul

5 which makes it slow to deduce what is required, and a blaze which is set off in it and prevents it from deducing what is required. Excellence and strength of the mind is a mean between excessiveness in the contemplation of what follows necessarily from the antecedent, which leads away from it to something else, and deficiency in this contemplation which falls short of the necessary consequence. Capacity for learning is a mean between proceeding to it with such ease that what is learned is not fixed in the mind, 10 and finding learning too difficult or impossible.

Temperance is a mean between two vices, namely: profligacy and frigidity. I mean by profligacy over-indulgence in pleasures and going to excess beyond the right limit, and by frigidity abstinence from the pursuit of the legitimate pleasure which 15 the body needs for its normal functioning and which is permitted by the Law and by reason. As for the divisions of temperance, modesty is a mean between two vices, one of which is shamelessness, the other excessive bashfulness. The extremes of the other virtues, which are vices, you can recognize by yourself. You may find names for them and you may not; but it would not be difficult for you to understand their meanings and to follow 20 in their regard the path we have taken.

When it comes to courage, we find it a mean between two vices: one is cowardice, the other is recklessness. Cowardice [28] is the fear of what should not be / feared, while recklessness is the venturing upon what should not be risked. Liberality is a mean between two vices, one of which is extravagance and prodigality, and the other avarice and stinginess. Prodigality is the giving of what should not be given to those who do not deserve it, while stinginess is the withholding of what should be given 5 from those who deserve it.

Justice is a mean between doing injustice and suffering injustice. One commits injustice when he acquires many possessions from the wrong sources and in the wrong way, and he suffers injustice when he is subservient and responds, with regard to his possessions, to the wrong people and in the wrong way. 10 For this reason, the unjust man has much wealth, since he acquires it by the wrong methods and such methods are numerous, whereas he who suffers injustice has few possessions and little wealth, since he refrains from acquiring them in the right way.

As for the just man, he is in the middle because he acquires wealth in the right way and abstains from acquiring it in the wrong way.

Justice is, then, a virtue which causes one to be fair to oneself
15   and to others, by refraining from giving, of the useful, more to himself and less to others, and, of the harmful, *vice versa*, i.e., less to himself and more to others. The just man applies equality, which is a proportionate relation between things, and it is from this meaning that his attribute, justice, is derived. [19] The unjust man, on the contrary, seeks, of the useful, more for himself and
20   less for others, and, of the harmful, less for himself and more for others.

We have now discussed in general those traits of character which are goods and virtues and their extremes which are evils
[29]   and vices. We have defined and sketched / those which could be so treated, and if it pleases God (exalted is He!), we shall later describe each one of them in detail.

Virtue can be achieved only by association

At this point, we should refer in a brief way to a doubt which may occur to the seeker of these virtues. So we say:–
5   We have made it clear, in the preceding pages, that man, of all the animals, cannot attain his perfection by himself alone. He must have recourse to the help of a great number of people in order to achieve a good life and follow the right path. This is why the philosophers have said: Man is a civic being by nature. This means that he needs to live in a city with a large population
10   in order to achieve human happiness. Every man needs other people by nature as well as by necessity. He must, therefore, be friendly towards others, associate well with them, and hold them in sincere affection, for they complement him and complete his humanity; and he himself plays the same role in their life. If, then, man is such by nature as well as by necessity, how could a rational person who knows himself choose to live in solitude and seclusion, and exercise by himself the virtue which he sees in
15   others? It is clear, therefore, that those who have sought virtue in asceticism and abstinence from association with other people and who have secluded themselves from them by living in

caves in the mountains, or building cells in the desert, or roaming about from one country to another—that such people do not realize any of the human virtues we have enumerated. For he who does not mingle with other people and who does not live with them in cities cannot show temperance, intrepidity, liberality, or justice. On the contrary, all the faculties and aptitudes with which he is equipped are nullified, since they are not directed towards either good or evil. And when they become nil and cease to / perform their own distinctive actions, those who possess them are reduced to the rank of inanimate objects or dead people.

Thus, they [the ascetics] think of themselves, and are thought of by others, as temperate and just, but they are neither just nor temperate. The same is true of them regarding other virtues. In other words, if they do not show the opposites of these virtues, which are evils, people think that they are virtuous. But virtues are not non-existences; they are actions and deeds which are manifested when one participates and lives with other people, and has dealings and various kinds of association with them. Indeed, we teach and learn the human virtues by the aid of which we live and mingle with other people, so that we may attain, from and by these virtues, other kinds of happiness when we pass to another state which does not exist for us at present.

Here ends the first discourse, with the praise of God and by His grace.

SECOND DISCOURSE

CHARACTER AND ITS REFINEMENT;
HUMAN PERFECTION AND ITS MEANS

/ SECOND DISCOURSE [1]

CHARACTER AND ITS REFINEMENT; HUMAN PERFECTION
AND ITS MEANS

Definition of character. Can it be changed by education?

Character is a state of the soul which causes it to perform its actions without thought or deliberation. This state is of two kinds. One kind is natural and originates in the temperament, as in the man whom the least thing moves to anger or who is aroused for the least cause, or in the man who is cowardly in
5 the face of the most trifling incident—who is afraid of a noise which strikes his ear or is terrified by news which he hears— or who bursts into excessive laughter at the least thing that pleases him, or is saddened and distressed because of the least trouble that befalls him. The other kind is that which is acquired by habit and self-training. It may have its beginning in deliberation and thought, but then it becomes, by gradual and continued practice, an aptitude and a trait of character.
10 It is for this reason that the ancients held different views regarding character. Some said that character belongs to the nonrational soul; others that the rational soul may have a share of it. Then people have differed on another point. Some have expressed the view that he who has a natural character does not lose it. Others have said: No part of character is natural to man, nor is it non-
15 natural. For we are disposed to it, but it also changes as a result of
[32] discipline and admonition either / rapidly or slowly. This last view is the one we favor because we observe its truth plainly and because the former view leads to the nullification of the faculty of discernment and reason, to the rejection of all forms of guidance, to the surrender of people to savagery and

29

neglect, and to the abandonment of youths and boys to the state in
5   which they happen to be without any direction or instruction.
This is manifestly very disgraceful.

The Stoics believed that all men are created good by nature,
but that they then become bad as a result of their association
with evil people, and as a result of their inclination to wicked
passions which cannot be tamed by discipline and are thus
indulged in and then sought in every way with no distinction
between the good and the bad among them.

10   Others, who came before the Stoics, maintained that men are
created out of the basest mud, which is the filth of the earth, and
that they are thus bad by nature but may become good as a result
of discipline and instruction. [They also believed that,] however,
some men are extremely bad and cannot be reformed by discipline, while others, who are not extremely bad, may become good
15   by discipline from boyhood on and by association with good and
virtuous people.

Galen, [2] on the other hand, observed that some men are
good by nature, others are bad by nature, and still others fall
between the two. He then showed the error of the first two views
which we have just mentioned. As regards the former, he did
so by saying that if all men are good by nature and then become
20   bad through instruction, then it necessarily follows that they
learn the evil either from their own selves or from others. If they
learn it from others, then those others who taught them are bad
[33]   by nature, and, consequently, all men cannot be / good by nature.
On the other hand, if they learn it from their own selves, then
either there is in them a faculty which causes them to desire the
evil only—and this makes them bad by nature—or they possess,
together with this faculty which desires the evil, another one
5   which desires the good, but the former dominates and overcomes
the latter—which, again, makes them bad by nature. The other
view he disproved by a similar argument. He said that if all men
are bad by nature, then they either learn the good from others
or from their own selves, and he went on to repeat precisely the
same argument as before. Having disproved these two views,
he verified his own view by clear and evident observations.
10   For it is quite evident that some people are good by nature:
they are few in number and do not later become bad. Others

are bad by nature: they are numerous and do not later become good. Lastly, there is the group which falls between these two: they may become good by accompanying good people and listening to their admonitions or turn bad by associating with bad people and being led by them to evil.

15 Aristotle made it clear in the *Book on Ethics*,[3] as well as in the *Book on Categories*, that a bad man may, by discipline, become good. But he did not consider this to hold absolutely, for he found that the repetition of admonitions and discipline and the good and virtuous guidance of people cannot but produce dif-
20 ferent results on different people: some are responsive to discipline and acquire virtue rapidly, while others are also responsive but acquire it slowly.

We put this in the form of a syllogism which goes as follows: Every character is subject to change. Nothing which is subject
[34] to change is natural./ Therefore, no single character is natural. The two premises are correct, and the conclusion of the syllogism follows according to the second mood of the first figure. The verification of the first premise, i.e., that every character is subject to change, we have already discussed and explained. It is clear from actual observation, from the evidence we have drawn
5 regarding the necessity of discipline, its usefulness, and its influence on youths and boys, and from the right laws by which God (mighty and exalted is He!) guides His creatures. The verification of the second premise, i.e., that nothing which is subject to change can be natural, is equally clear. For we never seek to change anything which is natural. Nobody wants to change the movement of fire which rises upwards by training
10 it to go downwards, nor to train the stone to move upwards and thus change its natural movement which is downwards. Even should one want to do it, it would not be within his power to change any of this or its like, i.e., the things which are natural.[4] So the two premises are sound, the composition [of the syllogism], which belongs to the second mood of the first figure, is also sound and has become a demonstrated proof.

Grades of receptivity to character improvement. Its means

15 People fall into many grades depending on their capacity

to acquire these good traits, which we have called character, their
eagerness to learn them, and their care for them. We can witness
and examine these differences in people, particularly in children.
For the character traits of children appear very early in their
life, and children do not try to conceal them deliberately or
consciously, as does the mature man who has attained, in his
growth and development, the point where he realizes for himself
20   those of his traits which are considered bad and conceals them
[35] by different devices and by actions which are contrary to / his
own nature. As you observe the character of boys and their
receptivity, or their aversion, to character improvement, and
as you see the impudence of some and the bashfulness of others,
and what they show of generosity or stinginesss, of kindness or
cruelty, of envy or its opposite, and of [other] varying traits, you
5   will realize therefrom the grades into which men fall with respect
to their readiness to acquire good character. You will recognize
that they are not all of the same grade in this respect, but that
there are among them the responsive and the unresponsive,
the docile and tractable and the rude and intractable, the good
and the bad, and those who occupy the middle ground between
these opposites in innumerable gradations. If innate nature is
neglected and not subjected to discipline and correction, every
man will grow up in accordance with his own nature and will
10   remain all his life in the condition in which he was in childhood,
following whatever suits him naturally: whether wrath, pleasure,
maliciousness, greed, or any other reprehensible disposition.

It is the Law which reforms the young, accustoms them to
good deeds, and prepares their souls to receive wisdom, seek
15   virtue, and attain human happiness through sound thinking and
correct reasoning. It is the duty of parents to train them to observe these and other forms of good conduct, by different methods
of discipline, such as flogging if necessary, or rebukes if availing,
or promises of favors or enjoyments which they like, or warnings
of punishments which they fear. Then, after they have become
20   accustomed to this conduct and have followed it for a long period
of time, they will be able to learn the proofs of what they
had adopted by tradition and will perceive the ways of virtues,
their acquisition, and the attainment of their ends by the art
which we are treating now. Verily, God is the Helper and the

Guide to success, and He is Sufficient unto us!

[36]   /In arranging these morals in order, and in directing them gradually towards final perfection, man has before him a natural way in which he imitates the course of nature. This way consists in finding out which of the faculties which are formed in us are first to appear, in beginning to reform them, and in proceeding then to those that come afterwards according to the natural order. This order is clear and obvious. For what is formed
5   in us first is that which is common to all animals and plants. Then it goes on to acquire one distinctive thing after another and to become thereby differentiated from one species after another until it achieves the human attribute. That is why we should begin with the desire that we feel for food and regulate it, and then proceed to the disposition which appears in us for anger and the love of honor and regulate that, and finally to the
10   desire which we experience for the sciences and for knowledge and regulate that also. We have called this order natural, and if we have judged it as such, it is because of what is produced in us successively from the beginning of our growth. I mean that we are first embryos, then children, and finally full men, and these faculties appear in us one after another in a definite order.

Superiority of the art of character training

15   That this art—I mean the art of character training, which is concerned with the betterment of the actions of man *qua* man— is the most excellent of all the arts becomes evident from what I say: –

As we have shown already, the human substance has a distinctive activity which it does not share with any other of the world's existents. Man is the noblest of these existents, but, when he does not perform the actions distinctive of his substance,
20   he resembles, as we have said, the horse which, if it ceases to perform completely the actions distinctive of a horse, is used
[37]   / as a donkey for carrying loads or as cattle for slaughter and is better dead than alive. In view of this, it must follow that the art which is concerned with the betterment of man's actions so that he may perform them completely and perfectly in accordance with his substance, and which aims at raising him from the rank

of the most debased, wherein he deserves to be detested by God
5 (mighty and exalted is He!) and to endure painful suffering
—it must follow that such an art is the noblest and the most
honorable of all the arts.[5] As for the other arts, their respective
ranks of nobility are in accordance with the ranks of the things
which they attempt to improve. This is very clear to anyone
who examines the [different] arts. For among them is [for in-
stance] the art of tanning, which is concerned with the improvement of the hides of dead animals, and the art of medicine and
10 treatment, [6] which attends to the improvement of valuable
and noble substances. So also are the various activities, some of
which are directed to the low sciences, while others seek the noble
ones. Thus, since the substances of existents, in the realms of
animals, plants, or inanimate objects, are of different degrees
of nobility (such as the difference, in the animal kingdom,
between the substance of worms and insects and that of man, as
15 well as the differences among the substances of the other existents
which are evident to anyone who desires to record them), it
must follow that the art and the activity which are directed to
the noblest of them are nobler than the arts and the activities
which are directed to the lowest.

You must realize that, although the name *man* is applied
to the highest as well as to the lowest of men, the difference
between these two extremes is greater than that between any
20 other two opposites.[a] You must realize also what the poet said:
[38]   / "I have known no such difference as that among men
          Searching for glory, when a thousand may count as
          one."
Although this poet considers himself to have exaggerated, he

(a)   In Mss. ﺝ and ﻝ there is a short addition with some variants, similar to
the one referred to on p. 20, n. (a) *supra*, which reads: "and [the meaning]
of God's Apostle (may the prayer and peace of God be upon him!)
when he said: 'There is no existent, other than man, of which one may
be better than one thousand,' or when he said (may peace be upon
him!): 'Like camels, out of a hundred of which one cannot find a single
one fit to be ridden,' or when he said: 'Men are as the teeth of a comb
(or, according to other reports, as the teeth of a donkey); their worth
varies according to their reason. There is no good in the company
of him who does not recognize your worth as much as you do his.'—and
many other similar traditions expressing the same meaning."

has really fallen short of the truth. The saying which is attributed to the Prophet (may the prayer and peace of God be upon him!), namely: "I was weighed against all my people, and I outweighed them,"[7] is truer and more correct.

5 This is true not only of man but also of many other substances, although the differences in the case of man are greater and wider. Thus, between the sword known as *al-ṣamṣām*[8] and the sword known as *al-kahām*,[9] there is a great difference. And the same is true of the difference between the thoroughbred horse and the despicable hackney. Therefore, whoever is able by his art to raise the lowest of these substances in rank to the highest is noble indeed, and so also is his art. How honorable and superior that art is!

The aim of this art is man's attainment of his perfection

Among these substances, man possesses different aptitudes for different ranks. Thus, the hope to improve him cannot always be on the same level. This is a thing which, God willing (mighty and exalted is He!), will become clear later on. What we should now know is that the existence of the human substance is due to the power of its Maker and Creator (blessed and sanctified is His name!), but that the betterment of this substance is entrusted to man and depends upon his will. Keep, therefore, this general statement in mind until, God willing (exalted is He!), we discuss it briefly in its proper place.

[39]   /At the beginning of this work, we said that it is necessary for us to know our souls: what they are, and for what purpose they exist. We said further that, for every existing substance, there is a perfection which is distinctive of it and a certain activity which, in so far as it is that individual thing, it does not share with anything else. This we explained fully in *al-Risālah al-Musʿidah*.[10]

5 If this is properly kept in mind, we ought then to know the perfection which is distinctive of man and the activity which, in so far as he is man, he does not share with anything else, so that we may become eager to seek and attain it and strive to reach its completion and end.

Now, since man is composite, his perfection and the activity distinctive of him cannot possibly be merely the perfection of his

10   simple elements and of their distinctive activities; otherwise, the existence of the composite would be absurd, as is the case with the ring or the bed. Thus, man, in so far as he is composite and man, has a distinctive activity which he does not share with any of the other existents. The best of men is he who is most capable of manifesting this distinctive activity and who adheres to it most strongly without any inconstancy or failure at any time. When the best of men is known, we can judge who would be the worst by considering his opposite.

The perfection of man: Its grades and its substance

15   The perfection which is particular to man is twofold, for he possesses two faculties, one of which is the cognitive and the other the practical. With the one he desires knowledge and the sciences and with the other the organization of things and their arrangement in order. These two perfections are the ones which were indicated by the philosophers. They said: Philosophy is divided into the theoretical part and the practical part. When

20   a man masters both parts, he gains complete happiness.

     Man's first perfection—through one of his two faculties,
[40] namely, the cognitive, that is the one with which / he desires knowledge—consists in his attainment in knowledge to the level where his perception becomes correct, his insight true, and his deliberation sound, so that he does not err in a belief or doubt a truth. In the knowledge of existents, in which he proceeds systematically, he reaches the divine science, which occupies the culminating rank among the sciences. He gains

5   trust in this science and reassurance by it; his heart becomes tranquil, his perplexity is dispelled, and the last object of desire becomes revealed to him until he unites with it. In other works of ours, we have indicated the path to this perfection and explained clearly the way leading to it.

     The other perfection—which is achieved through the other faculty, namely, the practical—is our aim in this work.

10   It is the perfection of character. It begins with the setting in order of one's faculties and the actions distinctive of them so that they do not combat one another but live in harmony within him, and so that his actions take place in accordance with his discerning

faculty and are organized and arranged in the proper way. It ends with civic organization, in which actions and faculties are properly regulated among the people in such a way that they attain the same kind of harmony [as in the individual], and the people achieve a common happiness, like that which takes place in the individual person.

15   Thus, the first, or theoretical, perfection is with respect to the other, or practical, perfection as form is to matter. Neither can be complete without the other, for knowledge is a beginning and action an end. A beginning without an end is wasted, while an end without a beginning is impossible. This [twofold] perfection of man is what we have referred to as an object. For object and perfection are in essence one and the same thing, 20   the difference between them being one of relation only. If we look at this thing when it is still in the soul and has not become actual, it is an object; when it is brought forth to actuality [41]   / and becomes complete, it is a perfection. The same is true with respect to all other things. When the house is [still] in the builder's conception and he knows its parts, structure, and various conditions, it is an object. But when the builder brings it forth to the realm of actuality and completes it, it becomes a perfection.

It follows from all that we have said that man attains his 5   perfection and is able to perform his own distinctive activity when he understands all the existents. By this I mean that he knows their universals and their definitions which make up their essences, and not their accidents and their properties which multiply them infinitely. For if you know the universals of existents, you come also to know their particulars in a certain way, since particulars do not separate from their universals. When you achieve this perfection, proceed to complete it by 10   organized action, and set your faculties and aptitudes in a scientific order, in accordance with the knowledge which you have already acquired. If you attain this rank, you will become a world by yourself and you will deserve to be called a microcosm. For then the forms of all the existents will have been present in you and you will have become, in a way, identical with them. By your actions you will have arranged them in order in the measure of your capacity, and you will thus become,

15 with respect to them, a deputy [11] of thy Lord, the Creator of all things. You will not err in them or deviate from His original and wise order, and you will then constitute a complete world. The complete existent is the everlasting one, and the everlasting is the eternally enduring. Thus, you will not miss anything from the abiding bliss, since your perfection will have made you ready to receive the divine emanation forever and always and you will have come so near to God that no veil should

20 then separate you from Him.

This is the highest rank and the extreme happiness. Were it not possible for the individual person to achieve this rank in himself, to perfect his form by it, and to rectify his defect by

[42] rising up to it, he would have been / in the same condition as the individuals of the other animals or as the individual plants, whose end is annihilation through the transformation which they undergo and the defects which can never be rectified. It would have been impossible for him to achieve eternal existence and everlasting bliss by coming close to the God of the worlds

5 and entering His Paradise. The person who is mediocre in knowledge and who cannot conceive this state nor reach an understanding of it, feels certain doubts and supposes that, when man's bodily constitution is destroyed, man vanishes and disappears as is the case with the other animals and the plants. Such a person deserves to be called an unbeliever and deviates from the mark of wisdom and from the path of the Law.

Man's perfection not in sensual pleasures

10 Some people have thought that man's perfection and his end consist in sensual pleasures and that the latter constitute the *summum bonum* and the extreme happiness. They have also thought that all the other faculties of man have been created in him only for the sake of these pleasures and their attainment, and that the noble soul, which we have called the rational, has been granted him for no other reason than to arrange and discriminate his actions by means of it, and then to direct them towards such

15 pleasures with the view that the final end is his enjoyment of these pleasures to the last and extreme limit. According to these people also, the faculties of the rational soul—I mean remembrance,

retention, and deliberation—are all meant for this end, because, so they have said, when man remembers the pleasure which he derived from food, drink, or sexual intercourse, he longs for it and seeks to enjoy it again. Thus, the usefulness of memory and retention
20   becomes nothing other than pleasure and its enjoyment. Because of such opinions which they have come to hold, these people have reduced the discerning and noble soul to the level of the despised
[43]   slave and of the hireling employed in the service / of the other, the concupiscent, soul in order to help it with food, drink, and sexual intercourse and to arrange them for its sake and to prepare them completely and agreeably.

This is the opinion of the masses, the common mob, and the ignorant and degraded people. It is precisely for these goods, which they consider their ends, that they long when they think
5   of Paradise and of proximity to their Creator (mighty and exalted is He!) in their invocations and prayers. Whenever they give themselves up to worship and abandon and forsake the world, they do so only by way of trading and of trying to gain more of these same pleasures. It is as if they abandon the meager among these pleasures in order to achieve the abundant and shun the ephemeral in order to gain the everlasting. Yet
10   you find that, in spite of these beliefs and these actions, whenever one mentions in their presence the angels and the highest and noblest creatures and says that they are free of such filth, the same men realize that these creatures are as a whole nearer than men to God (mighty and exalted is He!), superior to them in rank, and free from any of the human needs. Indeed, they realize also that their Creator and the Creator of everything (sublime is He!), who
15   has brought all into being, is free from these things and exalted above them and is not characterized by pleasure and enjoyment, although it is within His power to possess them, and that men share these pleasures with the beetles, worms, small insects, and wild animals even while they resemble the angels in reason and discrimination. Now, how they reconcile this latter belief with the former one [i.e., that pleasure is the end of life] is, indeed, most
20   astonishing! For they clearly see the pain that they must feel from hunger, nakedness, and the various deficiencies, and their needs to treat them and to be freed from them. When the traces of these deficiencies disappear and they are delivered from them,

[44] they delight in this condition / and find pleasure in their relief. They do not realize that, whenever they desire the pleasure of food, they have thereby desired first the pain of hunger, for, if they do not suffer the pain of being hungry, they cannot derive any pleasure from eating. The same is true of all the other pleasures, but in some it is more manifest than in others.

5   We shall state in another place that the nature of all [pleasures] is the same, that they are all experienced by man only after certain pains which affect him, and that every sensual pleasure is a deliverance from some pain or suffering. It will appear then that he who is content to seek the bodily pleasures and makes them his goal and his extreme happiness has consented to place himself in the meanest servitude to the meanest of lords,

10 since he makes his noble soul, wherein he resembles the angels, a slave of the base soul wherein he resembles the pigs, worms, and the lowest of animals that share this condition with him.

    In his work entitled *The Character of the Soul* [*Akhlāq al-Nafs*],[12] Galen expressed his astonishment that people can hold such a view and deemed as very ignorant those who are in this grade

15 of reason. But then he said that whenever these hypocrites, whose conduct is the worst and most detestable of conducts, find a man who holds this same opinion or view, they support and praise him and call people to follow him so as to make it appear that they are not alone in this way. For they think that, when they describe the virtuous and noble people as being like them, they are furnished with an excuse and are able to deceive

20 others who follow the same way. These are the people who corrupt youths by making them believe that virtue consists in the pleasures to which they are called by the nature of the body,

[45] / that those other, kingly, virtues are either false and absolutely nil or beyond the reach of anyone. As men are inclined by bodily nature to lusts, the followers of such people increase in number, and the virtuous among them become reduced.

5   One individual after another among such people may begin to perceive [the following facts:] that these pleasures arise only in response to the body's need; that the body is made up of opposite natures—I mean heat, cold, dryness, and moistness; that food and drink are but means to treat diseases which are caused in the body by decomposition so as to preserve, as far as possible,

its constitution always in the same state; that the treatment of a
disease does not constitute complete happiness and that the
relief from pain is not a desirable end or an absolute good; that
the completely happy person is he who is never affected by any
10   disease; that the holy angels, who have been chosen by God
to be near Him, do not experience these pains and so do not need
to remedy them with food and drink; and that God (sublime
is He!) is free from these attributes and exalted above them.
[If any one among these hypocritical people begins to perceive
and realize these facts,] they will contradict him by saying that
15   some men are nobler than the angels and that God is too exalted
above mankind to be mentioned in the same context. They will
dispute with him, treat his opinions as foolish, and create in him
false doubts until he gets to suspect the truth of what he has
perceived and what his mind has pointed out to him. And what
never ceases to be astonishing is that, in spite of this view which
they hold, whenever they find anyone who has abandoned the
mode of life to which they are inclined, who despises enjoyment
20   and pleasure, and fasts, and goes hungry, and eats only the vegetation of the earth, they extol him, admire him highly, deem him
worthy of lofty ranks, and assert that he is God's friend and intimate and that he is akin to the angels and superior to men. They
submit to him, humiliate themselves extremely before him, and
consider themselves miserable in comparison with him. The
[46]   cause of / this lies in the fact that, although they hold such stupid
and foolish views as you see, the other faculty that is in them,
i.e., the noble and discerning faculty, is still able, in spite of its
weakness, to make them appreciate the virtue of the virtuous so
that they are obliged to honor and extol them.

The ranks of the soul's faculties, and the consequent ranks of people

Since the faculties are three in number, as we have often
5   repeated, the lowest in the scale is the beastly soul,[13] the middle
is the leonine, and the noblest is the rational. It is only
in virtue of the best of these faculties, i.e., the rational, that man
achieves his humanity, partakes of the nature of the angels, and
differs from the beasts. He, then, is the noblest of men whose
share of this soul is the largest and who devotes himself to it

most completely and abundantly. As for the one who is overcome by either of the other two souls, he is degraded from the human
10 rank to the extent of his surrender to that soul. Consider, then, where you would place yourself, and in which of the ranks, which God (mighty and exalted is He!) has arranged for the existents, you would like to stand. For this is a thing that is entrusted to you and left to your choice. Place yourself, if you desire, in the rank of the beasts and you will be one of them, or occupy, if you want, the rank of the lions, or choose the rank of the angels and be one of them.
15   Each one of these ranks includes many grades, for some animals are nobler than others because they are apt to receive training. The horse is nobler than the ass only for this reason. Similarly, the falcon is superior to the raven. If you observe the animal kingdom as a whole, you will find that the animal which is apt to receive training—this being the sign of rationality (i.e., of the rational soul)—is better than the rest.
20 The animal species rises gradually on this scale until the animal which is in the realm of man is reached—I mean the most
[47] perfect of beasts, which stands in the lowest rank of / humanity. For the lowest of men are those who are poor in intellect and who stand near to the beast. They are the people who live in the extremities of the inhabited world and those who dwell in the farthest regions of the south and of the north. They differ from monkeys in a slight measure of discernment, and it is only in this measure that they deserve to be called human. Then they
5 become superior and possess more of this quality until we reach those who live in the central zones, where men acquire a moderate temperament which is disposed to assume the form of reason. There, we find the completely rational man and the person of full knowledge and discernment. They even differ further in this respect until they get to the limit of what can be attained in the acquisition of the intellectual and rational faculty. There, they stand in the [intermediate] realm between man and
10 the angel. Among them, we find the person who is worthy of receiving revelation and capable of engaging in philosophy and who then receives the emanation of the power of reason and has a glimpse of the light of truth. No higher state is possible for man, so long as he is man.

Go then backwards to examine the imperfect rank, which is the lowest of the human ranks, and you will find those 15 people whose rational faculty is weak. They are the people whom we mentioned as living in the realm of the beasts and in whom the beastly soul is strong and who are thus inclined to its desires which are reached through the senses, such as food, drink, clothing, and similar pleasures. They are the people who are driven to strong passions by their strong beastly souls with the result that they indulge in them instead of abstaining from them. But, in the measure which they possess of the rational 20 faculty, these passions evoke in them a sense of shame which causes them to hide in houses or under the cloak of darkness whenever they set themselves to enjoy one of their pleasures. This feeling of shame on their part is the proof of the vileness of this pleasure. For people usually show off that which is absolutely good and like to bring it forth and proclaim it. This vileness is nothing other than the imperfections which are neces-[48] sarily / attached to men and which they seek to remove. The most despicable of these imperfections are the most imperfect, and the most imperfect are those most in need of being concealed and buried.

Try to ask those who extol the value of pleasure and make it the desirable good and the human end: "Why do you conceal 5 the attainment of the highest goods, and why is it that you commend living according to them and yet hide them and consider their hiding and concealment as virtue and manliness and their proclamation and display among the virtuous people and in the assemblies of men as meanness and insolence?" If you ask them this question, you will become convinced, by their silence and hesitation to answer, of the baseness of their conduct and the wickedness of their life. Whenever anyone of them who has in him the least share of humanity meets a virtuous 10 person, he respects and reveres him, and wishes to be like him. But there are exceptions who reach such meanness of character, such want of humanity, and such insolence of face that they persist in defending their conduct without any aspiration to the rank of those who are superior to them.

The intelligent man's way to the attainment of his perfection

It is necessary, therefore, for the intelligent person to understand the bodily imperfections from which man suffers, and his
15 basic needs to remove and complete them. In the matter of food,
which keeps the balance of his constitution and his life's subsistence,
he should take of it only as much as is necessary for the removal
of his imperfection and should not seek the pleasure [of food]
for its own sake but rather for the sake of the subsistence of life,
which is prior to pleasure. Should he exceed this limit slightly,
let it be only in a measure that will keep his grade of manliness
and save him from being accused of meanness and avarice
relatively to his condition and rank among other people. In
the matter of clothing, [he should seek only] as much as will pro-
20 tect him from the harm of heat and cold and hide his nakedness. Should he exceed this limit, let it be only in such a measure
that will keep him from being despised and accused of stinginess
and from being degraded in the eyes of his fellows and those of
his class. Finally, in the matter of sexual intercourse, his practice
of it should go only as far as will preserve his kind and perpetuate
[49] /his image: in other words, the begetting of offspring. Should he
exceed this limit, let it be only to the extent that would not
violate the religious tradition or trangress what belongs to him
to what belongs to others.

The intelligent man should then seek virtue in his rational
soul (the soul by which he has become man), examine the
imperfections of this soul in particular, and strive to remedy
5 them to the extent of his capacity and effort. For these are the
goods which are not concealed, and when one attains them one
does not withhold himself from them by any sense of shame
or hide himself behind walls or under the cloak of darkness;
on the contrary, they are always exhibited among the people
and in the assemblies of men. It is because of them that some
people are better than others and the humanity of some superior
to the humanity of others. Further, the intelligent man should
give this soul the food which suits it and remedies its imperfections, in the same way as he gives the other soul [the beastly]
10 the food which is suitable to it. The proper food of the rational
soul is knowledge, the acquisition of intelligibles, the practice

of veracity in one's opinions, the acceptance of truth no matter where or with whom it may be, and the shunning of falsehood and lying whatever it may be or whence it may come.

15   He who has the chance in youth to be trained to follow the morality of the Law and to be required to observe its duties and requirements until they become as habits to him; who later studies first the works of ethics so that these morals and fine qualities become confirmed in him by rational demonstrations, and then the science of arithmetic and geometry so that he becomes accustomed to veracity in speech and correctness in demonstration and trusts nothing but these; and who then proceeds along the way, which we outlined in our work entitled *The Order of the 'Happinesses' and the Grades of the Sciences*, until

20   he attains the highest rank possible to man—he who follows this course, is indeed the happy and the perfect one, and it is his duty to praise God (mighty and exalted is He!) abundantly for this great gift and immense favor.

He, on the other hand, who does not have this chance in his early life and whose ill luck it is to be brought up by his parents to recite immoral poetry, to accept its lies, and to admire

[50] / its references to vile deeds and the pursuit of pleasures—as is found, for instance, in the poetry of Imru' al-Qays, al-Nābighah and their like; who later serves under chiefs who encourage him to recite such poetry or to compose its like and bestow generous gifts upon him; who has the misfortune of being associated with fellows that assist him in the quest of bodily pleasures,

5   and becomes inclined to covet excessively food, drink, vehicles, ornaments, and the possession of thoroughbred horses and handsome slaves, as was the case with me at certain times in my life; and who then indulges in them and neglects for their sake the happiness to which he is fitted—whoever leads such a life, let him consider all this as misery rather than bliss and loss rather than gain, and let him strive to wean himself from it gradually.

10   But what a difficult task this is! Yet it is, in any case, better than persisting further and further in the wrong way.

Let it be known to the reader of this work that I, in particular, have gradually succeeded in weaning myself [from these things] since becoming advanced in years with well-established habits. I have struggled hard against them, and I am

wishing for you, who are looking for the virtues and seeking
the genuine morality, precisely what I have accepted for myself.
I have even gone further in my advice by pointing out to you
15 what I myself missed at the beginning of my life so that you may
yourself achieve it, by showing you the way to safety before you
go astray in the wilderness of error, and by bringing the ship to
you before you sink in the sea of destruction.[14] In the name
of God, I call upon you to guard your souls, brethren and children!
Yield to the truth, cultivate the genuine morality rather than the
false, seek consummate wisdom, follow the straight path, and
20 consider the states of your souls and remember their faculties.

Let it be known to you that the best analogy made of your
three souls, which were mentioned in the first discourse, is that
[51] of three different creatures[15] assembled / in one place: a king,
a lion, and a pig. Any of these three who overcomes by his strength
the strength of the others becomes their ruler. He who reflects
on this analogy should recognize that, since the soul is not a bodily
substance and since it possesses none of the capacities or accidents
of the body—as we have pointed out in the beginning of this
work—its union and its attachment must necessarily differ
from the union of bodies and their attachment one to
5 another. Thus, when these three souls are mutually attached,
they become one, yet, in spite of their being one, they remain
different and preserve their respective capacities, revolting one
after another as if they had not been attached to, or united
with, one another. Again, each one of them seeks the help of
10 another as if it were itself non-existent and did not have its own
capacity. This is because the union of these souls does not consist
in the sheer joining of their ends or the coincidence of their
surfaces, as is the case with bodies. It is rather that they become
one in certain conditions and remain different in others according
to whether the capacities of some are agitated or quiescent.

It is for this reason that some people assert that the soul
15 is one but has many faculties, while others maintain that it is
one in essence but many in accident and in subject. But this is a
matter the discussion of which would lead us beyond the object
of this work, and which you will find in its proper place. However,
it does not do you any harm to hold, at this moment, any of these
views you wish, provided you realize that one of these [souls

or faculties] is by nature noble and moral, another is degraded and lacking morality, also by nature, and incapable of acquiring
20 it, and the third is lacking morality but capable of acquiring it and ready to yield to the moral soul. The one which is by
[52] nature noble and moral is the rational soul; / the one lacking morality and at the same time incapable of acquiring it is the beastly soul; and the one lacking morality but capable of acquiring it and of yielding to it is the irascible soul. This last soul in particular has been bestowed upon us by God (mighty and exalted is He!) in order that we may make use of it in rectifying the beastly soul which is incapable of acquiring morality.

5 The ancients likened man and his condition with respect to these three souls to a person mounted on a vigorous beast and leading a dog or a hunting panther. Now, if he is the one who tames his horse and dog—if he commands them and they obey him in the course which he takes and in his hunting and other activities—there is no doubt that the common life of the three of them will be happy and fine. The man will get
10 what he wants comfortably; he will let his horse, as well as his dog, run wherever he likes and as he likes, and when he dismounts and takes some rest, he will allow them to rest with him and will take good care of them and satisfy their need for food, drink, safety from enemies, and in other ways. But should the beast have the upper hand, the three would be in a bad condition. The man would become weak with respect to the
15 beast, which would not obey its rider but would itself be master: if it saw some grass from a distance, it would run towards it haphazardly and deviate from the main road; it would rush heedlessly into valleys, pits, thorns, and trees that come across its way, and get itself into trouble in them; the rider would suffer as any similar person would in the same circumstances; and all three of them would meet such evils and such dangers of destruction as is obvious to all. The same would be true if the
20 dog became strong. It would cease to obey its master. If it saw from a distance some prey or what it takes to be prey, it would rush towards it, dragging the rider and the horse along with it and causing all three of them to suffer harm and injury many times more than what we have described.

[53] /When one grasps this analogy, which was cited by the an-

cients, one's attention is called to the condition of these souls
with respect one to another, and he is furnished with an indication
of what God (mighty and exalted is He!) has bestowed upon
man and what He has laid within his power and offered him.
[He gets to know] also what man loses by disobeying his Creator
(exalted is He!) when he neglects to follow guidance, obeys
5 the decrees of these two faculties, and becomes enslaved by
them whereas they should follow him by being subject to his
command. Is there, then, a more miserable condition than that
of the person who disregards the guidance of God (mighty and
exalted is He!), who forfeits the favor which He has bestowed
upon him, who permits these two faculties to be roused
and agitated within him and to fight each other letting the
master among them become a subject and the king a slave, and
who allows himself to be involved with them in all sorts of perils
until he, as well as they, are torn asunder? May God protect us
10 from a relapse in character, which is caused by obedience to
Satan and acquiescence to the devils! By these we mean nothing
but those faculties which we have described and whose nature we
have depicted. We ask from God His protection and His assistance
in the refinement of these souls so that we may achieve, in what
relates to them, obedience to Him, which is our welfare and in
which lies our salvation and our attainment of the greatest triumph
and the everlasting bliss.
15   The philosophers have likened the person who fails to tend his
rational soul and allows the sway of passion and the love of honor
to gain mastery over it to a man who possesses a precious red
ruby, priceless in terms of gold and silver because of its magnifi-
cence and high value, and who throws it in the blaze of a kindling
fire near him, thus turning it into useless lime and losing it as
well as all the profits that could be derived from it.
20   We know now that, if the rational soul realizes its own
nobility and perceives its rank with respect to God (mighty and
exalted is He!), it will fulfill well its task as His deputy in
ordering and tending these faculties and will rise up with the
help of the power bestowed upon it by God to its place in His
[54] / esteem and to its own level of sublimeness and honor. It will
not submit either to the lion or to the beast, but will rather
discipline the irascible soul, which we have called leonine, and

lead it to morality by compelling it to good obedience. It will arouse it when the beastly soul is excited and moved to its
5   desires, in order that, with its help, it may subdue the latter, discipline it, and repress its revolt. For this irascible soul is, as we said, capable of morality and able to subdue the other or beastly soul, while the latter lacks morality and is incapable of it. As for the rational (i.e., the intelligent) soul, it conforms to what Plato said in the following words: "This is like gold in its
10   softness and suppleness, while that [the leonine soul] is like iron in its hardness and toughness." If, then, you choose to perform a good deed and the other faculty draws you to pleasure and to the opposite of what you intend, seek the assistance of the irascible faculty, which is roused and excited by a sense of indignation and enthusiasm, and subdue the beastly soul by its help. And even though, in spite of this, the beastly soul should triumph over you, if you later repent and feel indignant, then you will
15   be in the path of righteousness. Your duty then is to build up your resolution to the utmost and to be careful lest it [the beastly soul] should come back again at you to entice and over-come you. If you are not so careful and the issue does not result in your victory, you will conform to what the first philoso-pher said: "I observe that most people claim that they love [to do] good deeds but, although they are convinced of their value, they do not wish to suffer the trouble which is involved in them and are overcome by the pursuit of luxury and the inclination to idleness. If they do not suffer to be patient and come to know exactly what they have chosen and esteemed, there will be
20   no difference between them and those who do not love [to do] good deeds." Keep in mind the example of the well in which there fell a blind man and a man who is able to see. Both equally met death, but the blind man had a better excuse.

Now, he who has attained in [the acquisition of] these morals a rank of which one may be proud, and has acquired
[55]   through it / the virtues which we have enumerated, has necessarily the obligation to educate other people and to pour out to his fellow men the gifts which God (exalted is He!) has bestowed upon him.

A section on the education of the young, and of boys in particular, most of which I have copied from the work of 'Bryson.' [16]

We have said previously that the first faculty that appears in man when he is first formed is the faculty with which he desires the
5 food that keeps him alive. He instinctively asks for milk and seeks if from its source, the breast, without any previous instruction or direction. Along with this, he comes to possess the faculty by which he asks for it with the voice, which is his resource and the sign with which he shows pleasure or pain. Then this faculty grows in him, and it induces him to continually desire its growth and to use it in the pursuit of all sorts of pleasures. Following
10 this, he acquires the faculty with which he seeks those pleasures through the organs which are formed in him, and this is followed by the desire to perform the actions which give him those pleasures. Then he obtains through the senses the faculty of imagination, and he begins to desire the images which are formed in it. Next comes the irascible faculty by means of which he tries to ward off what injures him and to resist what hinders him from his benefits. If he is able by himself to take his revenge from what injures him,
15 he goes ahead and does it; otherwise, he seeks the assistance of others or asks the help of his parents by shouting and crying.

Following this, he acquires gradually the desire to discern those actions which are characteristically human, until he reaches his perfection in this respect, at which stage he is called a rational being.

20 These faculties are many in number, and some of them
[56] are necessary for the formation of others, / until one attains the final end, the one which is sought by man *qua* man. The first feature of this faculty which occurs in man is bashfulness, which is fear on his part lest he commit anything disgraceful. This is why we have said that bashfulness is the first sign which
5 should be looked for in a boy and taken as a symptom of his reason. For it shows that he has begun to perceive what is disgraceful and, at the same time, to be on his guard against it, to avoid it, and to be cautious lest it appear from him or in him. If, then, you look at the boy and find him bashful, with his eyes lowered towards the ground, neither having an insolent face nor staring at you, take this as the first evidence of his intelligence and as

the testimony that his soul has discerned what is good and what
10   is bad, and that his bashfulness is no more than self-restraint caused
by his fear lest anything disgraceful should come out of him.
This, in turn, is no more than the choice of the good and the
abandonment of the disgraceful through judgment and reason.
Such a soul is apt to be educated and fit to be taken care of. It
should not be neglected or left to association with people of opposite character who would corrupt, through companionship and
15   intercourse, anyone who has this fitness to receive virtue. For the
boy's soul is still simple and has not yet received the impress of any
form, nor does it possess any view or determination which would
turn it from one thing to another. Should it, however, receive
the impress of a particular form and assume it, the boy would
grow in accordance with it and become accustomed to it.

It is appropriate, therefore, that such a soul be roused to
the love of honor, especially that which comes to the boy through
religion and the observance of its traditions and duties, rather
20   than through money. Further, good men should be praised in
his presence, and he himself should be commended for any good
thing which he may perform and warned of reproach for the
least disgraceful thing which he may demonstrate. He should be
blamed for any desire on his part for food, drink, or splendid
[57] clothes, and he should hear the praise of / self-restraint and of disdain of greed for food in particular and pleasures in general.

He should be trained to like giving others preference over
himself in food and to be content with what is moderate and
frugal in seeking it. He should be taught that the people who are
5   most fit to wear colored and embroidered clothes are, first, women
who adorn themselves for the sake of men and, second, slaves
and servants, and that the dress which is most becoming to noble
and honorable people is white or its like. Thus, being brought
up on these teachings and hearing them repeatedly from everybody around him, he should also be prevented from mixing with
those who tell him the contrary, especially if they happen
to be his companions or his associates and playmates of the same
10   age. For, in his early life, the boy is generally bad in all or most
of his actions: he is a liar, telling and relating what he has not
heard or seen; he is jealous; he steals and slanders; he is importune, meddlesome, spiteful, and malicious; and he is most

harmful to himself as well as to everything that touches him. Later, under the constant influence of education, age, and ex-
15 perience, he changes from one state to another. That is why he should be trained as long as he is a child along the lines which we have described and are describing.

He should then be required to learn by heart good traditions and poems which corroborate what he has practiced in his education, so that by reciting, learning, and discussing them, all that we have described may become confirmed in him. He should
20 also be put on his guard against the study of frivolous poetry and what it contains about love and lovers, and against the impression which its authors give that it is a form of elegance and of refinement. For this kind of poetry has, indeed, a strong corrupting influence on youth.

[58]   /The boy should also be praised and honored for any good trait or any good deed which he may show. If, at times, he violates what I have described, it is preferable that he not be reproached for it or openly told that he has committed it. One should feign not to have noticed it, as if it would not occur to him that the boy would ever dare such a thing or attempt to do it. This is es-
5 pecially necessary when the boy conceals it and endeavors to hide what he has done from other people. If he repeats it, let him be reproached for it secretly, shown the seriousness of his action and warned against doing it again. For if you accustom him to reproach and disclosure, you will make him impudent and incite him to repeat what he has detested. It will become easy for him to hear blame for indulging in the detestable pleasures to which his nature urges him. And these pleasures are very
10 numerous.

The training of the soul should begin with [the formation of] good manners in eating. The boy should first be made to understand that eating is meant only for health and not for pleasure and that all the kinds of food have been created and prepared for us solely to make our bodies healthy and to sustain our life. They should be considered as medicines with which we remedy hunger
15 and the pain resulting from it. Just as we do not seek medicine for pleasure and are not driven by greed to take more and more of it, so it is also with food: we should take only as much of it as would preserve the health of the body, remove the pain

of hunger, and guard against disease. Thus, the boy should be made to despise the value of food, which gluttonous people extol, and to disdain those who covet it and take more of it than is necessary for their bodies or indulge in what does not agree with them. In this way, he would get to be satisfied with only one course of food and would not desire many courses. When he sits in the company of others, he should not be the first to start eating, nor should he stare constantly and fixedly at the courses of food but should be content with whatever is near him. He should not eat in a hurry or take rapidly one mouthful after another. The mouthfuls should not be too big or swallowed before they are well chewed. He should not soil his hands, or / his clothing, or his table companions, nor follow with his eyes the movements of their hands in eating. He should be trained to offer to others the food that lies near him if it is the kind that he prefers, and to control his appetite so as to be content with the least and poorest of food, eating once in a while dry bread without anything else. These manners, if commendable when shown by poor people, are even more commendable when shown by the rich.

The boy should have his full meal in the evening, for, if he has it during the day, he will feel lazy and sleepy and also his understanding will become slow. If he is forbidden to eat meat most of the time, the result will be favorable to him in [stirring] his activity and attentiveness, in reducing his dullness, and in arousing him to liveliness and agility. As for sweets and fruits, he should abstain from them entirely if possible; otherwise, let him take as little of them as possible because they become transformed in his body, thus hastening the process of dissolution, and, at the same time, they accustom him to gluttony and to the desire for excessive food. He should be trained to avoid drinking water during his meals. As for wine and the different kinds of intoxicating beverages, let him indeed beware of them, for they injure him in his body and in his soul and incite him to quick anger, foolhardiness, the performance of vile deeds, impudence, and the other blameworthy dispositions. Nor should he attend drinking parties, except when the company is well-bred and virtuous; otherwise, he might hear vile speech and silly things that usually take place in such parties. [Finally,] he should

₂₀ not begin to eat until he has performed the educational tasks which
he is pursuing and has become sufficiently tired.

[60] Furthermore, the boy should be forbidden to do anything
which he hides or conceals, for, if he / hides anything, it is only
because he either thinks or knows that it is disgraceful. He should
not be allowed to sleep too long because too much sleep makes
him flabby,[17] dulls his mind, and deadens his thinking. So much
for night sleep; as for sleep during the day, he should never
become accustomed to it. Similarly, he should not be given a
₅ soft bed or any other means of luxury and flabbiness, so as to
harden his body and to habituate him to a rough life. For the
same reasons, he should be denied moistened canvas [to cool
off the air] and living underground in summer, and camel furs
and fire in winter. Let him develop the habits of walking, movement, riding, and exercise lest he succumb to their opposites.

The boy should be taught not to uncover the extremities of his
body, nor to walk fast, nor to hang his hands loose but to join them
together at his chest. He should not let his hair grow long, nor
₁₀ adorn himself with dresses fit for women, nor wear a ring except
when necessary. Let him not boast to his companions of something
which his parents possess, or of his food, clothing, or the like. On
the contrary, let him be humble towards everybody and honor
all those who associate with him. Should he possess any honor,
or any power derived from his kin, he must not arouse the anger
of those who are below him, or attempt to guide those whom he
₁₅ cannot divert from their whims, or deal with them high-handedly.
[61] If, for instance, his maternal uncle / happens to be a vizier or
his paternal uncle a sultan, this must not lead him to do injustice
to his companions, or to defame his friends, or to seize the property of his neighbors and acquaintances.

He should be taught, when in the company of others, not
to spit, or blow his nose, or yawn, or cross his legs, or beat his
chin with his forearm, or support his head with his hand, for
₅ this is an indication of laziness and a proof that he has become
so flabby that he is no longer able to carry his head without the
help of his hand. Further, he should be trained not to tell lies
and never to swear, whether truthfully or falsely, for swearing
is disgraceful to men, though they may need it at times, but it is
never needed by boys. He should also be taught to keep silent,

10 to talk sparingly, and only to answer questions. If he is in the
company of older people, his duty is to listen to them and to
keep silent in their presence. He should be forbidden to utter
vile or improper speech, to insult, curse, or talk nonsense. On
the contrary, he should be taught to utter good and elegant
speech and to greet gracefully and kindly, and should not be
allowed to hear the opposite of this from others. He should also
15 be accustomed to serve himself, his master, and older people.
The children of the rich and of those who live in luxury need,
more than others, to cultivate these good manners.

If the boy is beaten by his teacher, he should not cry or ask
the intercession of any one, for such is the conduct of slaves and
those who are feeble and weak. He should not reproach others
except for disgraceful and bad manners. He should be accustomed not to treat other boys harshly, but to show kindness to them
20 and to repay their favors with bigger ones lest he make it a habit
[62] to seek gain from boys / and from friends. He should be made
to detest silver and gold and to fear them more than he does lions,
snakes, scorpions, and serpents. For the love of silver and gold
is more harmful than poison. He should be allowed from time to
time to play nice games in order that he may thus rest from the
5 toil of education, but his play should not involve pain or intense
fatigue. And, finally, he should be trained to obey his parents,
teachers, and educators and to honor, extol, and revere them.

The benefits of the education of the young

These good manners which are useful to boys are likewise
useful to older people, but to the young they are more useful
10 because they train them to love virtue and allow them to grow up
accordingly. It then becomes easy for them to avoid vices, and
later to follow all the prescriptions of philosophy and the regu-
lations of the Law and of Tradition. They thus get accustomed
to control themselves in the face of the wicked pleasures towards
which their natures urge them. [These good manners also] restrain
them from indulging in any of those pleasures or giving much
thought to them. They lead them to the high rank of philosophy
and promote them to the lofty grades which we described in
15 the beginning of this work, such as seeking proximity to God

(mighty and exalted is He!) and the vicinity of the angels, as well as enjoying a good condition in this world, leading a pleasant life, gaining a fine reputation, and having few enemeis, numerous praisers, and many who seek their friendship, particularly among the virtuous. If one goes beyond this grade and attains in his life to the understanding of the aims of men and the conse-quences of actions, one will realize that the final end of what
20　people desire and care for — such as wealth, the acquisition of
[63]　estates, slaves, / horses, furniture, and the like — is nothing else but to secure the well-being of one's body, to preserve its health and keep its balance for a certain period of time, to guard it against diseases or sudden death, to cause it to enjoy the grace of God (mighty and exalted is He!) upon it, and to prepare it for the eternal world and the everlasting life. He will realize also that all bodily pleasures are in reality deliverance from pain
5　and relief from fatigue.

　　When the boy understands this and grasps its truth, and then becomes accustomed to it by continuous practice, the next step should be to train him in those exercises which stir up the innate heat, preserve health, banish laziness, drive dullness away, arouse liveliness, and kindle the soul. He who is rich and leads a luxu-rious life will find these things which I have just prescribed harder for him to perform than they are for others because of
10　the large number of those who surround and tempt him, the fact that these pleasures agree with the nature of man at the begin-ning of his life, and the unanimous desire of the mass of the people to obtain as much of them as they can and to seek with their utmost effort that which lies beyond their reach. With the poor, on the other hand, it is an easier matter. Indeed, they are close to the virtues, capable of acquiring them, and able to achieve and gain them. As for the middle class, their condition in this
15　respect is intermediate between the two.

　　The virtuous kings of Persia were in the habit of not bringing up their children among their retinue and their intimates for fear that they get into some of the conditions which we have described or hear what I have cautioned against. They used to send them with people whom they trusted to distant regions where those who took charge of their education were rough and hard-living people
20　who did not experience ease or luxury. Their stories in this

regard are famous, and even in our present day many of the
chiefs of the Daylam remove their children, when they begin
to grow up, to their own country so that they may acquire this
[64] character there and be kept away / from flabbiness and the
customs of the people of evil countries.

Now that you know these laudable methods of educating
the young, you also know their opposites. I mean that whoever
grows up according to a different way or form of education
has no hope of success, and one should not strive to improve
5   or correct him. For he is in the same rank as the wild boar which
nobody hopes to discipline. His rational soul has become the
servant of his beastly and irascible souls and is busy trying to
satisfy their whims. As it is impossible to discipline the wild
beasts which do not respond to training, so also it is impossible
to discipline the person who grows up in this way, gets accustomed
10 to it, and becomes a little advanced in years, unless he is, in all
his conditions, aware of the vileness of his conduct, disapproving
of it, blaming himself for it, and determined to desist and to
repent. For such a man, one may entertain the hope that he
will depart gradually from his former character and return to the
ideal way by repentance, association with good and wise men,
and the diligent pursuit of philosophy.

The genesis and evolution of the faculties of existents

15   Having described the laudable character and what youths
and boys should be taught, we will start to describe all the faculties that appear one after another in the animals until we come
to the extreme perfection in humanity. For it is very necessary
that you know this in order to begin rectifying them one after
another in the natural order. So we say: –
20   All physical bodies share the definition which is common to
them, and then differ in rank according to their respective abilities
to receive the noble impressions and the forms which take
[65] place / within them. Thus, if the inanimate object takes on a
form which is acceptable to people, it will become thereby
superior to the original clay which is not capable of assuming
such a form, and, if it attains the point where it receives the
form of the plant, it will become, by the addition of this form,

superior to the inanimate object. This addition consists of [the
5 powers of] nutrition, of growth, of spreading, and of drawing
from the soil and from water what suits its nature, abandoning
what does not suit it, and discharging from the body, in the
form of gums, the excretions which are formed in it from its
food. These are the differences between plants and inanimate
objects. They represent a condition added to the mere physical
state which we have defined and which exists in the inanimate
object.
10   This additional condition in the plant, by virtue of which
it becomes superior to the inanimate object, is of various grades,
for certain plants, such as coral and the like, differ only slightly
from the inanimate object. Then the plants advance gradually
from one grade to another and appropriate more and more of
that addition. Thus, some plants grow without cultivation or
sowing, fail to preserve their kind by fruits or seeds, and do not
need for their formation anything beyond the combination of
15 the elements, winds, and sunshine. That is why they are in the
realm of the inanimate objects and akin to them. Then this
quality of the plants is enhanced, and some plants become superior to others in a systematic and orderly way, until there
appears in some of them the power of bearing fruit and of preserving their kind by means of seeds through which they produce
their like. This condition represents an addition to, and a distinction from, the species that come before them. Then [as
we pass from some plants to others], this quality grows further
20 so that the third [species] becomes as superior to the second as
the second is to the first, and the [species] keep on rising in rank
and some surpassing others until they attain the [end of] their
realm and enter that of the animal. Here are the superior trees such
[66] as the olive tree, the pomegranate tree, the vine, / and the various
fruit-bearing trees. But, even here, the faculties are still mixed —
I mean that the faculties of their males and their females are
still mixed and not distinct each from the other, that is, these
plants bear and reproduce their like. They have not yet attained
the limit of their realm which joins that of the animal.
But some species advance still further in this realm until
they reach the realm of the animal and cannot receive any
5 addition, for any slight addition would make them animals

and would take them out of the realm of the plant. Here their faculties become distinct, male and female qualities are produced in them, and they come to possess animal characteristics which distinguish them from the rest of the plants and trees. An example of this is the palm tree which touches the realm of the animal by virtue of the ten properties which are enumerated in their proper places. Only one grade separates it from the animal, and that is the capacity to uproot itself from the soil and to go in search of food. Tradition has preserved an allusion to, or a symbol of, this truth in the words of the Prophet (may the prayer and peace of God be upon him!): "Honor your aunt the palm tree, for it was created from the remains of the clay of which Adam was made."[18] Should a plant develop the capacity to move, to uproot itself from its realm and to seek its food instead of being tied down to its place and having to wait for its food to be brought to it, and should also other organs be formed in it by which it can obtain what it needs to remedy its deficiencies — should a plant develop such capacities, it would become an animal.

These organs develop in the animal from the beginning of its realm and grow better, and some animals become thereby nobler than others — exactly as was the case with plants. They go on achieving one quality after another until they develop the faculty of feeling pleasure and pain. Here the animal is pleased when it attains its benefits and is pained when harms befall it. Then it advances to the stage in which it receives the inspiration of God (mighty and exalted is He!), and thus recognizes what is good for it and what is bad, seeking the former and avoiding the latter. Those animals which stand at the beginning, near the realm / of the plant, such as worms, flies, and the lower kinds of insects, do not copulate or beget their kind, but reproduce asexually. Then the ability to acquire qualities develops in the animals — as was equally the case with the plants. They come to acquire the faculty of anger by which they rise to defend themselves against anything that is harmful. They are given weapons in accordance with their strength and with their ability to use them. If this irascible faculty is intense, their weapons are powerful and complete; if it is deficient, the weapons are deficient also; and if it is very weak, they are not given any weapons at

all, but are merely equipped with the means to flee, such as
swiftness in running and the ability to use cunning to escape
dangers. You can see this clearly when you observe the animal
10   that is equipped with horns which serve it as spears, the one that
is given teeth and claws which serve it as knives and daggers,
the one that possesses a shooting organ which serves it as darts
and arrows, and the one that is equipped with hoofs which
serve it as a mace or a battle-axe. Concerning the animals that
are not given any weapons [at all], this is because of their
inability to use them, their lack of courage, the deficiency of
15   their irascible faculty, and because, should they have been given
them, such weapons would have become a burden to them.
These animals (such as hares, foxes, and the like) are equipped
with means which serve them to flee or to deceive, like swiftness
in running, agility, craftiness, and cunning. And if you examine
carefully the conditions of such existents as beasts of prey, wild
animals, and birds, you will find this wise law constant in all
of them. Blessed be God, the Supreme Creator!
20   As for man, he is compensated for all these organs by being
guided to their use and given the capacity to control them all.
[68] On this point we shall speak / when it is due. As for the causes
of all these things, and the doubts which arise regarding their
mutual destruction and infliction of pain and injury, this is
not the place to discuss them, and I shall mention them — should
God lengthen the term of my life — when we reach the proper
place.
5   Let us come back now to the mention of the various ranks
of animals. So we say: Those animals that find their way to
copulation, the begetting of offspring, the protection and bringing up of the young, and the concern to keep them safe in a
shelter, nest, or den (as we observe in those that reproduce and
lay eggs) and finally to feed them, either with their milk or
with the food that they bring to them — such animals are superior
to those that are not able to do any of these things. Then these
conditions are enhanced among the animals until some of them
10   come close to the realm of man. Here they become responsive
to training and, as such, superior to other animals. This quality
goes on growing so that some animals become thereby preeminent
in various ways, as in the case of the horse and the trained falcon.

Finally, we pass from this rank to the rank of the animals which imitate man of their own accord and follow his example without any instruction, such as apes and the like. These attain such a degree of intelligence that it is only necessary for them, in order to be trained, to see a person perform a certain act and then to do something like it, without giving man any trouble or obliging him to discipline them. This is the furthest point in the animal realm. If any animal crosses it and receives a slight addition, it will leave this realm and pass to the realm of man, who is capable of acquiring intelligence, discernment, and rationality, the organs which these capacities use, and the forms which are appropriate to them. When he attains this rank, he proceeds towards knowledge, desires the sciences, and acquires faculties, capacities, and gifts from God (mighty and exalted is He!) which enable him to progress and advance in this / rank as was the case with the other ranks which we have described.

The first rank in the human realm, which touches the limit of the animal realm, is the rank of the people who dwell in the farthest parts of the inhabited world both to the north and to the south, such as the remotest Turks in the countries of Gog and Magog and the remotest Negroes and similar nations which are distinguished from apes to a slight degree only. Then the faculty of discernment and understanding grows in men until they reach the central regions where intelligence, quickness of understanding, and the ability to acquire virtues are produced in them. At this point ends the work of nature which God (mighty and exalted is He!) has entrusted with the sensible existents. With this ability, man becomes prepared to achieve virtues and to earn good traits by resolution, endeavor, and diligence, as we described above, until he reaches the limit of his realm.

The highest human rank

When man reaches the limit of his realm, he touches the beginning of the realm of the angels. This is the highest rank possible for man. Here the existents are unified, and their beginnings become joined to their ends and *vice versa*. This is called the circle of existence, for the circle is that which has been defined as one line which moves from a certain point and ends at

it. The circle of existence is the unified circle which creates unity out of multiplicity and which is a correct and demonstrative proof of the unity, wisdom, power, and munificence of its Creator
20 (may His name be blessed, His majesty exalted, and His remembrance sanctified!).

[70]   /Were it not that the explanation of this point does not fall within the scope of the art of the refinement of character, I would readily explain it. But you will come to know it if, God willing, you will attain this rank. If now you imagine and understand as much as we have alluded to, you will realize the condition for which you were created and to which you are summoned, the realm which touches your own, and your advance-
5 ment from one rank and one class to another. You will have genuine faith and will behold what the masses have failed to see. You will be able to progress gradually to the noble and hidden sciences, beginning with the study of logic, which is the instrument for the corrrection of understanding and of instinctive reason. You will proceed with the help of this science to earn the knowledge of all the creatures and of their natures, and then to become attached to this knowledge, to advance
10 in it, and to attain thereby the divine sciences. Here you will be ready to receive the favors and gifts of God (mighty and exalted is He!). His divine grace will descend upon you and you will be free from the agitation of nature and its movements towards animal passions. You will note the ranks of the existents through which you evolved gradually, and you will know that each one of the ranks could not have existed without the preceding ones. You will know also that man does not achieve
15 his perfection until he has passed through all that lies before him, and that when he becomes a perfect man and reaches the end of his realm, the light of the highest realm will shine upon him and he will become either a complete philosopher, who receives inspiration in the philosophical attempts which he makes and heavenly support in his intellectual conceptions, or a prophet, confirmed [by God], who obtains divine revelation in accordance
20 with the various grades which lie with God (mighty and exalted is He!). He will then become an intermediary between the higher world and the lower, as a result of his conception of the condition of all existents and of the condition to which he is pro-

moted from the merely human one, and as a result of sighting the realms which we have described. Then also he will understand the words of God (mighty and exalted is He!): "No soul knoweth what delight of the eyes is hidden in reserve for them." [19] And
[71] he will realize the meaning of the saying / of the Apostle of God (may the prayer and peace of God be upon him!), "There, there is what no eye has ever seen, nor an ear ever heard, nor ever occurred to the heart of a man." [20]

Having reached in our discussion the mention of this high and noble rank to which man is designated, and having set in proper order the conditions through which he advances, and having explained that this advance begins first with the desire for
5 knowledge and the sciences, it is necessary to clarify and explain this point further. So we say: –

This desire may lead a person in a straight path and in the right direction until he attains the end of his perfection which is his complete happiness. But this seldom occurs. It may, on the other hand, divert him from the highest objective and the right path, as a result of many causes which it would take us
10 too long to enumerate and which you do not need to know at this point while you are in the process of refining your character. For, just as the physical nature which manages bodies may, as a result of certain defects which are produced in the physical body or certain evils which befall it, cause it to desire what does not complete it — such as in the case of those who desire to eat mud and the like which do not perfect the nature of the body,
15 but destroy and corrupt it — so also the rational soul may desire the kind of study and discernment which would not perfect it nor induce it to seek its happiness, but which would rather impel it towards the things that hinder it from its perfection and cause it to fall short of it. In this case, a person needs a mental and spiritual remedy, just as in the former he needs a physical and bodily medicine. That is why there is such a great need for those who train and cultivate, for the educators and those who
20 guide to the right path, since superior natures that are led to happiness by themselves and without assistance are hard to find; they do not exist except [rarely] in the course of extended times and distant periods.

In this genuine education, which brings us to our goals,

[72] we must / observe the principle which plays the role of the end,
so that, having observed the end, one can come down gradually,
by way of analysis, to the physical things, and then start from
the bottom and proceed, by way of synthesis, until one reaches
again the end which had been observed before. It is this fact
5 which caused us, at the beginning of this work and in other
chapters as well, to state certain advanced truths which do not
properly fall within the scope of this art, in order to stir those
who are worthy of them to desire them. For it is not possible for a
person to desire what he ignores completely, while, if one who
has an aptitude and a concern for these truths comes to observe
them, he will have some knowledge of them and will, consequently, desire them, strive to attain them, and suffer toil and
hardship for their sake.

The duty of the manager of cities

10   You should know that any person who is prepared for a particular virtue is thereby nearer than others to it and has a greater
chance to attain it. Consequently, the happiness of one person
is different from the happiness of another, except for the one
who is endowed with a pure soul and a superior nature and
who thus attains the ends of things and the limit of these ends,
in other words, the extreme happiness beyond which there is
no happiness. It is for this reason that the manager of cities
15 should induce every person to seek his own particular happiness.
He should then divide the care and attention which he gives
to the people into two parts: the first consisting in guiding them
aright and reforming them by means of the intellectual sciences,
and the second in guiding them towards the practical arts and
sensible activities. In the first part — in which he guides them
to intellectual happiness — he should start with the ultimate
end and lead them gradually, by way of analysis, to the faculties
20 which we have described, while in the second part — in which he
guides them to practical happiness — he should start with these
faculties and proceed from them to those ends.

[73] / *Conclusion and introduction to the following discourse*

Inasmuch as our object in this work is [that we acquire]

moral happiness and that all the deeds which we perform should be good, as we stated at the beginning of this present work — which is written especially for lovers of philosophy rather than for laymen— and inasmuch as theory precedes practice, it is incumbent upon us to discuss the absolute good and the human happiness in order

5   that the ultimate end may be noted and then sought by the voluntary actions which we have summed up in the first discourse. It is with this point that Aristotle began his work,[21] which he prefaced by a discussion of the absolute good so that this good could be known and desired. We shall now state what he said and add to it what we have taken also from him in other sections so as to bring together what was mentioned by him in different places. We shall also, in the measure of our capacity, add what we have taken from the commentators of his works and the followers

10   of his philosophy. It is God who grants success and support, for all goods are in His hands. Sufficient is He for us, and an excellent guardian indeed!

THIRD DISCOURSE

THE GOOD AND ITS DIVISIONS;
HAPPINESS AND ITS GRADES

/ THIRD DISCOURSE [1]

THE GOOD AND ITS DIVISIONS;
HAPPINESS AND ITS GRADES

Definition of the good and of happiness

   With the help of God (exalted is He!), we begin this discourse
by stating the difference between the good and happiness, after
quoting the words of Aristotle in imitation of him and in acknowledgment of what is due to him. So we say: *The* good, as he
defined it and according to the view of the ancients which he
approved, is that towards which all things aim, i.e., the utlimate
end.[2] And anything which is useful towards that end may be
5 called *a* good. As for happiness, it is the good in relation to its
possessor and constitutes to him a perfection. Happiness, then, is
a good. The happiness of man may be different from the happiness
of the horse; and the happiness of everything lies in its particular
completion and perfection. As for *the* good, which is desired by
all, it is an object which can be sought and which has an essence;
it is the good common to all men *qua* men and which all of them
10 share. Happiness, on the other hand, is *a* good with respect to
one man or another; it is then relative, and has no definite essence.
It differs in accordance with those who seek it, but there is no
difference concerning the absolute good. Happiness is sometimes
thought to belong also to the non-rational beings. If this is
true, then happiness is only those beings' aptitudes to achieve
15 their completions and perfections without intention, or delib-
[76] eration, or will. These / aptitudes correspond to desire, or
what is similar to desire, in the case of the rational beings who
use their will. As to what animals get from their food, drink,
and relaxation, it should be called luck or chance, and does

69

not deserve the name of happiness. The same is true in the case
of man.

5   The above-mentioned definition of the absolute good is
deemed right because reason does not admit of effort or motion
that goes to no end. This is a first [principle] of reason. For
example: Every art, every aspiration, and every voluntary measure
aims at some good [3] and that which does not aim at some good
is futile and is denied and forbidden by reason. Necessarily,
10   therefore, the absolute good becomes that towards which all
people aim. It remains, however, to know what it is and what its
final end is—that is, the end of all goods to which they all lead—
so that we will may make it our object, direct ourselves towards
it, keep our thoughts from being diffused among the many goods
which lead directly or indirectly to it, and [finally] so that we
will not mistake what is not good for what is good and spend the
whole of our lives seeking it and toiling for it. All this we shall
15   explain, God willing and helping.

The divisions of the good

Aristotle's division of the good, as reported by Porphyry
and others,[4] is as follows: – He said: Some goods are noble,
some are praiseworthy, others are potential goods, and still
others are useful in achieving what is good. The noble goods are
those whose nobility is derived from their very essence and which
20   ennoble whomsoever acquires them. These are wisdom and
reason. Examples of praiseworthy goods are the virtues and the
fine voluntary deeds. Examples of potential goods are the readiness
[77] / and the aptitude to obtain the above-mentioned things. Useful
goods are all the things which are sought not for themselves, but
in order to attain thereby the [other] goods.[5]

Another division: Some goods are ends, and some are not
ends. Of those which are ends, some are complete and some
5   are not complete. An example of the former is happiness, for
when we attain it we do not need anything else in addition.
Examples of the latter are health and wealth, for even if we
attain them we are still in need of more [goods], so we acquire
other things. Goods which are not ends at all are such things
as medical treatment, learning, and exercise.[6]

10   Another division: Some goods are in the soul, some are in the body, and some are external to them.

Another division: Of the goods, some are chosen for themselves, some as means to others, some both for themselves and as means to others, and some neither for themselves nor as means to others.

15   Another division: Of the goods, some are absolutely so, while others are goods only in case of necessity, or because of certain coincidences which occur to some people, or only at certain times and not at others. Also: Some are goods to all people in all respects and at all times, while others are not goods to all people or in all respects.[7]

20   Another division: Of the goods, some are so in substance, some in quantity, some in quality, and so on in the other categories. Some are like faculties and aptitudes, others like states, [78] and still others like actions. / Some are like ends, others like matter, and still others like tools. The existence of the goods in the various categories is as follows: In substance—I mean what is not accident—God (exalted and blessed is He!) is the First Good, because all things turn towards Him in desire for 5 Him and so as to obtain from Him such divine goods as immortality, eternity, and completion. Goods in respect to quantity are the moderate number and the fair amount; in respect to quality, [such goods] as pleasures; in respect to relation, as friendships and authorities; in respect to the where and the when, as the mild place and the lovely and pleasant time; in respect to position, as comfortable sitting, lying down, or reclining; in respect 10 to possession, as money and benefits; in respect to being acted upon, as hearing good music and the other moving sensations; and [finally] in respect to acting, as the effectiveness of one's commands and the spread of one's action.[8]

Another division: Of the goods, some are intelligible, while others are sensible.

As for happiness, we said that it is *a* good. It is the completion and the ends of goods. Completion is that [end] which, once 15 it is attained, we do not need anything else in addition. This is why we say that happiness is the best of goods, but in order to attain this completion, which is the ultimate end, we need other kinds of happiness, some of which are related to the body, while others are external to it. Aristotle said: It is difficult for man to do noble deeds without any means such as ample resources, numerous friends, and good fortune.[9] He said: It is for this [79] reason that / wisdom needs the art of government in order to show its superiority. And he added: This is why we said that if anything is a gift from God (exalted is He!) and a favor to men, happiness must be it, for happiness is a gift from Him (mighty is His name!) and a favor which is in the noblest rank of the goods and in their highest grade.[10] It belongs only to the complete man, and, for this reason, nobody who is not complete, 5 such as boys and their like, can share it with him.[11] These are the divisions of the goods.

The divisions of happiness

According to this philosopher, the divisions of happiness are five in number. The first consists of the health of the body and the tenderness of the senses, which are due to moderate temperament, i.e., when one's senses of hearing, sight, smell, taste, and 10 touch are good. The second consists of the possession of fortune, associates, and their like, so that one may have the possibility of spending money wherever one should, to realize with it the various goods, to aid with it the good people in particular and all the deserving ones in general, and to perform all that enhances his virtues and brings him commendation and praise. The third consists in one's enjoyment of good reputation and of widespread fame among the virtuous people, so that he is commended and greatly 15 praised by them because of his charity and munificence. The fourth is to be successful in one's affairs, that is, to realize all that one deliberates and decides to do, and to attain all that he expects therefrom. The fifth consists in having good judgment, sound thinking, and sane beliefs in the domain of religion and in other domains, and in being free from error and fault and able to give good counsel. Thus, according to this honorable man 20 [Aristotle], whoever can claim all these divisions together is a happy and perfect man, and whoever possesses only some of them has only a proportionate share of happiness.

[80]   /The philosophers who preceded this man, such as Pythagoras, Socrates,[12] Plato, and their like, agreed that all

the virtues and happiness belong to the soul alone. Thus, when
they divided happiness, they confined it all to the faculties
of the soul which we mentioned at the beginning of this work,
5   that is, wisdom, courage, temperance, and justice. They were
unanimous also in holding that these virtues are sufficient for
happiness and that one does not need beside them any other
virtue, whether pertaining to the body or external to it; further,
that when one obtains these virtues, his happiness would not
be impaired even if he were sick, or lacked any organ, or were
afflicted by all the diseases of the body, unless the soul itself
10   were thereby hurt in its particular activities—such as when the
mind is vitiated, or the intellect spoiled, or the like. As for poverty,
obscurity, lowliness, and the other defects which are external
to us, they are not, according to these philosophers, detrimental
to happiness in any way.

The Stoics and a group of the Naturalists, on the other
hand, included the body as a part of man and did not regard
15   it a mere tool as we have explained above. Thus, they were obliged
to consider the happiness of the soul as incomplete unless it is
coupled with the happiness of the body and of what is also external to the body, such as the things that exist as a result of
fortune and good luck.

Philosophers who are thorough investigators look down
upon fortune and all that exists through it, or with it, and do
not deem these things worthy of the name of happiness, for hap-
20   piness is something fixed, abiding, and unchanging, and is the
worthiest, noblest, and most exalted of things. Thus, according to
[81]   these philosophers, the lowest of things—that which / changes, is
not fixed, is not produced by deliberation or thought, and does
not result from reason or virtue—cannot partake of it.

Is happiness realizable in this world? The views of the ancients

For this reason, the ancients differed in regard to the supreme
happiness. Some thought that it cannot be achieved by man
until he is separated from the body and all physical things. They
5   are the people who, as we said earlier, considered the supreme
happiness to lie in the soul only and confined the attribute of
humanity to this substance alone, to the exclusion of the body.

They concluded, therefore, that so long as the soul is attached
to nature and its impurity, to the body's contaminations and
necessities, to man's needs of the body, and to its own numerous
wants—so long as the soul is in this state, it cannot be absolutely
happy. Furthermore, as they realized that it does not attain
the perfection that corresponds to the existence of intellectual
10   things because these are concealed from it by the darkness of
matter—in other words, as they realized its shortcoming and
deficiency—they held that when it abandons this turbidity, it
will abandon all forms of ignorance, become purified and refined,
and receive illumination and divine light—by which I mean
the perfect intellect. It follows, according to the view of these
people, that man cannot attain complete happiness except in
15   the next world after his death. So long as he is man, he cannot
be completely happy.
      The other school, however, said: It is disgraceful and un-
becoming to believe that, so long as man is alive, performing
good deeds and professing right beliefs, striving to achieve virtues
first for himself and then for his fellowmen, and conducting
himself, by these good deeds, as the deputy of the mighty Lord
(may the mention of His name be exalted!)—so long as man is
20   in this state, he remains miserable and imperfect, but that when
[82] he passes away and loses all these / things, he becomes happy in
a complete way. Aristotle held this view. For he spoke of the
happiness of man; and man to him is the being that is composed
of both a body and a soul and that is thus defined as the rational
mortal, or the rational, two-legged, erect being, or the like. This
5   school, which is headed by Aristotle, believed that human happiness is possible for man in this world if one strives for it and
toils in its pursuit until he reaches its end. When the philosopher
[Aristotle] saw this and saw also that men differ in regard to
this human happiness and that it constitutes for them a very
difficult problem, he felt it necessary to exert himself to clarify
10   it and to discuss it at length. For the poor man thinks that the
greatest happiness consists in fortune and wealth, the sick man
sees it in health and well-being, the lowly man in honor and
dominion, the dissolute man in the satisfaction of all the various
desires, the lover in winning his beloved, and the virtuous man in
the shedding of benefits to those who deserve them. [Finally,]

15 the philosopher believes that all of these are different kinds of happiness, provided they are ordered according to the requirements of reason, i.e., [they are sought] when they are needed, at the right time, and in the right way. He believes also that what is desired for the sake of some other thing is less worthy than that thing of the name of happiness.

The author's view: The two grades of happiness

As each of these two schools held a certain view, it is neces-
20 sary that we state in this regard what we deem is right and what
[83] combines the two views. So we say: / Man possesses a spiritual virtue, by which he is akin to the good spirits that are called angels, and a bodily virtue, by which he is akin to the animals. He is made up of both of them. Consequently, on account of the bodily part by which he is akin to the animals, he abides in this lower bodily world for a short period of time in order to
5 build it up, organize it, and set it in order. But when he attains perfection in this grade, he moves to the upper world and abides in it eternally and everlastingly in the company of the angels and the good spirits. By the lower world and the upper world, one should understand what we stated earlier, for we said there that we do not mean by the upper world the upper plane in
10 the realm of sense nor by the lower world the lower plane in the same realm, but that all that is sensible belongs to the lower world, even though it may be perceived on the upper plane, and all that is intelligible belongs to the upper world, even though it may be conceived on the lower plane.

Further, you should know that one does not need, when in the company of the good spirits, i.e., those that are free from bodies,
15 any of the kinds of bodily happiness which we have mentioned, but only the happiness of the soul, that is, only the eternal intelligibles which in fact constitute wisdom. Thus, so long as man is man, he cannot have complete happiness unless he achieves both states, and these can be completely obtained only by means of the things which lead to eternal wisdom. The happy man, therefore, is
20 in one of two ranks: either he is in the rank of the bodily things, attached to their lower states and happy in them, while, at the same time, regarding the noble things, looking for them, desiring

them, directing his efforts towards them, and rejoicing in them;
[84] or else he is in the rank of the / spiritual things, attached to their
higher states and happy in them, while, at the same time,
observing the lower things, learning from them, reflecting on
the signs of divine power and the evidences of consummate wisdom [in them], following their example, regulating them, pouring
out goods on them, and leading them gradually to what is better
and better to the extent of their readiness and according to their
5   capacity. Whoever is not in either of these two ranks is in the
rank of the animals—indeed, he is even further astray, for the
latter are not exposed to these goods, nor given the capacity
to seek these high ranks, but are only able with their faculties
to move towards the perfections proper to them. Man is exposed
and called to these high ranks, and well equipped for them; yet,
10   he does not obtain them, nor does he strive towards them, but
rather prefers their opposites and uses his noble faculties in the
pursuit of base things. They [the animals], on the other hand,
achieve their own perfections. Thus, if they are denied the human
goods [and] deprived of the opportunity of being in the vicinity
of the good spirits and of admission into the Paradise promised
to those who fear God, they may be excused, but man is inexcus-
15   able. The former are like the blind man who deviates from
the road and falls into a well; he is to be pitied, and not blamed.
The latter is like a person who is able to see, but who nevertheless
deviates and ends by falling into a well; he is to be detested and
blamed, and not pitied.
    Now that it is evident that the happy man must necessarily
be in one of the two ranks [the bodily and the spiritual] which we
have mentioned, it becomes also evident that the one happy man
20   is imperfect and falls short of the other, and that the imperfect one
is thereby not free or exempt of pains and sorrows, on account of the
deceits of nature and the sensual allurements which present themselves to him in his contacts, hindering him from what he is considering, preventing him from progressing as he should in these mat-
[85] ters, and keeping him busy / with his bodily attachments. He who
is in this rank is not absolutely perfect nor completely happy.
    [On the other hand,] the person in the other rank is the
one who is completely happy. He has an abundant share of
wisdom, and, by virtue of his spirituality, he abides among the

5 higher beings from whom he derives the subtleties of wisdom; he is illuminated by the divine light; and he seeks to add to his virtues in the measure of the attention he gives to them and the lack of hindrances from them. Thus, he is ever free from those pains and sorrows of which the one in the first rank is not exempt, and he is always happy in himself, in his condition, and in the overflowing of the light of the First One which he constantly
10 receives. He delights only in these pleasures and rejoices only in these beauties. Nothing pleases him except the demonstration of this wisdom among the wise, and nothing gives him comfort except the company of those who are akin or near to him and wish to learn from him. Whoever attains this rank has attained the final and extreme happiness. He is the one who does not mind being separated from his beloved in this world, nor does he regret the enjoyments which he misses in it. He is the
15 one who regards his body, fortune, and all the goods of this world (which we have enumerated and placed among the kinds of happiness related to his body or external to it) as a burden upon him in all but the necessary needs of his body to which he is attached and from which he cannot be set free until his Creator so wills. He is the one who longs to associate with his kindred and to meet
20 the good spirits and the chosen angels who are akin to him. He is the one who does nothing but that which God wants him to do, who chooses only that which brings him near to Him, who does not disobey Him by following any of his whims or base desires,
[86] / who is not deceived by the deceits of nature, who does not pay attention to anything that hinders him from his happiness, who is not grieved at the loss of a beloved, and who does not regret his failure to attain a desire. But this last rank is one in which people
5 differ greatly. I mean that those who attain it fall into numerous and divergent classes.

Aristotle's statement on the grades of happiness

These two ranks are those which the philosopher [Aristotle] discussed in his work entitled *The Virtues of the Soul*,[13] and of which he chose the second one. I shall cite his very words, which have been translated into Arabic. He said: "The first of the ranks of virtues which are called happiness is that in which man directs his will

10 and efforts towards his interests in the sensible world including
those things pertaining to the soul and to the body and those
states of the soul which are closely attached to them and associated with them. In this case, man's conduct in the sensible states
does not go beyond the moderation which is appropriate to
these states. This is a condition in which man may be affected
15 by desires and passions, but only to a moderate, not excessive,
degree—a degree rather nearer to what ought to be than to
what ought not to be. For, although one in this condition comes
in contact with the sensible things and deals with them, he
follows the right conduct which keeps to the mean in virtue and
does not transgress the judgment of reason."

"Then comes the second rank in which man directs his will
20 and efforts to the best improvement of his soul and body without,
at the same time, being affected by any of the desires or passions
[87] or / caring for any of the sensible possessions except inasmuch
as he is drawn to them by necessity. Then the rank of man rises
gradually in this kind of virtue, for the grades and ranks in such
virtues are many in number, some being higher than others.
This is due to the differences among people: first, in natural
5 dispositions; second, in habits; third, in their ranks and their
shares of science, knowledge, and understanding; fourth, in
their aspirations; and fifth, in their desires and concerns, and,
some say also, in their fortunes."

"From the extreme end of this rank—I mean this kind of
virtue—one steps into the purely divine virtue. This is the rank
10 which is not accompanied by any longing for something that
is to come, or looking back to something that is on its way, or
bidding farewell to a past, or any expectation of what is remote,
or any wish to keep what is near, or any fear or alarm from a
particular state or attachment to it, or any desire for any human
fortune or even for the fortunes of the soul or for any necessary
bodily need, physical faculty, or faculty of the soul. [In this rank,]
15 the intellectual part [of man] rather operates in the uppermost
ranks of virtues, i.e., it gives its full attention to divine matters,
strives for them, and attempts them without seeking any return.
I mean that its attention, striving, and attempt are all precisely
for the sake of the very essence of these matters. This rank is
enhanced in people according to their aspirations, their desire, the

value of their striving and attempt, the strength of their nature,
[88] and the firmness of their confidence, / and depending upon the
readiness of those who have attained this level of virtue, in the
conditions which we have enumerated, to follow the example
of the First Cause and to imitate Him and His activities."

"The last rank in virtue is that in which the activities of man
5   are all divine. Such activities are absolute goods; and when
an activity is an absolute good, it is not performed by its doer
for the sake of anything other than the activity itself. For the
absolute good is an end sought for its own sake. In other words,
it is the object which is itself desired and aimed at for its own sake.
And that which is an end, especially if it is a supremely excellent
end, does not exist for anything other than itself. Thus, when all
10 the activities of man become divine, they will all proceed from
his inner and true self, which is his divine reason and his real
essence. The various vicissitudes of his bodily nature will disappear, be shed, and pass away, through the various accidents
that occur to the two beastly souls as well as the accidents of
the imagination, which itself originates from these two souls and
15 from the vicissitudes of the sensible soul. Then he will cease to have
any will or aspiration independent of his activity, for the sake of
which he does whatever he may do. On the contrary, he will
undertake his activity without any will or aspiration except for
the activity itself, i.e., his aim in his activity is nothing but the
activity itself. This is the way of the divine activity."

"This state is the last rank of the virtues, the rank in which
man's actions come to resemble those of the First Principle,
the Creator of all (mighty and exalted is He!). I mean that he
20 gets to the point where he ceases to seek, by what he does, any
[89] fortune, or reward, or return, or increase, / but where his activity
itself is his aim, i.e., where he does not act for the sake of any
other thing besides the very essence of the activity and his own
essence, or [in other words] he does not perform anything for
any reason other than for this activity itself and for his essence
itself. His very essence is the divine intellect itself. So does God
5   (exalted is He!) act for His own sake and not for anything outside
Himself. Man's activity in this state becomes, as we have said, an
absolute good and absolute wisdom. He initiates it only for the
sake of bringing it out and not for any other end which he seeks

thereby. So also the characteristic activity of God (mighty and
exalted is He!) is not primarily intended for the sake of something
outside Himself. I mean, it is not performed for the sake of the
10 government of the world of which we are a part. For if this were
the case, then His actions would have been performed and would
be performed and accomplished in the light of the things that
are outside [Himself], for their management and the management of their conditions, and because of His interest in them.
In this way, the things which are outside [Himself] would become
reasons and causes for His actions. But this is both disgraceful
and unbecoming, and God is highly exalted above it. The care
15 that He (mighty and exalted is He!) takes of the things which
are outside [Himself] and the activity with which He manages
and supports them come both as a secondary purpose. He does not
do this for the sake of the things themselves but, again, for the
sake of His own Self. For His Self is superior on its own account,
and not on account of that over which it is superior or of anything
else whatsoever."

[90]   /"Such is the way of man when he attains the extreme end
of the capacity to imitate the Creator (mighty and exalted is
He!). The actions which he performs become primarily for the
sake of his own essence, which is the divine intellect, and for
the action itself. Whenever he performs an action by which
5 he supports and benefits others, he does not do so, primarily,
for the sake of those others. What he performs for others he rather
does for a secondary purpose, while the primary purpose of his
activity is his own self and the activity itself, i.e., the virtue and
the good themselves. For such activity is a virtue and a good,
and is done for the sake of the activity itself, not for securing
benefit, or preventing harm, or taking pride, or seeking authori-
10 ty, or coveting honor. This is the object of philosophy and the
culmination of happiness. However, man cannot attain this
state until he loses all his will in regard to the outside world and
all the accidents that affect the soul, and until his thoughts arising
from these accidents die away and he is filled with a divine flame
and a divine aspiration. He can thus be filled only when
he becomes absolutely free from what is physical and is
15 totally purified from it. Then he will be filled with a divine
knowledge and a divine desire and will become certain of the

divine things, as a result of what becomes established in himself, i.e., in his very essence, which is reason, in the same way as the first propositions, which are called the primary intellectual sciences, had been established in it. But, in this case, reason's conception and its vision and ascertainment of divine things take place in a manner which is nobler, finer, more pronounced, more
20 manifest to it and more evident than [that of] the first propositions which are called the primary intellectual sciences."

These are the words of this philosopher [Aristotle], which I have quoted exactly. They come from the translation of abu-
[91] 'Uthmān / al-Dimashqi,[14] who is a man well-versed in both languages, namely Greek and Arabic, and whose translation has won the approval of all those who have studied these two languages. At the same time, he has tried hard to reproduce the Greek words and their meanings in Arabic words and meanings
5 without any difference in expression or substance. Whoever refers to this work, i.e., the one called *The Virtues of the Soul*, will read these words as I have quoted them.

Wisdom is the way to complete happiness

These ranks, through which the completely happy man progresses, cannot be achieved until he has acquired a sound knowledge of all the parts of philosophy and mastered them gradually in the order which we set forth in our work entitled *The*
10 *Order of the 'Happinesses'*. Whoever thinks that he can attain them by any other method or any other plan has judged falsely and deviated very far from the truth. Let him remember at this point the great error into which some people fell when they believed that they could attain virtue by impeding and neglecting the cognitive faculty, by disregarding the investigation which is proper to reason, and by being satisfied with deeds that are
15 neither civic nor in accordance with the demands of discernment and reason. Some have called these people the practical and the toiling.[15] This is why we have arranged this work to come after the former one, in order that from both of them one may perceive the final happiness, which is sought through consummate wisdom, and so that the soul may be educated for it and made ready to receive it by what has been called a cleansing and a purification from

physical things and bodily desires. And this is why I have also called this work *The Book on Purification.*

[92]   /In his work called *Ethics*, Aristotle said: Neither the young nor those who have the nature of the young will derive much benefit from this work. And he added: I do not mean by the young here those who are young in age, for age is of no significance in this respect. What I mean is the conduct which is
5   pursued by the people of passion and sensual pleasure.¹⁶ As for me [Miskawayh], I say that I have not mentioned this last grade of happiness in the hope that the young may attain it, but only in order that they may hear of it and that they may know that here is a grade of wisdom which is attained only by its own people who occupy the highest rank. [I have mentioned it also] so that every one who studies this work may seek the first grade of happiness through the cultivation of the character which I have
10   described. In case he succeeds afterwards and is aided by a strong desire, a full eagerness, and all that we have cited and reported from the philosopher [Aristotle], let him tread up the steps of philosophy and endeavor to climb them, and God (mighty and exalted is He!) will help him and lead him to success. If one attains the end of this happiness and abandons, together with his coarse body, the lower world, and keeps only his
15   fine soul which he has taken care to purify and cleanse from physical impurities for his sublime future life, he will have succeeded and prepared himself spiritually to meet his Creator (mighty and exalted is He!). He will have become free from any longing or any desire for those faculties which had hindered him from his happiness, for he will have been cleansed and freed from them and rid himself of any wish or care for them. He will have purified his self to prepare it to be in the vicinity of the Lord of the universe and to receive His favors and the overflowing of
20   His light for which he had not been formerly prepared and to whose gifts he had not been receptive. In this stage, he will get the blessing which was promised to the God-fearing and the righteous—and to which we have alluded many times earlier— in the words of God (mighty and exalted is He!): "No soul knoweth what delight of the eyes is hidden in reserve for them," ¹⁷ and in the saying of the Prophet (may the prayer and peace of
[93] God be upon Him!): "There, there is what an eye / has never seen,

nor an ear ever heard, nor ever occurred to the heart of man."

Having discussed, in summary form, these two stages of the extreme happiness, it has become sufficiently clear that one of them comes with respect to us first, while the other comes second, and that it is impossible to attain the second without

5 passing through the first. We should now go back to where we started, namely, to the first grade of the final happiness, and we should complete our discussion of it as well as of character, which lies at the basis of this work, leaving the explanation of the second grade to another occasion. So we say: He who attends to some of the faculties which we have cited to the exclusion of the others, or who attempts to improve them at a certain time only and at no

10 other, cannot achieve happiness. Such would be the condition of a person in the management of his home if he attended to some parts of it, or if he did so at a certain time only, for he would not be a [true] home manager. The same would apply in the case of the manager of a city if he gave all his attention to a single group or at a single time only, for he would not, by any means, deserve the title of chief. Aristotle used an analogy wherein he said that the appearance of only one swallow does not prove

15 the coming of spring, nor does one mild day bring the tidings of its arrival.[18] The seeker of happiness should, therefore, strive for the life that is delightful to him and so be pleased by it always, for this life is one and is delightful in itself, and this is why we have said that he should always desire it and keep firmly attached to it forever.

As the types of life, being distinguished by the three ends

20 towards which men aim, are three in number (I mean the life of pleasure, the life of honor, and the life of wisdom) and the life of wisdom is the noblest and the most complete, and as the virtues of the soul are many in number, it is necessary that man's superiority

[94] and nobility be the result of the most superior / and the noblest of these virtues. Thus, the life of the virtuous happy men is a life which is delightful in itself because all their deeds are voluntary and deserve praise. Each one takes pleasure in what is dear to him; the just man delights in justice and the wise man in wisdom. The good deeds and the ends that are attainable through the virtues are delightful and lovable. For happiness is the most

5 delightful of all things.[19]

Aristotle said: Divine happiness—even though it is as noble
as we have stated and even though its life is more delightful
and noble than any other life—is still in need of other external
kinds of happiness in order that it may be manifested
through them; otherwise, it will remain hidden and invisible.
In such a case, its possessor will be like a good man who is
10   asleep and whose action is not brought to light, and who, consequently, will not differ from any other man. This is in accord
with our description of this type of happiness earlier in this
work.

The pleasure of this happiness is a genuine pleasure

He, then, who knows the reality of this happiness and who
is capable of expressing his activity through it is the one who
enjoys it, who experiences a pleasure which is real, unadul-
terated, and unembellished with falsehood, and who passes
15   beyond love to rapture and ecstasy. In this condition, he
refuses to allow the high ruling power in him to be subject to
the ruling power of his belly and lower organs and does not let
the noblest part of him serve the basest part. By the pleasure
embellished with falsehood, I mean those pleasures which we
share with the irrational animals, for those pleasures are sensual.
They last for a short time, and the senses get tired of them soon.
Whenever they last a long time, they become disagreeable to the
20   senses and may even turn painful. And just as the senses have a
[95] distinct accidental pleasure, so also / reason has a distinct essential
pleasure. The difference is that the pleasure of reason is essential,
while that of the senses is accidental. How can one, therefore,
who does not know real pleasure, delight in it, and how is it
possible for him, who does not know essential authority, ever to
yearn for it? This is why we have discussed it at an early stage and
have evoked the desire for it by speaking of it again and again.
This is also why we have said that whoever does not know the
5   absolute good and the complete virtue and has not learned
practical wisdom, i.e., the preference for the best, the practice
of it, and persistence in it—such a person cannot be keen about
it or find comfort in it. How can such a person derive pleasure
and enjoyment out of those goods which we have indicated

and discussed?

The wise men of old had a parable which they used to quote
10   and inscribe in their temples (which were their places of worship
and prayer). It goes as follows: The sovereign entrusted with
this world says: Here is good, there is evil, and there is what
is neither good nor evil. Whoever has a true knowledge of these
three will be delivered from me and will escape safely, but he
who does not know them I will kill in the most terrible way,
for I will not inflict on him a swift death by which he will be
released from me, but will kill him little by little. He who
15   considers this parable and reflects on it will understand from it
all that we have stated above.

The happy man's attitude towards misfortunes

You should know that so long as the happy man, whose
condition we have described, is living under this celestial sphere
revolving with its stars, its degrees, and its harbingers of good
and of bad fortune, he is subject to the same disasters, calamities,
and the various kinds of tribulations and misfortunes which
befall others. But he is not frightened by them, nor does he suffer
[96]   /as much hardship as others in bearing them. For he is not apt
to be quickly affected by them through the habit of terror and
fright, nor is he subject to the effect of troubles and griefs caused
by accidental conditions. In case he is afflicted with any of
these pains, the affliction will be only to an extent that will
not remove him from happiness to its opposite or ever draw
5   him outside of the realm of happiness in any way. Never
will he be so drawn, even though he may be smitten by
all the misfortunes of Job (may the peace of God be upon
him!) or many times their number. The reason is that he finds
himself able to abide by the requirements of courage and endurance in the face of what frightens those who are weak in character.
Thus, he is pleased, first with himself, and then because of the good
reports that are spread about him. He sees that the murderer
10   who boasts of cleverness, or the wrestler who craves for victory,
endures great distress, such as dismemberment and the abandonment of desires within his reach, for the sake of the victory and
the wide reputation which he might gain. He deems that there is

more reason and justification for him to exercise endurance, for his object is nobler and his reputation among the virtuous is greater, wider, and more honored, and because he achieves
15 inward happiness and then becomes a model for others.

Aristotle said: Some of the effects of ill-luck are slight and easy to endure. If they befall a person and he endures them, this will not be an indication of his high-mindedness and strong determination. He who is not happy and has not practiced this
20 noble art of the refinement of character will be greatly moved and, when misfortunes befall him, he will find himself in one of two conditions: either going through excessive agitation and intense suffer-
[97] ing / which reach the point where one feels pity and compassion for him, or following the example of the happy men and listening to their admonitions, in which case he will show endurance and tranquility but will be inwardly afraid and his conscience will be in pain. For, just as the paralysed limbs go to the left when moved to the right, so also go the movements of the souls
5 of the wicked. These souls move away from the good towards which they are urged. I mean that if they follow the example of the temperate and practice their actions, their souls will move in a direction opposite to that towards which they urge it; and if they follow the example of the brave and the just, they will also be in the same condition.[20]

The happy man's condition after death

An indication, from Aristotle's discussions, that he believed in the immortality of the soul and in the other world is the one
10 which he takes up in the *Book on Ethics* and which goes as follows:–
Said he: We have concluded that happiness is a fixed, unalterable thing. We also recognize that man is subject to many changes and various coincidences, since it is possible for the person who leads the most pleasant life to be afflicted with great misfortunes, as is said symbolically of Priam.[21] Now, nobody would
15 consider a person happy who suffers such misfortunes and dies as a result. On the basis of the same reasoning, no one should be called happy so long as he is still alive, but we should rather wait until the end of his life before we can judge whether he was happy or not. It follows, therefore, that man becomes

happy only when he is dead; but this is an abominable thing to say since we have maintained that happiness is an activity.[22]

20 Aristotle added: There is here also a doubtful point. One might
[98] /think that good and evil befall the dead man inasmuch as they befall the living man without his being aware of them; for example: honor, disgrace, and the success or hardship of children and children's children. This may arouse a certain confusion, for it is possible for one who lives happily all his life until old

5 age, and who dies in the same condition, to have such changes occur to his children in the sense that some are virtuous and lead good lives, while others prove to be the opposite. It is evident that there may be variation and difference of every kind between parents and children. Now, it would be odd if, on account of changes in others, the dead man were to become happy at one

10 time and unhappy at another. Still, it would also be odd if the conditions of children did not, at any time, affect their parents.[23] But we must return to the point in doubt.

The doubt which Aristotle raised for himself here is the doubt of those who believe that man passes after his death through various states and that he is by necessity variously affected by the conditions of his children and of his children's children

15 depending upon the character of their lives. Would that I knew what we should say of a man who dies happy but is then overtaken by the misfortunes of some of his children and the bad conduct of his descendants which are contrary to his own conduct while alive! It would be hideous if this affected his happiness, but it would be equally hideous if it did not do so in any way.

[99] / Then Aristotle resolved these doubts by saying in substance the following: Man's conduct should be laudable. For he chooses, in all that occurs to him, the best of deeds: practicing endurance at one time, seeking, at another, the better and the

5 still better, and disposing of his fortune if he has a large one, or showing good fortitude if he has none—all of this in order that he may be happy in all situations and in no way departing from happiness. If very bad luck befalls a happy man, it will make his life happier because he will bear it well and exercise good patience in the face of hardships and tribulations. Should he not do so, it would trouble and disturb his happiness and cause

10 him such grief and sorrow as would prevent him from performing

many deeds. The good which is shown by happy men in these conditions is brighter and fairer than in other conditions. It is so if the happy man endures easily great and grave misfortunes, not through insensibility and lack of understanding but because of manliness and greatness of soul.[24] Aristotle said:

15 If activities are, as we have said, the basis of life, then no happy man can become miserable, for he does not act disgracefully at any time. This being the case, the happy man always feels blessed even if he suffers the misfortunes that befell Priam. Never is he miserable, or rapidly changeable. For he does not lose

20 happiness easily, or as a result of slight afflictions, or even because of many grave ones. Nor indeed is he happy if he suffers these things for a short period, but only if he succeeds in achieving good things over a long time.[25]

[100]   /Then, a little further, he added: As for the condition of man after death, to say that the afflictions which befall all his children and friends do not, in any way, affect him would be to state something which is absolutely inadmissible and which is contrary to what all men believe. As the accidents which

5 happen to these people are many and different, and as some of these accidents pass from them to the dead man and affect him more than do others, to try to divide them into particulars would lead us to no end. But if we were to speak in general and by way of outline, it would suffice us to say as follows: As some of the afflictions which befall the dead man before his death are hard to endure and damaging to his life, while others are

10 easily endured, so would be the case, as far as he is concerned, with what befalls his children and friends. Every one of the accidents which happen to people when they are alive differs from what happens to them after their death more than any example can show. It seems likely that if any of these things penetrate to the dead—be they good or bad—they must be some-

15 thing small and trifling which does not make the unhappy man happy, nor deprive the happy man of his happiness. This is how Aristotle resolved the doubt which he brought out.[26]

The pleasure of happiness is active, essential, and complete [27]

Having stated that happiness is the most pleasurable, the

best, the most excellent, and the most genuine thing, we ought
now to explain more completely than we did before the pleasur-
20 able aspect of it. So we say: – Pleasure is of two kinds: the one
[101] is passive and the other active. Passive pleasure / is like the
pleasure of females, while active pleasure resembles the pleasure
of males. Thus, passive pleasure is the one which we share with
the irrational animals, for it is accompanied by passions and
the love of revenge, which are the agitations of the two beastly
souls. The other pleasure, which is the active one, is characteristic
5 of the rational animal. Not being material or subject to its own
agitations, it is thus complete and essential, whereas the former
is incomplete and accidental. By essential and accidental, I
mean that sensual pleasures which accompany passions pass
rapidly and end quickly: they change to non-pleasures and even
10 turn to pains, or become detestable, horrid, and repulsive. These
are the contraries and opposites of pleasure. Essential pleasure,
on the other hand, does not become at any other time non-
pleasant. It does not change its condition, but remains always
constant. If such is the case, then our judgment that the pleasure
of the happy man is essential and not accidental, intellectual
and not sensual, active and not passive, divine and not beastly,
is correct and evident.
15   For this reason, the philosophers have said that pleasure, when
genuine, leads the body from deficiency to completion and from
illness to health. Similarly, it brings the soul from ignorance to
knowledge and from vice to virtue. However, there is here a
secret which the learner should come to know. It is that the
inclination of our nature to sensual pleasure is very strong and
20 our desire for it very troublesome, and that habit does not add
much to the strength of this nature because of the strength and
[102] the desire which are born in us from the beginning. / Thus,
when the sensual pleasure is vile, and when one's nature
becomes excessively inclined to it and strongly moved by it,
one comes to look upon all that is bad in it as good, to
consider all that is difficult in it as easy, and to fail to see what
is faulty or disgraceful until he is enlightened by wisdom.
5   The case of the fine intellectual pleasure is, however, quite
the opposite, for one's natural disposition dislikes it, so that,
when one turns to it with his knowledge and judgment, he

needs both patience and training. But upon reflection and practice, he will discover its beauty and splendor and will attain a condition opposite to the one in which he was in [the world of] sense. From this, it has become clear that man is in need, at the beginning of his life, first of his parents' guidance, then of the
10   divine law and the right religion to reform him and set him straight, and then to consummate wisdom to assume his direction to the end of his life.

The relation of happiness to generosity has also become clear, for we have shown that happiness is an active pleasure, and the pleasure of the one who acts consists always in giving, while
15   that of the one who is acted upon consists always in taking. And the pleasure of the happy man is obtained only when he brings forth his virtues and demonstrates his wisdom and sets it in its proper places. For, as the accomplished writer is pleased by demonstrating his writing—as is also true of the clever mason, the fine jeweler, the proficient musician and, in general, of every clever and excellent artisan who is pleased by demonstrating
20   his excellence in his art—so, also, the possessor of happiness is indeed pleased to demonstrate his virtues and to diffuse them
[103] / among those who recognize and deserve them. This is exactly the meaning and reality of generosity, with this provision: that to be generous in the highest and most honored things is better and nobler than to be so in the lowest and meanest of them. The first sort of generosity, though noble and high in rank, is affected contrarily to the other sort, though this other is insignifi-
5   cant and trifling. For the fortune of the owner of money and of all external possessions decreases with spending and is impaired by giving and his treasures vanish by dissipation, whereas the fortune of the possessor of complete happiness does not decrease because of spending, but increases, and his treasures do not vanish by dissipation, but rather multiply. The one fortune is exposed to many dangers on the part of enemies, thieves, and other trespassers, while the other is guarded from every danger, and evil men and enemies can find no way to it by any method
10   or means.

Happiness is loftier than any praise

The pleasure of the happy man has thus become clear: How it comes to be, whence it begins, and whereto it leads; and what is the nature of the real and essential pleasure. It has also become clear that this pleasure is eternal, complete, and divine, and that its opposite, which is essential misery, has the opposite and contrary attributes. I mean that its pleasures are all acciden-
15 tal, that they change to what is contrary to their nature and thus become painful or detestable, that they are not divine but satanic, and finally that they are not praiseworthy but reprehensible. It remains to examine whether happiness is to be praised, for Aristotle said that the most excellent things are not praised because they are too excellent and exalted to be praised. Said
[104] he: / We ascribe happiness to the deserving and good people, but we do not find any man who praises happiness itself in the same way as he praises justice. On the contrary, he exalts and honors it as something divine. Superior to praise are God and
5 the good, for all other goods are ·praised by being related to God (exalted is He!) and to the good. Praise belongs to virtue and its exercise. There ended Aristotle's discussion of this point, but further on he said: God (exalted is He!) is too high and noble to be praised. Instead, He is glorified, and we glorify Him greatly (exalted is He!). And because happiness and the happy are divine, everything else is done for its sake. Therefore, it is
10 also glorified. Consequently, happiness should not be praised, for it is higher than all praise, but should be, rather, glorified in itself, and all other things should be praised on its account and in accordance with their share of it.[28]
This is the end of the third discourse of the work entitled *The Refinement of Character* and also *The Purification of the Soul*.

FOURTH DISCOURSE

JUSTICE

/FOURTH DISCOURSE[1]

False virtues and real virtues

We have said earlier that happiness is demonstrated in such activities of man as justice, courage, temperance, and the other virtues which come under these genera and which we have enumerated and defined. But these activities may be performed by one who is neither happy nor virtuous. For some people may act like

5 the just, the courageous, or the temperate and yet may not themselves be just, or courageous, or temperate. For instance, those who deny themselves the pleasures of eating, drinking, and the like in which other people indulge, either because they hope for more than what they are getting at the time or because they do not know these pleasures and have never experienced them—such as the villagers who live far from the cities and the shepherds

10 in the wilderness and the summits of mountains—or because they are satisfied with what they find and are getting, or because they lack the desire and are imperfect in their constitution, or because they are afraid of enjoying them and of suffering an adversity on account of them, or [finally] because they have been forbidden to partake of them—all of those people act like the temperate, but are not truly temperate. For to be called truly temperate, one must fulfill the definition of temperance which

15 we have previously stated and must choose temperance for its own sake and not for any other purpose. He must prefer it because it is a virtue, and then satisfy each of his desires according to

[106] his need, / in the right way, at the right time, and in the right condition.[3]

The same is true of the man who acts like the courageous,

95

but is not himself courageous. For he who goes to war and exposes himself to frightful dangers for the sake of some things which 5 may be secured with money, or for one or more innumerable desires—such a man acts like the courageous, but the nature of his action is one of greed rather than of the virtue which is called courage. And whoever is bolder and more undaunted by dangers in this case must necessarily be greedier and more insatiable rather than more courageous. This is because he risks his noble 10 soul and endures great adversities for the sake of money or what can be gotten with money.

We have observed how crafty people act like the temperate and the courageous, and yet are as far from every virtue as one can be. They abstain from all desires, endure the punishments of the ruler, suffer to be whipped with lashes, to have the members of their bodies cut off and to receive incurable wounds, and 15 reach the extreme of endurance even in such tortures as crucifixion, the gouging of eyes, the amputation of arms and legs, and various sorts of mutilation—all for the sake of acquiring a name and a reputation among people who resemble them in poor discrimination and lack of virtue.

One may also act like the courageous because he fears the reproach of his kinsmen, or the punishment of his ruler, or the loss 20 of his prestige, or the like. Another may do the same if he happens [107] to triumph frequently over / his opponents; so he ventures, trusting in what he has become accustomed to and ignorant of the workings of chance. Lovers may also act like the courageous; they run the risk of terrible dangers in seeking their beloved, or in being impelled by immorality, or in their eagerness to enjoy the sight of the beloved—not, as do the truly courageous, in seeking virtue 5 or in preferring a commendable death to a wicked life.

As for the courage of the lion, the elephant, and their like among animals, it resembles courage, but it is not real courage. For these animals are confident in their strength and its superiority over that of others, so that, when they attack, they do so, not by the nature of courage but by a sense of complete strength and power and of self-confidence in victory. Those 10 of them that are beasts of prey are well-equipped with weapons which other animals lack. They are like an armed person attacking one who is unarmed. This is not courage, since it is not

accompanied by that choice which the courageous person takes. Such a person is more afraid of the disgraceful act than he is of death itself, and it is for this reason that he prefers a
15 commendable death to a disgraceful life. However, the courageous man does not find any pleasure at the start of his undertakings— for these are harmful to him—but rather in their consequences. These consequences last all during his life and even after his death, especially if he defends his religion, his true beliefs in the unity of God (mighty and exalted is He!), and the Law which represents God's guidance and his just way, in which lie
20 mankind's interests in this world and in the next. For if such a man thinks of the brevity of his life and realizes that he is in-
[108] evitably bound to die after a few days, / and if he also loves what is good and keeps to the true belief, he will undoubtedly defend his religion and prevent the enemy from abusing his women and conquering his city. He will refuse to flee and will know that the coward, in choosing to run away, only attempts to spare something which is ultimately doomed to perish and pass
5 away, even though this may be delayed for a limited number of days, and that in this altogether short life the coward is de- tested and insulted and his life is troubled by humiliation and various sorts of disgrace. This is how the courageous man conducts himself with respect to the faculties of his soul—I mean in his resist- ance to his passions or in his submission to them. His conduct here is exactly the same as his conduct in the former case.[4]

Hear the words of the most eminent *Imām* [5] (may the peace of
10 God be upon him!) which proceed from real courage, for he said to his companions: "O ye people! If you are not killed, you are anyhow bound to die. By Him—in Whose hands rests the soul of Ibn-abi-Ṭālib—a thousand strokes of the sword on one's head is indeed preferable to a death in bed." [6] Whoever knows the definition of courage will see clearly that all [the kinds of behavior] which we have enumerated are not included in it, although they resemble it in appearance. For not
15 every one who risks dangers, or fears disgrace, is courageous. He who is not fearful of losing his honor, or of the abuse of his wom- enfolk, or at the occurence of tremors, earthquakes, thunderbolts, or incapacitating diseases, or when he loses his brethren and friends, or while in the midst of a stormy sea or raging waves—he

who is not afraid in such circumstances would be more appropri-
20   ately described as either mad or impudent rather than as courageous. The same is true of the man who takes risks in times of
[109] safety and tranquility, / such as by jumping from a high roof,
or climbing a difficult ascent, or attempting to wade through
deep water without knowing how to swim, or attacking an angry
camel or an unruly ox or an unbroken horse, without any necessity
calling for such actions but merely in pretentious display of courage
and in imitation of the courageous. To call such a person boast-
5   ful and foolish would be more appropriate than calling him
courageous. As for the one who strangles himself from fear of
poverty or humiliation, or who kills himself with poison and the
like because of a wrong which is coming to him, he would more
fittingly be characterized by cowardice than by courage. For
whatever boldness he shows is of the nature of the former and not
10   of the latter. The courageous man endures admirably the misfortunes which befall him and performs deeds which, as we explained before, are worthy of that state. For this reason, he should
be honored, and [on his part] he should be sparing of himself.
And it befits the ruler particularly and the guardian of religion
and of government to be proud of such a man, to exalt his position,
to enhance his importance, and to distinguish him from all
those whom we have described as trying to act like him.
15   From all that we have already stated, it becomes evident
that the courageous man is he who disdains hardships for the
sake of what is good, and who endures dangers and scorns what the
masses deem serious, even death itself, for the sake of choosing
the best. He does not mourn anything for which no one is responsible or become agitated by any misfortunes which befall
him. When he is angry, his anger is in the right measure, directed at
20   the right person, and at the right time; and so also is his revenge.
For the philosophers have said that the man who does not
[110] take his revenge / withers, but when he takes his revenge, he
regains his vigor. Revenge is laudable when it fulfills the requirements of courage; otherwise, it becomes reprehensible.
Tradition has preserved for us many tales of persons who defied
powerful rulers and sought revenge from them only to ruin
5   themselves without hurting the rulers. The same consequence
befalls the man who defies a strong rival or an inveterate

foe whom he cannot match. His attempt to avenge himself against him turns out badly for him and adds to his disgrace and incapacity. Thus, the requirements of courage and temperance are fulfilled only in the case of the wise man who uses every means in its proper place and in accordance with the prescription of reason. Consequently, every courageous and temperate man
10 is wise, and every wise man is courageous and temperate.

The case is exactly the same when one acts like the liberal, but is not himself liberal. For he who spends his money for his pleasures, or in order to gain fame, or to show off, or to win the favor of the ruler, or to ward off a harm from himself, his womenfolk, or his children; or he who gives it away to those who do not deserve it (such as wicked people, entertainers, and
15 buffoons); or he who uses it with the expectation of getting more through trade or gainful business—all of these act like the liberal, but are not themselves liberal. Some of them are induced to spend their money by greed, and others by boastfulness and hypocrisy; some do it for the sake of getting more money and of gaining by it, and others by way of dissipation and in ignorance of the value of money. The last type of spending occurs mostly
20 in the case of heirs and those whose acquisition [of money] has been without toil and who thus do not realize its difficulty. For money is hard to acquire, but easy to spend. Philosophers have likened this [rule] to [what happens when] a man raises a
[111] heavy burden to the summit of / a mountain and then pushes it downwards; to ascend with it and carry it up is difficult, but to send it down from there is easy.

Money is necessary for living, and it is useful in bringing wisdom and virtue to light. Whoever tries to earn it in the right
5 way will find it difficult to earn, for the fair gains are few and their ways are not many for the just and liberal man. As for the man who is neither good nor liberal, he does not care how he acquires money or how it gets to him. Consequently, there are many liberal and virtuous men whose share of it is small and whom we find blaming luck and complaining of it. Their opposites, however, because
10 they acquire money by treacherous means and do not care how they attain it, are found rich in it, lavish in their expenditures, grateful for their good fortune, and envied and regarded with a jealous eye by the masses. But when the rational man sees him-

self free from blame and his honor untarnished by evil, and finds
that he has not defiled himself by any shameful gain or sought
such gain by treachery, theft, or injustice to those who are of
15   his own class or below, and sees also that he has avoided its
disgraceful and dishonorable ways—such as pandering, deceit,
selling base commodities to kings, inducing them to give their
money away through cunning and craftiness, helping them in their
immoralities, praising what is vile to satisfy their desires, and
similar means including calumny, slander, backbiting and the
various iniquities which are committed by those who go after
20   money in the wrong way through various forms of fraud and
injustice—when the rational man sees himself in this light, he
is pleased with himself, finds in the tranquility and the praise
which he wins a substitute for money, and does not blame his
luck, or hate the vicissitudes of fortune, or envy those who have
acquired money by other than fair means. This is how people
acquire money and how they spend it.[7]

[112]   /*Real justice*

The same is also true of the man who acts like the just,
but who is not himself just. For when he acts justly in certain
matters, through hypocrisy in order to obtain thereby honor,
money, or any other desire, or for any other purpose such as
those which we have enumerated before, he is not just, but only
5   acts like the just for the sake of the object which he pursues. His
act must be thus ascribed to his purpose, for, as we have already
stated and explained, it is only in accordance with this purpose
that he performs that act. The truly just man is he who harmonizes
all his faculties, activities, and states in such a way that none
exceeds the others. He then proceeds to pursue the same end
in the transactions and the honors which are external to him, desiring in all of this the virtue of justice itself and not any other object.
10   He can achieve this only if he possesses a certain moral disposition
of the soul out of which, and in accordance with which, all his
activities come forth. And justice, being a mean between extremes and a disposition by which one is able to restore both
excess and deficiency to a mean, becomes the most perfect of
virtues and the one which is nearest to unity. By this I mean

that to unity belongs the highest honor and the most eminent rank, and that any multiplicity which is not regulated by the meaning of its own unification is devoid of subsistence or stability. Excess and deficiency, multiplicity and paucity—these are detrimental to things whenever there does not exist a relation between them which preserves their equilibrium in some way. For equilibrium is what restores to them the shadow of unity and its meaning, and invests them with its dignity. It removes from them the vices of multiplicity and discrepancy, and of that confusion which cannot be limited or controlled by equality, the substitute of unity in all multiplicities.

[113] /*Justice through the preservation of equality or the other proportions*

The etymology of the word [equality] indicates to you its meaning. For counterbalance ['idl] in loads, equilibrium [i'tidāl] in weights, and justice ['adl] in actions are all derived from the meaning of equality [musāwāh].[8] Equality is the noblest of the proportions treated in the art of music and other arts. Thus, it is not divisible and does not fall into genera. In its [basic] meaning, it is unity or a shadow of unity. When we cannot find that equality which is true sameness within multiplicity, we resort to the aforesaid proportions which can be resolved into it and are really derived from it. We are then obliged to say: "The relation of this to that is as the relation of this [other] is to that [other]." Thus, proportion exists only between four terms, or three in which the middle one is repeated and which thus also become four terms. The first kind of proportion is called discrete, the second continuous. As an example of the first, we take the first four [terms] and say: "A is to B as C is to D." To give an example of the second, we take B as common and say: "A is to B as B is to C." This kind of proportion is found in three forms: the numerical, the geometrical, and the proportion of harmony. All of this is shown and explained in the compendium which we wrote on the science of arithmetic.[9] The other proportions go back to it, and it is for this reason that the ancients honored it and derived by it the five noble sciences.

As the proportion of equality is rare—being comparable to unity—we have recourse to the maintenance of the other propor-

[114] tions in the many cases in which it is involved, / since these proportions are based upon it and do not depart from it. So we say: – Justice which is external to us is exercised in three areas: first, the division of money and honors; second, the division of voluntary transactions such as selling, buying, and exchange; and third, the divi-
5 sion of things in which injustice and violation of rights have been committed.[10] Justice in matters which fall in the first division takes the form of a discrete proportion which exists between four terms, i.e., wherein the relation of the first to the second is as the relation of the third to the fourth. For example, we say: "This man is to this honor or to this money as any one in the same rank is to the same share [of honor or money]; therefore, this
10 share must be kept for him and delivered to him."[11]

On the other hand, in matters which fall in the second division—i.e., transactions—justice takes the form sometimes of a discrete, and sometimes of a continuous, proportion. For instance, we say: "This clothier is to that shoemaker as this clothing is to that shoe." Then, again, there is nothing which
15 prevents us from saying: "The clothier is to the shoemaker as the shoemaker is to the carpenter," or: "The clothing is to the shoe as the shoe is to the chair." From these two examples, it becomes clear to you that the former [or discrete] proportion occurs in depth only, while the latter [or continuous] proportion occurs in both breadth and depth. I mean that the former occurs between the two universals and the two particulars which is more like depth, while the latter occurs in breadth between the
20 two sets of particulars and may also occur between the two universals and the two particulars.

As for the justice which is exercised where injustices and oppressive acts have taken place, it is nearer to the geometrical proportion. For when a certain relation exists between one man
[115] / and another, and the former annuls it by doing injustice or harm to the latter, justice requires that he receive a similar harm so that the relationship between them may be restored. The business of the just man is then to bring equality to the things which are unequal. For example: If a line is divided into two
5 unequal parts, he takes from the longer and adds to the shorter, so as to secure equality in the line and to remove from it the attributes of paucity and multiplicity and of excess and deficiency.

The same is true of lightness and heaviness and all other similar matters. But the just man should be aware of the nature of the mean in order to be able to restore both extremes to it. For instance, both gain and loss are extremes in the sphere of transactions, one
10 being an excess and the other a deficiency. Thus, if one takes less than he should, he is on the side of deficiency, and if he takes more, he goes over to the side of excess.[12]

In all these cases, it is the Law which establishes intermediateness and equilibrium. As men are civic by nature and cannot live without cooperation—some having to serve others and
15 some taking from, or giving to, others—they seek proportionate compensation. Thus, when the shoemaker takes from the carpenter the latter's product and gives him his own, the exchange between them is a barter if the two articles are equal in value. But there is nothing which prevents the product of the one from being superior in value to that of the other. In this case, money is what sets things aright and establishes equality between
20 them.[13] Money, then, is just and intermediate, but it is mute. The rational man uses it and regulates with it all that takes place in transactions so that they may be carried on in a straightforward and orderly manner and in a right and just proportion. That is why when money, which is a mute establisher of justice, fails to settle the differences between two opponents, we have recourse to a ruler who is an articulate [14] establisher of justice.

[116] /The three laws

Aristotle said that money is a just law (nāmūs). Law in his language denotes administration, management, and the like.[15] In his work known as Nicomachea,[16] he said: The highest law is from God (blessed and exalted is He!), the ruler is a second law
5 on His behalf, and money is a third law. The law of God (exalted is He!), i.e., the [Religious] Law, is the model for all the other laws. The ruler, who is second, imitates it and money is a third imitator. Different objects are valued in terms of different prices in order to make partnerships and transactions possible and to show how receipt and payment may be carrried on. Thus, money is the equalizer of things that differ, adding to some and taking
10 away from others until equilibrium is established between them

so that business may be carried on fairly, as between, for example, the farmer and the carpenter. This is civic justice. By civic justice cities have flourished, and by civic injustice they have been destroyed.[17] There is nothing to prevent a small labor from being equal to a considerable labor [of another kind]. For instance, the engineer does little supervision and labor, 15 but his supervision is worth a considerable amount of labor on the part of people who toil under him and carry out his plans. The same is true of the commander of an army. His management and supervision are slight, but they equal many labors on the part of those who fight under his command and perform the heavy and gross work. The unjust man annuls equality and, according to Aristotle, he is of three different grades. The most unjust man is he who does not accept the Law and refuses 20 to abide by it; the second in the order of injustice is he who does not accept, in his transactions and all his affairs, the decision of the just ruler; and the third is he who does not earn money, but usurps it, giving himself more than what is his due and others less than what is due to them.

[117]   /Aristotle said further: He who abides by the Law acts according to the nature of equality and gains both the good and happiness through the various ways of justice. For the Law, being from God (mighty and exalted is He!), commands men to perform praiseworthy deeds and does not prescribe anything but the good and whatever leads to happiness. It also prohibits all kinds of bodily 5 wickedness and prescribes courage, the preservation of order, and perseverance in struggle. It prescribes temperance and forbids profligacy as well as slander, insults, or foul language. In short, it prescribes all virtues and forbids all vices. Thus, the just man exercises justice towards himself as well as towards his fellow citizens, while the unjust man exercises injustice towards 10 himself, his friends, and all his fellow citizens.[18]

Aristotle added: Justice is not a part of virtue, but the whole of virtue; nor is injustice, which is its opposite, a part of vice, but the whole of vice.[19] Some kinds of injustice are apparent and done voluntarily such as what takes place in selling, buying, securities, loans, and borrowings; some are hidden but also done voluntarily 15 such as theft, profligacy, pandering, the slaves' deceit, and the giving of false testimony; and some are oppressive for the sake of domina-

tion such as torture by stocks, fetters, shackles, and sticks (?)[20]. The just *imām*, who rules according to equality, abolishes these kinds of injustice and acts as the deputy [*yakhluf*] of the Custodian of the
20   Law[21] in preserving equality and in refusing to assign more goods to himself than to others. Hence the tradition that says: "The Caliphate (*al-Khilāfah*) purifies a man."[22] Said Aristotle: The
[118] common people think that the rank of the *Imāmah*, / which is the Caliphate, belongs to those who are of noble heritage and descent; others qualify for it those who possess a large fortune. Rational men, however, deem it to be the prerogative of the wise and virtuous, for only wisdom and virtue bestow real authority and sovereignty, and it is they that have placed the first and the sec-
5   ond in their proper rank and [conferred upon them] their virtue.

Causes of harm

     The causes of all harm fall into four different kinds: first, passion resulting in baseness; second, wickedness resulting in injustice; third, error resulting in grief; fourth, misfortune resulting in anxiety which includes humiliation and grief. As for passion,
10 it causes a person to harm others without being himself in favor of the harm or delighting in it, but merely in order to attain the object of his desire. He may even be pained on account of it and may loathe it, yet the power of passion impels him to commit it. The wicked man, on the other hand, performs the harm deliberately because he likes it and takes pleasure in it, such as, for instance, the one who approaches the ruler and induces him to discontinue a favor of which he himself gets
15 nothing, simply because he takes pleasure in the misfortune which befalls others. As for error, its author does not intend to cause injury to others, nor does he like it or delight in it, but he aims at a certain act and this leads to another. He is grieved and distressed on account of the error which he happens to commit. [Finally,] misfortune is not due to the person who causes it, nor does he deliberately have any share in it; he falls rather
[119] into it as a result of some outside cause / such as, for instance, when a person's unruly mount hits and kills one of his friends, or when he shoots his arrow towards a prey but hits his child. Such a person should be called unfortunate; he should

be pitied and excused rather than blamed or punished. But if
an intoxicated, or furious, or jealous person performs a bad
5 action, he deserves both blame and punishment because he is
responsible for causing it. For the intoxicated man has, by his
own choice, done away with his reason, and the men of anger and
jealousy have chosen to be led by these two faculties whenever
these are agitated in them.[23]

The divisions of justice. First is what is due to God

Resuming our discussion of justice, we say: Aristotle divided
justice into three categories. The first is what people perform
10 towards God, the Lord of the universe. It consists in one conducting himself towards the Creator (mighty and exalted is
He!) in the right way, according to his obligations to Him, and
in the measure of his capacity. For, since justice consists indeed
in giving to the right person what ought to be given in the right
way, it would be inconceivable that men should not owe God
(exalted is He!), who granted us all these immense goods, an
15 obligation which they should fulfill. The second is what people
perform, one towards another, such as the payment of what
is due to others, the honoring of chiefs, the discharge of trusts,
and fairness in transactions. The third is the discharge of obligations towards ancestors, such as the payment of their debts,
the execution of their wills, and the like. This is what Aristotle
said.

Although what he said concerning the duties towards God
20 (mighty and exalted is He!) is clear, to substantiate it we shall
state on the subject what is fitting at this point. It is as follows:
[120] As justice / manifests itself in receipt and payment and in the
various honors which we have mentioned, it is necessary that, in
return for the gifts and the innumerable favors which reach us from
the Creator (mighty and exalted is He!), He should have on us a
claim that must be fulfilled. For whoever is given a certain good,
no matter how slight it may be, and does not see the necessity
5 of repaying it in some way is an unjust man. What would he be,
then, if, after being given a great deal and after receiving constantly, he paid absolutely nothing in return? Moreover, the
effort of man to repay should be commensurate with the favor

which he receives. For instance: If a just king safeguards roads, spreads justice, expands construction, protects womenfolk, defends property, prevents acts of injustice, and insures to people their chosen interests and ways of life, he thereby gives every one of his subjects a benefit which is his individually—although the good is done universally to all—and he deserves that every one of them repay him in some way. He who fails to fulfill this obligation is unjust, since he receives the favor of the king, but does not offer him anything in return. The subjects' repayment to their virtuous king takes, in effect, the form of sincere prayers [for him], widespread praise of [his] good deeds, honest gratitude, exercise of obedience, abstention from opposition either secretly or openly, true love, fulfillment of his [the king's?] life in the measure of one's capacity, and pursuit of his example in the management of one's home, household, children, and kindred. For the king stands in the same relation to his city and subjects as the head of a family stands to his home and family. Whoever does not repay that beneficence with this obedience and love does wrong and acts unjustly. Such wrongdoing and injustice become more abominable and disgraceful when they are shown in return for plentiful favors. For injustice, though disgraceful in itself, is of many different grades, and the return for any favor should be in accordance with its rank and standing, in the measure of its usefulness and benefit, / and in relation to its quantity. If, then, the favors are many in number and high in standing, what kind of a man is he who does not observe any obligation in return for them or does not feel that they should be repaid with obedience, or gratitude, or sincere love, or honest endeavor?

If this [repayment of favors on our part] to our kings and chiefs is an undeniably good act and an avowed duty, how much truer is it that we should have towards the King of kings—from whom we receive every day, or rather every twinkling of the eye, the various uncounted and innumerable forms of His beneficence pouring forth on our bodies and souls—obligations which we should perform and endeavor to fulfill? Would we be ignorant of the first favor which He bestowed upon us—i.e., that of bringing us into existence—and of the successive favors which followed and which pertain to the formation of our bodies, concerning which

10   the author of the two works *Anatomy* and *The Uses of the Organs*[24]
filled about one thousand pages without covering even a part of the
essence of the subject? Or would we forget His favor in granting
us our souls, in equipping them with an endless number of faculties and aptitudes, in supplying them with reason's emanation,
light, splendor, and blessings, and in entitling us to the eternal
15   kingdom and the everlasting bliss? No! By my life! Only cattle
would be ignorant of such favors. As for man, his observance of
his conditions at all times forces him to know about them.

Although the Creator (exalted is He!) is beyond the need of
our assistance and efforts, it is disgracefully absurd and abomi-
nably unjust not to observe any obligation towards Him nor to
20   offer Him, in return for these benefits and favors, what would
remove from us the mark of injustice and of failure to fulfill
the stipulation of justice. But, in the discussion of this question,
Aristotle did not specify the kind of worship which we should
observe towards our Creator (mighty and exalted is He!). He
[122]   said, however, what can be rendered / as follows: "People have
different views with respect to what men should perform towards
their Creator (exalted is His rank!). Some think that it should
take the form of prayers, fasting, the service of temples and places
of worship, and the offering of sacrifices. Others are content with
the confession of His Godship, the acknowledgment of His beneficence, and the glorification of Him in the measure of their
5   capacity. Still others try to win His favor by doing good, first
to their own souls, in purifying them and tending them well,
and then to the deserving ones among their own people, in
giving them comfort and helping them with wisdom and good
counsel. Some believe that to set one's mind constantly on the
divine, to look for the means by which man can add to his knowledge of God (mighty and exalted is He!) until his knowledge
of Him and of the reality of His unity becomes complete, and to
10   direct one's efforts towards Him—that this is man's obligation
towards his Creator. Others believe that men's duty towards
God (mighty and exalted is He!) does not follow one single way,
and is not one definite thing which all people should fulfill in the
same fashion, but that it differs in accordance with the different
classes of people and their ranks in knowledge." These are
Aristotle's words as translated into Arabic.

15   As for the later philosophers, they hold that the worship of God (mighty and exalted is He!) is of three kinds. The first consists of what is due to Him on the part of bodies, such as prayer, fasting, and seeking the noble stations in order to commune silently with Him (mighty and exalted is He!). The second consists of what is due to Him on the part of souls, such as true beliefs (for example, the knowledge of the unity of God and of the praise and glorification that are due to Him), reflection upon

20   what He has poured forth on the world through His generosity and wisdom, and the further cultivation of this knowledge. The third consists of what is due to Him when people associate with one another in cities, that is, in transactions, common farming, marriages, the discharge of trusts, the mutual

[123]   tendering of advice / and assistance in various ways, and also in waging holy war against the enemies, protecting womenfolk, and defending property. They [the later philosophers] said that these kinds of worship are the ways that lead to God (exalted is He!) and constitute His creatures' obligations to Him. Others said: The worship of God consists of three things: true belief,

5   right speech, and good action. Action is divided into the bodily, such as fasting and prayer, and the non-bodily, such as transactions and holy war. Further, transactions are divided into exchanges, marriages, and ways of mutual assistance.

        Though these kinds [of worship] are few and limited in number, they fall into many kinds and innumerable divisions. And, as a result of them, man acquires a variety of stations and

10   positions with God (mighty and exalted is He!). The first station is that of the men of certitude and is the one to which the philosophers and eminent scholars belong. The second station is that of the men of good deed, and to it belong those who act in accordance with what they know, i.e., such as we have described in this work regarding virtues and their application. The third station is that of the righteous; it is the rank of the reformers, who are the true deputies of God (mighty and exalted is He!) in the

15   improvement of peoples and countries. The fourth station is that of the victors, and to it belong those who are sincere in love. It is the climax of the rank of union [with God]; no creature can attain any position or station beyond it. Man achieves happiness in these positions if he has acquired four qualities:

first, eagerness and vigor; second, true sciences and ascertained knowledge; third, shame of ignorance and deficiency of mental
20 alertness which are due to neglect; and fourth, [persistence in the practice of] these virtues and continued progress in them in the measure of one's capacity. These, then, are the causes of attachment [to God].

[124]   / There are also separations from God (mighty and exalted is He!) and falls which are known as curses. The first of these is the fall for which one deserves avoidance by others and then their contempt; the second is the fall for which one deserves seclusion followed by disdain; the third is the fall for which one deserves expulsion followed by loathing; and the fourth is the
5 fall for which one deserves disgrace followed by hatred. Man is miserable if he has acquired four attributes: first, laziness and idleness resulting in the loss of one's time and the passing away of one's life without any human benefit; second, stupidity and ignorance caused by failure to investigate and to exercise one's soul with the teachings which we have enumerated in our work,
10 *The Order of the 'Happinesses'*; third, impudence resulting from the neglect of the soul when it pursues passions and the failure to restrain it from committing sins and evil deeds; and fourth, abandon caused by the persistent performance of disgraceful deeds and the failure to repent. In the Law, these four attributes are given the four following names: the first is deviation [*zaygh*], the second is submission [to passion] [*rayn*], the third is veil
15 [*ghishāwah*], and the fourth is seal [*khatm*].²⁵ To each of these miseries, there is a special remedy which we shall mention when we treat the diseases of the soul in order that it may regain its health, God permitting (exalted is He!). The philosophers and the custodians of the Law do not disagree on the things which we have just mentioned; the only difference is in the terms and in the indications according to the [different] terminologies.

Justice is intermediateness; it encompasses all the virtues

20   Plato said: When man acquires justice, every part of his soul illuminates every other part, for all the soul's virtues are
[125] achieved / in it. Then the soul rises and performs its particular activity in the best possible way. This is the happy man's nearest

approach to God (sanctified is His name!). He said [further]:
Justice is intermediateness, not in the same way as the other virtues
which have been mentioned, for it is in the middle while injustice
is at both extremes.[26] Injustice is at the two extremes, because
it is both an excess and a deficiency. It is in the nature of injustice
to seek the one and the other: to seek an excess of whatever is
useful, and a deficiency of whatever is harmful. Thus, the unjust
man practices both excess and deficiency. Of the useful, he seeks
excess for himself and deficiency for others, while in the case of
the harmful, he acts in a contrary and opposite manner, seeking
deficiency for himself and excess for others.[27] The virtues which
we have said are means between the vices are also limits and ends.
For the mean in this case is an end to the vices on all sides and
is at the extreme distance from all of them, so that, when one
goes beyond the mean's distance, one approaches, as we have
already said, one of the vices.

It now becomes clear, from all that we have already said,
that all virtues are types of equilibrium and that justice is a name
which embraces them and includes them all. It becomes evident
also that as the Law determines the voluntary acts which are
the result of reflection and of divine ordinance, it follows that
the one who adheres to it in his transactions is just, while the
one who violates it is unjust. This is why we have said that justice
is a designation for the one who adheres to the Law. But we have
also said that justice is a disposition of the soul from which this
virtue proceeds. If you consider this disposition, you will see
clearly that its possessor inevitably obeys / the Law voluntarily
and does not oppose it in any way. For if he observes the proportionate relations which we have mentioned, because they are
[forms of] equality, and if he chooses them after careful consideration and on the basis of his own preference and desire,
then he will necessarily have to act in accordance with the
Law and refrain from violating it.

Equality cannot be established between less than two, but
it also involves a transaction common to both of them. This is
the third thing; but this third may be two things as we have
said, in which case the proportionate relations would be, as
we have explained, between four things.

Justice is a disposition of the soul

You should realize that this disposition of the soul is neither activity, nor knowledge, nor capacity. It is not activity because
10 we have shown that activity may take place without a disposition of the soul—such as in the case of the man who performs the acts of justice but is not himself just, or the man who performs the acts of courage but is not himself courageous. It is also different from capacity and from knowledge because each of these is the same for two opposite things, i.e., the knowledge of two opposites is the same, and so also is the capacity for two opposites. On the other hand, the disposition which is favorable to one of two opposites is different from that which is favorable to the other.
15 For instance, the disposition of the courageous is different from that of the coward, and, similarly, the disposition of temperance is different from that of intemperance, and that of justice from that of injustice.[28]

Moreover, both justice and liberality are exercised in the area of transactions, receipt, and payment, with the difference that justice occurs in the acquisition of money according to the
[127] conditions / which we have already stated, whereas liberality occurs in the spending of money in accordance with the conditions which we have also mentioned. It is in the nature of the man who acquires to take and, thus, he is more like the passive, while it is in the nature of the man who spends to give and, thus, he is more like the active. For this reason, people's love of the liberal
5 is stronger than their love of the just, although the good order of the world is based more on justice than on liberality. The characteristic of virtue resides in doing what is good, not in avoiding what is evil; and the characteristic of the people's love and praise resides in the spending of money rather than in its acquisition. The liberal man does not honor money; he gathers it not for its own sake, but in order to spend it in the ways which earn for him love and praise. It is characteristic of him that he neither accumulates a large fortune, since he spends lavishly,
10 nor becomes poor, since he acquires money in the right way and never slackens in earning it. As it is by money that he achieves the virtue of liberality, he neither wastes or dissipates it, nor is stingy and miserly with it. Thus, every liberal man is just,

but not every just man is liberal.

A difficult question

At this point, we face a difficult question which the philoso-
15 phers asked themselves and to which they gave a convincing
answer. But another, and more convincing, answer can be given
to it, and we must state both of these. The question is this: One
may entertain some doubt and say that if justice is a voluntary
act which the just man performs and by which he aims at acquiring virtue for himself and praise from others, it follows
necessarily that injustice is a voluntary act which is performed
20 by the unjust man and by which he aims at acquiring vice for
himself and blame from others. But it is mean and improper
to think of the intelligent man as intending, after reflection and
by choice, to injure himself.
[128] /They [the philosophers] then answered and resolved this
doubt by saying that he who commits an act which brings
him harm or pain would be acting unjustly towards his own
self and hurting it while believing that he is benefiting it,
because of his bad choice and his failure to follow the counsel
of reason in what he does. An example of this is the jealous man
5 who may bring evil upon his own self, not because he prefers to
injure it, but because he thinks that he is giving it immediate
benefit in being delivered from the harm which calumny causes
him. This is the answer of these people [the philosophers].[29]
The other answer is the following: As man possesses many
faculties by virtue of the aggregate of which he is called an individ-
10 ual man, it would not be inadmissible that different actions
should issue from him in accordance with these different faculties.
What would be inadmissible is that the one and simple thing,
possessing only a single faculty, should perform with this faculty
various actions which differ, not in accordance with the different
organs nor in the measure of its own different dispositions, but
only by virtue of that single faculty itself. This, indeed, would be
inadmissible and improper. But it has become evident from
man's condition that he possesses many faculties and performs
15 with each faculty acts which contradict one another. I mean
that he who is prone to anger chooses, when he flares up, acts

which contradict those which he performs when he is calm and
composed. The same is true of the man who is possessed by an
agitated passion, or of the one who is seized with elation and rapture. It is in the nature of such people to use the noble reason as
their servant and to refrain from consulting it. That is why you find
that when the intelligent man is freed from those states and turns
20   from anger to satisfaction and from intoxication to sobriety,
he is surprised at himself and says: "Would that I knew how I
chose those vile acts!" He then repents; and this is because the
faculty that was agitated within him, in order that it might take its
full course, induced him to commit an act which he, in that state,
[129]   considered to be fitting and proper. But as soon as / he is free from
it and consults his reason, he perceives the vileness and the corruption of that act.

The faculties of man, which prompt him to the various passions
and to the love of honors which he does not deserve, are many
in number. Accordingly, his acts are also many. Thus, if a man
5   becomes accustomed to leading a virtuous life and does not perform
any act except after following the counsel of pure reason and
observing the right Law, his acts will all be well-ordered, not
varying among one another nor violating the rules of justice.
By justice, I mean the equality which we have discussed earlier.
This is why we have said that the happy man is the one who has
the chance in his childhood to become familiar with the Law, to
give himself up to it and to get accustomed to follow all its com-
10   mands, and who, when he attains the stage in which he is able to
comprehend motives and causes, takes up the study of philosophy
and finds it in agreement with what had become ingrained in him
by habit, with the result that his judgment becomes firm, his
insight penetrating, and his determination effective.

Another difficult question

Now, there is an even more difficult question. Benevolence
is a very laudable thing, but it does not come under justice.
15   For justice is, as we have stated, an equality, while benevolence is an excess. But we have [also] concluded that justice
embraces all the virtues, that there is nothing beyond it, and that,
on the contrary, any excess over it, just as any deficiency from it,

should be considered as blameworthy, in order that the dignity of the mean, which we have already described in respect to the various aspects of character, may be realized by justice. The answer to this question is that benevolence is [a sort of] circumspection on the part of the benevolent person in exercising justice
20 so as to ensure that he has not missed any of its conditions. Moreover, the condition of the mean between two extremes of
[130] character is not always the same. For an excess in liberality /
—if it does not reach the stage of dissipation—is better than a deficiency in it and more like the observance of its conditions, becoming in this way a form of circumspection and of resoluteness in the practice of this virtue. In the case of temperance, however, a deficiency from the mean is better than an excess over it and more like the observance of the conditions of the mean, thus constituting a greater circumspection in it and a stronger resolute-
5 ness in holding on to it. Yet, there is no benevolence where there is no justice. By this I mean that he who gives his money to those that do not deserve any of it and fails to assist those who deserve it is not called a benevolent man but a waster. He is only bene-volent if he gives to those who deserve all that they deserve, plus some more by way of benevolence. This excess is not the same as the one which we have mentioned under liberality.
10 For that excess is a shift to the extreme which is called dissipation and which is blameworthy. That it is blameworthy may be known from its definition, which is the giving of what is improper to the improper person and in the improper way. Benevolence, then, does not violate the conditions of justice, but is rather circumspect in it. For this reason, it has been said that the benevo-lent man is nobler than the just. It has, then, become clear that benevolence is not something different from justice, but, on the
15 contrary, it is justice plus circumspection in its exercise. It is like an exaggeration which does not divert justice from its mean-ing, for this disposition of the soul is not different from that dispo-sition but is precisely the same.

As for the extremes which are vices—i.e., the excess and the deficiency which we have already discussed—they are all blame-worthy dispositions and different from the laudable ones. It
20 is by the definitions of these things that you seize their meanings and the similarities and the differences among them. Moreover,

[131] the Law prescribes justice / in a universal way and does not go down to particulars. By this I mean that justice, which is equality, occurs sometimes in the realm of quantity, sometimes in the realm of quality, and so on for the rest of the categories. To make this clear: The proportion of water to air, for instance, is not in quantity but in quality, for if it were in quantity, the two substances would have had to be equal in measure. But in that case they
5 would struggle with each other and one of them would reduce the other to its own substance. The same is true of fire and air. Should all these elements reduce one another [in this way], the world would vanish in a short time. But the Creator (sanctified is His name!) has distributed power justly among them. They struggle with one another, but none of them is able to overcome another in totality. It is only that some part of them reduces another part at the extremes, in other words, where their ends
10 meet. But their totalities cannot overcome one another, for their powers are equal and equivalent to the utmost. It is of this kind of justice that he[30] (may peace be upon him!) said: "By justice stand the heavens and the earth." If either of them had surpassed the other by a slight amount of power, it would have been able to reduce and overwhelm it, and the world would have vanished.
15 Praise be to Him who upholds justice. There is no God but He!

While the Law prescribes universal justice, it does not prescribe universal benevolence. It only urges people to practice benevolence, and this in particulars which cannot be specified because they are endless. On the other hand, Law is definitive in [prescribing] universal justice because it is limited and can be specified.

20 It has also become clear, from what we have already stated, that benevolence is exercised in the kind of justice which pertains to man himself—I mean in first dealing with equality between
[132] / himself and others, and in then showing discretion and circumspection in this fair dealing as would constitute benevolence. But, if he is a judge among a community and he himself does not possess any share of what is being judged, he should not practice benevolence; his only duty is that of pure justice and right equalization without either excess or deficiency. Moreover, it has become evident that the disposition from which just

5 acts proceed is called virtue when considered in relation to its possessor, justice when in relation to the person with whom he deals, and an aptitude of the soul when considered in itself. So the first imperative and duty of the intelligent man is to exercise justice with respect to himself. We have explained already how he does this and how he harmonizes his many faculties when some

10 of them agitate him. We have pointed out the genera to which these numerous faculties belong, and the fact that some of them are related to the different passions and others to the seeking of the numerous honors, and that, when they combat and agitate one another, their disturbance produces in man the various kinds of evil and each one of the faculties attracts him to what is suitable to it. Such is the condition of every composite which is made up of many [elements], if they do not have one head to regulate and unify them.

15 Aristotle likened the person who is in such a state to one who is pulled from two directions and who is thus divided between them and split in two, or who is pulled from different directions and is thus cut into pieces according to the directions [from which] and the faculties [by which] he is pulled. There is nothing which can regulate this multiplicity of which man is made up except the one head which has been bestowed on him by nature. By this I mean reason, which distinguishes man from the animals

20 and which is God's deputy in him. Thus, if reason directs all these faculties, they will reach a state of equilibrium and will be freed from the disorganization which is caused by multiplicity. All that we have mentioned with regard to the refinement of character is based on this.

If a person succeeds in achieving that [which we have been describing], namely, in being just towards himself, and if he acquires this virtue, then he has necessarily to be just towards

[133] his friends, his relatives, / his kinsmen, and then towards those who are remote, and, finally, towards all animals. If this be true and manifestly evident, it follows therefrom that the worst of men is he who is unjust, first towards himself, then towards his friends and kinsmen, and finally towards all men and animals. For the knowledge of one of two opposites is the same as the knowledge

5 of the other. Thus, as we have said, the best of men is the just man, and the worst of them is the unjust.

Justice or love? Introduction to the following discourse

There are those who have said that the good order of all existents and the soundness of all their conditions depend upon love.
They have also said that man is forced to acquire this virtue,
i. e., the disposition from which justice in dealings proceeds,
only because he fails to achieve the dignity of love, and that, if
10 those who deal with one another are bound by love, they will
be fair to one another and no disagreement will take place
among them. For a man loves his friend and wishes for him
what he wishes for himself; and no confidence, or cooperation,
or mutual help can take place except among those who love one
another. Thus, if people cooperate and are bound by love, they
will attain all the desirable things and will not fail to secure the
objects of their search, even though these objects may be hard and
difficult. They will then bring forth sound opinions, their minds
15 will collaborate in deducing any right measures which may be
obscure, and they will strengthen themselves in order to gain
all the goods by cooperation. Aristotle was one of those who
supported and confirmed this opinion.

These people [who spoke thus about love] had in view the
virtue of unification which is realized in a collectivity. Indeed, this
is the noblest end for the people of a city. For if the citizens love
one another, they will be in close relation, and each man
will wish for his companion what he wishes for himself. Their
20 numerous capacities will become one, and none of them will
fail to arrive at a sound opinion or a right action. In all that they
attempt to do, they will be like the person who wants to move
[134] a heavy weight by himself and is not able to do so, but if / he is
assisted by others he can then set it in motion. Indeed, the
manager of the city aims, in all his measures, at binding its
people by ties of affection. If he succeeds in attaining this aim
in particular, he will achieve all the goods which will be difficult
for him, or for the citizens, to achieve individually. He will then
overcome his rivals, build up his country, and live happily with
5 his subjects. But this desirable and coveted type of unification can
be accomplished only by means of sound opinions on which sane
minds will be expected to agree, and by means of strong beliefs
which result only from religions directed towards the Face of God

(mighty and exalted is He!). The kinds of love are many in number, but they all ascend to one object.[31] With God's help, we shall state in their regard as much as opportunity affords in what follows this discourse.

10   This is the end of the fourth discourse. To God belong praise and gratitude!

FIFTH DISCOURSE

LOVE AND FRIENDSHIP

/FIFTH DISCOURSE [1]

LOVE AND FRIENDSHIP

Need for cooperation and harmony

We have already spoken of the need which people have for
one another, and it has become clear that every one of them finds
his completion in his friend and that necessity requires that they
should seek one another's assistance. The reason is that men are
born with deficiencies which they have to remedy and, as we
have explained before, there is no way for any single individual
5 among them to become complete by himself. There is, then, a
genuine need and a demanding necessity for a condition in which
diverse persons are brought together and combined so that they
become, by agreement and harmony, as one single person all
of whose [bodily] organs associate in the performance of the single
act which is useful to him.

Love: Its kinds and causes

Love is of various kinds, and has as many corresponding
10 causes. The first of these kinds is that which is established quickly
and dissolves quickly; the second, that which is established quickly
but dissolves slowly; the third, that which is established slowly
but dissolves quickly; and the fourth, that which is established
slowly and dissolves slowly.

Love is divided into these kinds only because the ends at
[136] which men aim / in their desires and conducts are three in number
and join together to form a fourth. They are pleasure, the good,
the useful, and their composite.[2] Since these, then, are the ends
which men seek, it follows inevitably that they are causes of the

123

love of those who help to achieve them and who are means to
5   their attainment. The love which is caused by pleasure is the
kind that is established quickly and dissolves quickly because
pleasure itself, as we have explained already, changes quickly.
The love which is caused by the good is the kind that is established
quickly but dissolves slowly; the love which is caused by the
useful is the kind that is established slowly but dissolves quickly;
and [finally] the love which is caused by their composite — if
this composite includes the good — is the kind that is established
10   slowly and dissolves slowly. All of these kinds of love occur dis-
tinctly among human beings because they involve will and deliberation and lead to requital and reward.

As for what takes place among irrational animals, it should
more appropriately be called affinity. It takes place chiefly
among those animals that are similar. When it comes to objects
that have no souls, such as stones and the like, all that they possess
15   is a natural predisposition to the centers which pertain to them.
There may be also some discordance or similarity among them
according to their temperaments which are formed by their primary elements. These temperaments are many in number. If there are
among them any which are related by a proportion of harmony,
a numerical, or a geometrical proportion, various forms of
similarity occur among them; but if the opposites of these proportions occur, discordance takes place. They also come to possess
20   properties which are fine, strange powers, and which are called
the secrets of the natures [of things]. These occur especially in
the case of the proportions of harmony, which are the noblest
[137]   of proportions after / the relation of equality. These proportions
have their opposites which are explained and clearly demonstrated in the art of arithmetic and later in the art of harmony.
The temperaments which are based on these proportions and the
knowledge of them are hidden from us and difficult to seek,
5   although some people claim to have attained them. The powers
and properties which occur in the temperaments as a result of the
said proportions are not found in the [primary] elements themselves. To discuss them would lead us beyond our object, and
we have mentioned them here only because they resemble the
similarities and the discordances which appear to take place
among animals. They do not resemble those [similarities and

discordances] which take place among men by [the exercise of] will. It is the latter which are the subject of our discussion, and which involve reward and requital.

Friendship and its kinds

10   Friendship is a kind of love, but it denotes something more particular than love. It is affection in its very essence, and it does not take place among a large group, as is the case with love. Passionate love is the excess of love, and is more particular than affection because it takes place between two persons only. It is not motivated by either the useful or that which is composed of the useful and something else, but occurs only in the case of the 15 lover of pleasure to excess or the lover of the good to excess. The former, namely pleasure, is blameworthy; the latter, namely the good, is laudable.[3]

Friendship among the young, and those who have a nature similar to that of the young, is motivated by pleasure. Thus, such people become friends quickly and their friendship is severed also quickly. This may occur among them many times in a short 20 period. Their friendship may endure so long as they are confident of the duration of pleasure and of its return time after time. But when this confidence in the return of pleasure ceases, their friendship [also] ceases immediately and at the [same] time.[4]

Friendship among old people, and those who have a nature [138] similar to that of the old, takes place only / when there is a possibility of benefit: they become friends because of that benefit. Thus, if the benefits are common to them and mostly of long duration, their friendship lasts. But when the bond of benefit which is common to them is severed, and their expectation of it ceases, their affections cease also.[5]

5   Friendship among virtuous people is for the sake of the good and is caused by the good. Since the good is something stable and has an unchangeable essence, the affections of those who are bound by such friendship are lasting and unchangeable.

Divine love

Further, since man is made up of opposite natures, the

result is that the disposition of any one of these natures is different from the disposition of any other, and the pleasure which is
10 agreeable to one nature is different from the pleasure of its opposite. Thus, man does not experience any pleasure that is pure and free from pain. But as he also possesses within him another substance—one that is simple, divine, and not mixed with any of the other natures—he can experience a kind of pleasure which is unlike any of the other pleasures in that it, also, is simple. The love which is caused by this pleasure is the kind that is carried to
15 excess until it becomes a complete and pure passionate love akin to rapture. This is the divine love of which we hear and which some of those who seek to become one with God claim to achieve. It is the one of which Aristotle, quoting Heraclitus,[6] speaks when he says: Things that differ are not akin to one another and they
[139] do not come together in / good harmony. On the other hand, those things which are akin find pleasure in, and long for, one another.[7] So I say that when the simple substances are akin to, and long for, one another, they harmonize, and when they harmonize they become a single thing and admit of no otherness
5 within themselves. For otherness is due to matter only. Things made up of matter, namely, bodies—though they may have a certain longing for harmony—do not, and can not, unite. For they meet at their extremities and on their surfaces, and not in their essences. When they meet in this way, they are bound to separate quickly one from another, since [real] union is impossible in their case and they unite only in the measure of their capacity, i.e., in the meeting of their surfaces.
10   If, then, the divine essence within man is freed from the turbidity which comes to it from contact with nature, and if it is not lured by the various kinds of desires and pursuits of honors, it will long for its like and will perceive, through the eye of its intelligence, the First Pure Good, which is not contaminated with matter, and will hasten towards It. The light of that First Good will pour upon it, and the pleasure which it will experience
15 thereby will be beyond comparison to any other kind of pleasure. Whether it makes use of the bodily nature or not, it will attain the meaning of union which we have described. However, it will be more worthy of this high rank after freeing itself totally from the bodily nature, because it will not achieve complete purity

until it leaves the worldly life. Among the virtues of this divine
love are: that it does not admit of diminution, is not impaired
20   by slander, is not opposed by the sovereign[8], and takes place
among virtuous people only.

[140]   / *Fellowship originates love and is developed by the Law*[9]

As for the kinds of love which are motivated by benefit or
pleasure, they may take place among the wicked as well as among
the virtuous[10]. But with the disappearance of the useful and the
pleasant, these kinds of love dissolve and disappear because they
are accidental.[11] Often they occur when people meet in strange
5   places—such as on a ship or the like—but they cease as soon as
people leave those places. The cause of this love is fellowship
[*uns*], for man is, by nature, inclined to fellowship and not
savage or averse to others. From this word, the name "man"
[*insān*] is derived in the Arabic language. This is evident from
the rules of grammar, and is not as the poet said: "You are called
man because you are forgetful [*nāsi*]". This poet thought that the
10   word "man" was derived from "forgetfulness" [*nisyān*], but this
is a mistake.
You must realize that this fellowship innate in man is the
[value] that we must be eager to keep and to acquire in common
with our fellow men. We must exert our efforts and our capacities
so as not to miss achieving it, because it is the origin of all kinds of
love. It is indeed to help develop this fellowship that both the
Law and good custom have enjoined people to invite one another
15   and to meet in banquets. Possibly the Law made it an obligation
on people to meet five times a day in their mosques and preferred
communal prayer to individual prayer in order that they may
experience this inborn fellowship which is the origin of all love
and which exists in them in potency. In this way, this inborn
fellowship would become actual, and would then be strengthened
20   by the right beliefs which bind them together. Such a daily
meeting is not impossible for the inhabitants of any quarter or
[141]   street. That the Custodian / of the Law (may peace be upon
him!) aimed at what we have just mentioned is shown by the fact
that he made it incumbent upon all the people of the city to
meet together once every week, on a particular day, in a mosque

which is capable of holding them all, so that the inhabitants of
all the quarters and streets may assemble once every week in the
same manner as the members of the home or the household come
5   together every day. He decreed also that the inhabitants of the
city should gather twice a year with the people of the nearby
villages and countryside in a place of worship in the open outside
the city, so that the place will be large enough to hold them all,
and so that they may see one another and renew their common
fellowship and be embraced by the love that binds them together.
Further, he made it incumbent upon all, once in their lifetime,
to come from their countries to meet in the Holy Place at Makkah.
He did not specify a fixed time in their life in order to give them
10   ample opportunity. In this way, the inhabitants of the distant
cities can come together, as do the inhabitants of the same city,
and can achieve the same state of fellowship, love, and community
of good and of happiness as those who are brought together every
year, or every week, or every day. With this innate fellowship,
they meet to seek the goods common [to them], to renew their
devotion to the Law, to glorify God for His guidance, and to
15   rejoice in the right and straight religion which has united them
in piety and obedience to God.

    The *Imām* is the person who guards the observance of this
tradition and the other duties prescribed by the Law so that
they will not change from their [original] conditions. His art is
the same as that of the king, and the ancients did not give this
name to anybody except to the one who guarded religion and
20   took charge of the keeping of its grades, commandments, and
prohibitions. Anyone who neglected this [duty] was called by
them a usurper and was not deemed worthy of the name of king.
For religion is a divine condition which leads men voluntarily
to supreme happiness, and the king is the guardian of this divine
condition and the one that watches the people's observance of
[142]   their obligations. / The wise man and king of Persia, Ardashīr,[12]
said: Religion and kingship are twin brothers, and neither is
complete without the other. Religion is a foundation and kingship
a guardian; anything without a foundation is destroyed, and anything without a guardian is lost. This is why we enjoin the one
who has been set up to guard religion to be alert in his position,
5   to master his art, and to refrain from undertaking his duties in

a leisurely manner, or occupying himself with one of his own pleasures, or seeking honor and victory except in the right way. For, whenever he neglects any of his duties, disorder and weakness are sure to creep in. Then the conditions of religion will be changed, people will find a license [to indulge] in their passions, and there will be many who will help them to do so. The state of
10 happiness will turn to its opposite, disagreement and mutual hate will arise among them, and they will thus be led to dispersion and division. The noble purpose will be lost, the order which the Custodian of the Law sought through [the execution of] the divine prescriptions will be destroyed, and it will become then necessary to renovate the situation, to resume the endeavors, and to look for the true *Imām* and the just king.

The kinds of love differ according to their causes

Coming back to the discussion of the kinds of love and their
15 causes, we say: In all the kinds of love except the divine, if the causes are shared by the lovers and are one and the same, the two loves may be established together and dissolve together, or one of them may endure and the other dissolve.

To give an example: The pleasure shared by a man and a woman is the cause of love between them. The two loves may exist
20 together, since the cause is the same, namely, pleasure; or the one
[143] may cease and the other endure, since / pleasure, as we have already explained, changes and is almost never stable, and thus the cause affecting one of the two lovers may change while that affecting the other may persist. Moreover, there exists between a man and his wife common goods and mixed benefits, which they seek in cooperation. By this I mean the goods external to us, which
5 are the causes of the prosperity of home life. The wife expects these goods from her husband because it is he who earns and procures them; while the husband expects his wife to administer these goods because she is the one who keeps and manages them in order that they may become fruitful and not wasted. When either of them fails, their love changes and complaints begin to arise, and things continue in this way until love either ceases, or remains along with complaints and reproach.
10   What we have said about pleasure applies also to benefit,

when it is shared by people and is the one and identical [cause of love] among them. When we come, however, to the diverse kinds of love whose causes are also diverse, we find them more subject to quick dissolution. An instance of this is when the love of one of two lovers is for the sake of benefit, while that of the other is for the sake of pleasure, as happens among companions, one

15 of whom is a singer and the other a listener. The singer loves the listener for the sake of benefit, while the listener loves the singer for the sake of pleasure.[13] The same also happens to the lover and the beloved when the former finds pleasure in beholding the beloved, while the latter expects benefit. In this kind of love, mutual complaints and accusations of unfairness arise continually. This is because the seeker of pleasure receives it quickly, while the seeker

20 of benefit gets it only after some delay, and matters can hardly become even between the two. Thus, you see the lover complaining of his beloved and accusing him of unfairness, while in

[144] reality he himself is unfair and deserves to be accused / because he wants to get his pleasure of beholding without delay and does not pay attention to the reward which is due to his companion. Reproachful love is of many kinds, but its root lies in what I have stated. Reproach and rebuke may enter even into the love that exists between the chief and the subject, or the rich man and the

5 poor, because of the divergences of the causes, and because each of them expects from the other a reward which he does not get. Their mutual intentions become spoiled, they find each other slow [to give], and they blame each other. This condition ceases when the two parties observe justice, and when each of them is satisfied to get from the other only as much as he has a right to and each of them accepts to treat the other with the justice which lies between them. Slaves, in particular, are not satisfied unless

10 their masters give them more than what they deserve, while the masters find them too slow in the performance of their duties and in [showing] solicitude and goodwill, all of which leads to reproach and bad conscience. This is the reproachful love of which [one] can hardly ever be free unless one follows the stipulation of justice, and seeks the mean in what he deems to be his right and is satisfied with it. But this is difficult.

On the other hand, the mutual love of virtuous people is

15 not motivated by any external pleasure or any benefit, but is

due to their essential similarity, namely, in aiming at what is good and seeking virtue. Thus, when one of them loves another because of this similarity, no difference or dispute takes place between them. They exchange advice and agree to be just and equal in their desire of the good. This equal rendering of advice and desire of the good is what unifies their multiplicity. This is

20 why a friend is defined as another person who is yourself, but is other than you in person,[14] and this is why he is so rarely found. The friendship of the young, the common people, and those who are not wise is unreliable because such people love and befriend for the sake of pleasure and benefit. They do not know the good in reality and their motives are not sound.

[145] / Sovereigns show friendship as if they were being beneficient and charitable to those whom they befriend. They do not, therefore, fall within the definition which we mentioned. Their friendship admits of excess and deficiency, and equality is rarely found among them.

5 The same is true of the love between a father and his child, because this love is of different kinds and its motives are also, as we have said, different. However, though a father's love of his child and a child's love of his father differ in a certain way, there is an essential agreement between them. By essential here I mean that the father feels that his child is he himself, and that he has natu-

10 rally stamped his own human form on the personality of his child and really transmitted his own self to his. It is only proper that he should feel this way since God's planning, through the natural urge which is God's way (mighty and exalted is He!), is what helps man to bring forth his child and makes of him the second cause of the child's existence and of the transmission of his own human form. For this reason, a father loves his child to such an extent that he comes to desire for him all that he desires

15 for himself and strives to educate him and to endow him with all that he himself has missed throughout his life. If he is told: "Your child is superior to you," he will not be pained because he regards him as his very self. And as a man who himself progresses from one state to another, and who rises in virtue one grade after another is not pained—but is rather pleased—if he is told: "You are now better than what you used to be," so also does a father feel if he hears the same thing about his child [i.e., that the

child is better than he]. Moreover, the love of a father is superior
to that of his child in that he is the one who brings him into
existence, who knows him from the time he comes into being,
and who rejoices with expectation while his child is still an em-
bryo. Then as the child is brought up and grows, his father's
[146] /joy in him as well as his expectations for him are strengthened.
He becomes assured that his own form will endure in his child,
even though his material body may vanish. These meanings,
which the men of knowledge can see clearly, appear to the common people as if they lay behind a veil.

   A child's love of his father, on the other hand, falls below
5 this rank because he is the one who is brought into existence and
who knows neither himself nor the one who brought him into
existence until a long time has elapsed, and after he has ascertained
his father through sensation and drawn benefit from him over
a long period. Later he will come to understand his condition
truly, and the honor with which he will treat his parents and the
love which he will show them will depend upon his intelligence
and his insight into the nature of things. This is why God urged
children to take care of their parents, but did not urge parents
to take care of their children. As for love between brothers, it is
10 due to the fact that the cause of their coming into being and of
their descent is one and the same.

   The relation of a king to his subjects should be a paternal
one, while their relation to him should be filial and their relation
one to another fraternal. In this way, authorities will be kept in
conformity with their own genuine conditions. For a king's regard
for his subjects is the same as a father's regard for his children,
15 and so also is his dealing with them. We have already alluded
to this matter and will clarify it further when we discuss the
king's policy in another book. A king's concern for his subjects
should be identical to a father's concern for his children in solicitude, compassion, sympathy, and responsibility. He should follow
the example of the Custodian of the Law (may the peace of God
be upon him!) and, indeed, the example of the Prescriber of the
Law (may His name be exalted!) in tenderness, mercy, the
seeking of the subjects' interests, their protection against mischief,
20 and the preservation of order among them—briefly, in all that
brings good and averts evil. Then he will be loved by his subjects

as children love their solicitous father, and the relation which exists between the latter will exist between his subjects and himself.[15]

[147] / These kinds of love differ in rank in accordance with the magnitude of the benefits [which accrue from them]. Thus, a father should receive a paternal honor, a sovereign a royal honor, and people among themselves a fraternal honor. Each one of these ranks has a merit pertaining to it and a worth which

5 is its due. When this merit is not upheld by justice, it will increase or decrease, corruption will affect it, authorities will change, and things will be reversed. The authority of a king will become that of a usurper and, as a result, the subjects' love will turn into hate. The same will happen to the authorities of those who are

10 inferior to the king; and what was love among good men will become hate among wicked men. Concord will turn into aversion, mutual affection into hypocrisy, and each one will seek what he deems good for himself even though it may be harmful to others. Friendships and the common good will cease to exist. This will lead to anarchy which is the opposite of that order which God has instituted for His creatures, which He prescribed in the Law, and which He enjoined in [the dictates of] consummate wisdom.

The love which is not mixed with agitations nor subject

15 to evils is man's love of his Creator (mighty and exalted is He!). It belongs exclusively and particularly to the man learned in the knowledge of the divine, and is beyond the reach of anyone else except by false pretense. For how can man find the way to love God if he does not know Him, and if he is not aware of the varieties of favor which God pours down upon him and the forms of benefit which God continually grants him in his soul and

20 body—unless, of course, he pictures to himself an idol, presume it to be God (exalted is He above what the falsifiers presume!), and love and worship it ? Indeed, most men are as God said (mighty and exalted is He!): "And most of them believe not in

[148] God, without / associating other deities with Him." [16] By my life! We notice the common people pretending to know and to love, while imagining at the same time a figure or a ghost and worshipping it instead of God. This is far-reaching error. Those who pretend to experience this kind of love towards God are very many in number, but those who genuinely have it are very

5   few, indeed the smallest minority.
         Such a love is tied up with obedience and veneration. A
     man's love of his parents, and the veneration and obedience
     he renders to them, come near to this love [of God], but no other
     kind of love rises to the rank of these two, except the love of
     disciples for the philosophers. This last-mentioned love is in-
     termediate between the first love [that of God] and the second
10   [that of one's parents]. For the first love is beyond any other love,
     its causes are beyond any other cause, and the blessings which
     come from it are beyond comparison with any other blessings.
     The second love approximates it because its cause is the second
     cause of our sensible existence or, in other words, of our bodies
     and our coming into being. As for the third love, namely, [our]
15   love of philosophers, it is nobler and superior to love of parents
     because the philosophers' nobility and rank become reflected
     in our souls, they are the causes of our real existence, and with
     their help we attain perfect happiness. No one is able to repay
     or reward what is due to the first [the philosopher] or to the
     second [the parent], no matter how hard he endeavors and how
     far he goes; nor can one ever fulfill his obligations towards them
     even though he may serve them to his furthest capacity and
20   utmost power.
[149]   / The love of the seeker of philosophy towards the philosopher
     or of the good student towards the virtuous teacher is of the same
     sort and follows the same line as the first love. This is because
     of the great good which the student envisions and attains, the
     sublime hope which cannot be realized except by the philosopher's
     care nor be fulfilled except by his attention, and the fact that he
5   is a spiritual father and a human Lord and his beneficence is a
     divine beneficence. For he brings the student up on complete
     virtue, nurtures him with consummate wisdom, and imbues him
     with the desire for eternal life in the everlasting bliss. And since he
     is the cause of our intellectual existence and the educator of our
     spiritual souls, then, as the soul is superior to the body, [he,] the
     one who bestows upon us the former, should be deemed superior
10   to the one who gives us the latter; and so also is the one education
     superior to the other. It is proper, therefore, that the student's
     love of the teacher of philosophy be pure and similar to the first
     love.[17]

Now, since this love [of the philosopher] is of the same kind as the first love [love of God], and the same is true of obedience, and since the cause of both of these blessings, who exposes us 15 and leads us to them as well as to all other blessings, is the First Cause, who is also the cause of all goods, it follows that our love of Him should be in the highest rank of love and that the same should be true of our obedience to Him and our glorification of Him.

Whoever attains this grade of character should know the ranks of the various kinds of love, and what each person deserves 20 to get from the other so that he will not offer to a foreign chief the honor due to a father, nor to a sovereign that due to a friend, [150] nor / to kinsmen that due to a child, nor to a father that due to a mother. For every one of these and their like is entitled to a kind of honor and a right to repayment which are not appropriate to any other. If one does not discriminate among these obligations, confusion and corruption will affect them and reproaches will take place, but if he discharges to every one his due and his share 5 of love, service, and good counsel, he will be acting justly and his love and the justice manifested in it will obligate his friends and associates to love him in return. The same way should be followed in one's fellowship with one's friends, comrades, and companions; he should observe their rights and render to each one of them what is due to him.

The conduct of the good man and that of the wicked man

Whoever adulterates love or friendship is in a worse position 10 than he who counterfeits silver or gold coins. For the philosopher [Aristotle] stated that adulterated love dissolves quickly and degenerates rapidly just as counterfeited coins are spoiled in a short time. This holds true in all kinds of love. For this reason, the intelligent man, in seeking the good, follows always the same way and adheres to the same method. He performs all his acts 15 for the sake of his own essence and recognizes his good as lying with others as well as within himself. His friend is, as we said, he himself but differs from him only in person. He treats his other comrades and acquaintances as he treats his friends and as if he were striving to get them to attain the ranks of real friends although

this is not possible in the case of all of them. This is the conduct
of the good man towards himself, his chiefs, relatives, children,
20 kinsmen, friends, and sovereign.

[151]   / The wicked man, on the one hand, evades this conduct and
has an aversion to it because of the bad disposition which he has
acquired, his love of idleness, and his failure to exert himself to
gain a knowledge of the good and to discriminate between it,
on the one side, and both evil and that which is deemed good but
is not in reality so, on the other. The deeds of the person who is
5 in such a state of wickedness and of bad disposition are all bad
and his own self is also bad. And whoever has a bad self runs
away from it, for we run away from what is bad. He finds himself
obliged to befriend people who are compatible with him so as to
spend his life with them and thereby distract himself from his
own self and from the agitation and anxiety which he finds in it.
For whenever these wicked people are alone with themselves,
they remember their bad deeds, and opposite powers are
10 roused within them which induce them to commit opposite
evils. Hence, their own selves cause them pain, their souls are
thrown into all kinds of discord, and the powers which lie within
them, namely, those which they have not disciplined by a true
education, pull them in different directions, such as towards
bad pleasures, or the seeking of undeserved honors, or evil passions
which lead them to rapid destruction. When these forces pull
15 them in different directions, they produce many pains within
them, for it is not possible for a person to rejoice and be grieved
at the same time, or to be pleased and angry while in the same
condition, or to be pulled in different directions by a single
movement. Nor can he combine opposites and experience them
all. Thus, his misery induces him to run away from his own self
because it is bad and corrupt, suffers pain, and causes him much
20 trouble. He seeks the society and company of those who resemble
him or are worse than he, and he finds in them, for the time
being, rest and comfort on account of the similarity between
them. But very soon such people prove harmful to him and add to
his confusion and corruption; he suffers because of them and runs
[152] away from them. He has no one / to love him, not even his own
self, nor one to give him good counsel, not even his own soul,
and he gains nothing but repentance nor reverts to anything but

misery.[18]

The good and virtuous man, on the contrary, leads a righteous and lovable life. He loves himself and his deeds and is pleased with himself as others are also pleased with him. Every
5   one likes to establish relations and friendship with him. He is his own friend and the friend of other people. Only the wicked man is opposed to him.

Beneficence and the love resulting from it [19]

He who leads such a life becomes beneficent to others either intentionally or unintentionally, for his acts are pleasing and lovable, and whatever is pleasing and lovable is desired and sought by people. Thus, many welcome him, pay him honor, and follow
10   his example. This is essential beneficence, which lasts and does not cease and which grows rather than diminishes. Accidental beneficence, on the other hand, not being a part of character, nor a conduct constantly pursued, is bound to cease and to be mingled with reproach; and the love which results from it falls among the kinds of reproachful love. This is why the person who performs accidental beneficence is enjoined to cultivate it and is told that to cultivate kindness is more difficult than to initiate it.
15   The love which takes place between the beneficent and the beneficiary admits of excess and deficiency. By this I mean that the beneficient's love of the beneficiary is stronger than the latter's love of the former. Aristotle took as proof of this the fact that the creditor and the bestower of favor are each interested in the debtor and in the one on whom favor is bestowed. They watch
20   the interests of these and seek their well-being. The creditor desires the well-being of the debtor in order to be able to get his
[153]   money back rather than because of / his love of him. I mean that he prays for his well-being, long life, and ample prosperity and satisfaction in order that he may receive what is due to him. The debtor, on the other hand, does not take great interest in the creditor, nor does he pray for him in such fashion.

As for the bestower of favor, he truly and necessarily loves
5   the one on whom he bestows his favor even though he does not expect any benefit from him, for every one who performs a good and laudable act loves what he does, and when this, act is right

it must be loved to the extreme. It is evident, then, that the love of the beneficent man is stronger than that of the beneficiary. The latter, on the other hand, has a stronger and greater desire for the benefit than has the former.

10   Moreover, the love which one gains through beneficence and which he cultivates continually becomes like possessions which one toils hard to acquire. Possessions which are acquired with toil and exertion are loved more strongly and cherished more eagerly [than are others], while he who acquires money without toil will not care for it nor spare it but will spend it in the wrong

15   way, as do heirs and their like. He, however, who acquires it with toil, who travels in search of it, and who encounters hardships in gathering it will inevitably be very eager to keep it and will love it immensely. It is for this reason that the mother's love of her child is stronger that the father's and her longing and rapture are many times greater. Such also is the kind of love with which the poet loves his poetry and admires it more than others do. Similarly,

20   every one who toils in the performance of an act loves that act. Again, the one who is passive does not exert himself as hard as the one who is active. And he who takes is passive, while he who gives is active. Thus, from all these points of view, it becomes clear that the beneficent man loves intensely the recipient of his beneficence.

[154]   / Some people do good for the sake of the good itself; others do it for the sake of good repute; and still others do it out of sheer hypocrisy. It is clear that, of these, the highest in rank is the one who does it for its own sake, i.e., for the sake of the good itself. And whoever is in this rank will not fail to win good repute,

5   lasting praise, and the love of those who have not received his favor, although he does not aim at these things either by act or intent.

Since we made earlier an acceptable judgment which no one can refute, namely, that every man loves his soul, and since this love is necessarily divided into the three kinds which we mentioned, i.e., the love of pleasure, that of the useful, and that

10   of the good, it follows that the person who does not discriminate among these kinds so as to distinguish which of them is superior and which is even more superior will not know how to benefit his soul, which is the object of his love. He will fall into various

sorts of error because of his ignorance of the real good. Thus, it comes about that some people choose for their souls the life of pleasure and others the life of honor and of the useful, because they do not know what is superior to these sorts of life.

15 But he who knows the life of the good and its high rank will undoubtedly choose for his soul the best of lives and the most precious of goods. He will not choose the beastly pleasure or the pleasures that are external to his soul, because all of these are accidental and subject to change and dissolution. Rather he will choose for it the most perfect, the highest, and the greatest of goods, namely, that which belongs to it in essence—I mean that which is not

20 external to it, but which relates to the divine part in him. He who leads such a life and chooses it for his soul benefits the latter, raises it to the highest eminence, and makes it worthy of receiving the divine emanation and the real pleasure which he will never

[155] lose. In such / a state, he will inevitably perform all the other goods and will benefit others by giving money freely and being generous in all that people usually withhold stingily. In all of this, he will allot to his friends more than is within the power of those who lead the other lives, and he will thus come to be honored by everybody and especially by his friends.

The values of friendship

5 Furthermore, we have already shown that man is civic by nature and have explained what is meant by civic. It follows necessarily that man's complete human happiness is realized through his friends; and whoever finds his completion through others cannot possibly attain his full happiness in solitude and seclusion. The happy man, therefore, is he who wins friends and endeavors to distribute goods generously among them in order that he may attain with

10 them what he cannot attain by himself, and so that he may find pleasure in them all the days of his life and they also may find pleasure in him. We have explained the condition of this pleasure and the fact that it is enduring, divine, indissoluble, and unchanging. The number of such happy men among the majority and mass of the people is very small, whereas those who seek the beastly pleasures or the useful are very numerous. But only a few of the former are sufficient; they are like spices in food, or like salt

15   in particular.

Moreover, the first kind of friend which we have described cannot exist in great numbers because such a person is precious and he is loved excessively, for excess in love can take place and be achieved with a single person only. As for good comradeship, generous reception, and the endeavor to pursue with every one the course of real friendship—all of these are practiced for

20   the sake of acquiring virtue and because we have already stated that the good and virtuous man conducts himself in his association with his acquaintances as a friend, although it may not be possible to reach real friendship with them.

[156]   / Aristotle said [20]: A person cannot do without a friend in good fortune as well as in bad fortune, for he is in need of him in both situations. In bad fortune he needs the assistance of friends, and in good fortune he needs companionship as well as people to

5   whom he can be beneficent. And, indeed, even a great king needs people to whom he can accord favors and grant benefits, just as the poor man needs a friend who can accord him favors and bestow benefits upon him. [Furthermore,] Aristotle said: It is for the sake of the virtue of friendship that people participate in common, mix in pleasant company, joke with one another, and meet for exercise, hunting, and banquets.

10   As for Socrates,[21] he spoke in these words: "I am greatly astonished at those who teach their children the tales of kings and the fighting among them, and the stories of wars, hatred, revenge, and rebellion, but who forget the subject of affection, the accounts of concord, and the benefits which all people gain

15   through love and fellowship. For no man can live without affection, even though the world may favor him with all its attractions. Whoever thinks that affection is trivial is himself trivial, and if he believes that it is available and can be achieved with little trouble or attained with ease [he is completely misled], for [he should know] how hard such affection is [to come by], and how difficult it is for one to find a friendship which may be trusted in adversity." He added further: "But I believe and say that to me the value and significance of affection is superior to all the

20   gold of Croesus and the treasures of all the kings; and to all the jewels for which the people of the world vie; and to all that the world contains on land and sea; and to all the cultivated lands,

buildings, commodities, and furniture of which they dispose.
[157] / All of this is not worth the virtue of affection which I have chosen
for myself, for all I have enumerated is of no use to its possessor
when he is tormented by a misfortune befalling his friend. All
the things of this world cannot take the place of a friend whom one
trusts for assistance in an important affair or in winning happiness
in the near or far future. Blessed, therefore, is he who is granted
5   this great favor when he is devoid of authority, and exceedingly
blessed is he who is given it while in authority! For when the
latter takes in hand the affairs of his subjects, and seeks to know
their conditions and to study these affairs thoroughly, he will
find that two ears, two eyes, and one heart are not sufficient.
If he secures trustworthy friends, they will be for him eyes, ears,
and hearts completely, as it were, his own. They will bring his
10   outer limits close to him, enabling him to detect from the nearest
point the farthest and to see the absent in the form of the present.
Where can such a virtue be found except in a sincere friend, and
how can one hope to meet it except with a sympathetic comrade?"

Discrimination in the choice of friends[22]

Now that we know about this great and important blessing,
we should try to find out how to acquire it, where to seek it,
15   and, after obtaining it, how to keep it; otherwise, we may meet
with the same fortune as the proverbial man who, while looking
for a fat sheep, found a swollen one and was deceived by it taking
the swelling to be fat. The poet referred to this when he said:
"God forbid that your perceptive sight
Should discern fat where there is only swelling."
This is especially true since, as we have seen, man, unlike the
20   other animals, affects various attitudes in order to show what
is not true. He gives his money away, though he may be stingy,
so that it may be said that he is generous, and in some situations
[158] he ventures on certain fearful dangers / so that it may be said
that he is courageous. The character of the other animals, on
the other hand, is plain from the start and free from affectation.
Again, the same is true of the person who is ignorant of herbs
and plants. Since they look similar to him he may take one
of them thinking it to be sweet, but upon tasting it he finds it

5 bitter, or thinking it to be edible but it proves to be poisonous. Thus, it is necessary that we should be careful to avoid risks in seeking this great favor lest we involve ourselves in the friendship of the deluders and the deceivers who picture themselves to us as virtuous and good until they trap us in their nets and then devour us as wild beasts devour their victims.

The way to safety from this danger, according to what we learned from Socrates, is to inquire about the conduct of our prospective friend during his childhood towards his parents, brothers, and relatives. If his conduct was good, you can hope that he will be good; otherwise, keep away from him and do not have anything to do with him. Socrates said: Try then to inform yourself about this person's conduct towards the friends he had before you and add this to his conduct towards his brothers and parents. Then follow his behavior to find out whether he is grateful or ungrateful for the favors which he receives. I do not mean by gratefulness the offering of such reward as would actually be beyond his power, but I do mean that he may neglect to cultivate his inclination to show gratitude and thus fail to repay to the extent that lies within his power and capacity. He may also seize the favor that is accorded to him as if it were his right or not trouble himself to express his thanks in words. It is not too much for any one to publicize the favors which are bestowed upon him and to praise the bestower and give him credit for it. There is nothing which thwarts the granting of favors more than / ingratitude; and it is sufficient for you [to consider] the punishments which God has provided for those who are ungrateful of His favors even though He is too exalted to be harmed by ingratitude. [On the contrary,] there is nothing which attracts favor and confirms it as much as thankfulness, and it is sufficient for you [to consider] what God has promised to the grateful although He can dispense with their gratitude. Investigate, therefore, this trait of character in your prospective friend and beware lest you be afflicted with an ingrate who despises the favors of friends and the beneficence of the sovereign.

Consider then his inclination towards relaxation and his dislike of activity which may entail the least hardship. For this trait of character is bad: it results in inclination to pleasures and leads one to fail to fulfill such obligations as are incumbent upon

10 him. Observe definitely his love of gold and silver and whether he belittles their accumulation or is eager to keep them. For many companions affect love of one another and exchange gifts and advice until they come to a dealing among them which involves those two metals; they then growl at one another like dogs and end up with all sorts of enmity.

15 Observe, after this, his love of authority and excess of praise, because he who loves domination, authority, and excessive praise, will not be fair to you in his affection and will not be satisfied to get from you as much as he gives you. Arrogance and self-conceit will cause him to belittle his friends and to try to hold himself above them. But no friendship or bliss can be maintained with such an attitude, and inevitably his relationship with them will turn into enmity, rancor, and much hatred. Note also whether he is one of those who are excited by singing, melodies, and the vari-
20 ous sorts of entertainment and play as well as listening to buffoons
[160] and jesters. If he is such a person, / he will be too busy to help and console his friends and he will do his best to avoid recompensing benefit, or enduring toil, or getting involved in any favor entailing hardship. Consequently, if he is free from these traits, one should keep him and covet his friendship, and be satisfied with one [such friend] if he finds him, for perfection is rare.

5 Moreover, he who has many friends cannot fulfill all his obligations towards them and is forced to overlook some of his duties and to fall short of others. He may go through opposite states in succession. I mean that in helping one friend, he is driven to share his happiness, while in helping another he has to share his grief; he is led to strive with one and be idle with another,
10 and the same is true of many diverse states similar to these.[23]

You must not be led by what I have been urging upon you—i.e., to look for virtue in your prospective friend—to pay close attention to his small defects, thus ending with no one left to you and remaining without a friend. You must rather overlook slight defects from the like of which no human being can be free, and
15 consider the defect that you find in yourself and tolerate its equivalent in others. Beware of the enmity of your friend or of the one whom you have intimately treated as a friend. Heed what the poet says:

"From among your friends a foe might rise.
Too many friends, therefore, avoid.
Most mischief which your path doth cross
Is brought about by food or wine.²⁴

One's duties towards his friend

　　　Thus, when you gain a friend, you should pay much regard
20　to him and do your utmost in looking after him. Do not neglect
to fulfill [even] a slight obligation towards him whenever anything
serious befalls him or any accident happens to him. In times of ease,
[161] you should/meet him with a cheerful face and a generous disposition
and should show him, in your looks and movements, and in your
affability and joy at seeing him, what would make him, day by
day and in every situation, more confident of your affection and
5　more trustful in your absence. When he encounters you, he
should see joy in all the parts of your body in which it can be
expressed; for an intensely warm welcome at the appearance of a
friend cannot be concealed, and the joy of meeting one's like is
something which admits of no doubt. You should act in this
same way towards those whom you know to be the objects of his
care and love, be they friends, children, subordinates, or attendants. You should praise them, but not with such excess as to
carry you to flattery and cause him to loathe you and to perceive
10　your affectation. You can indeed accomplish this if you aim at
the truth in all the praise that you express to him. Follow this
method and be careful lest you neglect it in any way or at any
time. For it will bring sincere love, earn complete confidence,
and win for you the love of strangers and those with whom you
are not acquainted. And just as pigeons, when they become
habituated to our homes and like our company and rove about us,
15　bring us their kindred and their like, so it is with man when he
comes to know us and to associate with us as one who desires
us and delights in our company. He also has the advantage over
irrational animals in that he is able to describe well, to utter
good praise, and to propagate commendable qualities.
　　　Further, you should know that, if the sharing of your good
fortune with a friend is incumbent upon you lest you keep it to
yourself alone or consider any part of it as exclusively your own,

20   the sharing of his bad fortune is even more incumbent upon you
and its impression upon him is much deeper. Then if a calamity
[162] descends upon him or a misfortune affects him, or / ill luck over-
takes him, consider how you can comfort him with your own person
and your money and how you can show him your concern and
solicitude. Do not wait until he asks you either explicitly or im-
plicitly, but know what is in his heart, be quick to [catch] what is
in his soul and share with him the pain of what has befallen him
so that it may be easier for him to bear. Should you attain any
5   degree of power and wealth, let your friends partake fully of it
without any ostentation or arrogance on your part; and should
you observe that any of them shun you or show less attention to
you than usual, try to become more intimate with them, to seek
their company, and to attract them to yourself. For if you disdain
to do this or are seized by any sort of haughtiness or arrogance
towards them, the tie of affection will be broken and its strength
destroyed. And, in addition, you are not secure against the loss
[of that power and wealth], and [should you lose it] you would
10   feel embarrassed [upon meeting] them and would be forced to
break away from them so as not to see them.

Furthermore, you should cultivate these stipulations by
constant practice so that affection may remain unchanged.
This condition is not peculiar to affection alone; rather it applies
to all that pertains to you. I mean that if you do not pay continuous attention to your mount, your clothes, and your house,
15   they will be spoiled and destroyed. The form of your wall and
roof is subject to the same rule; if you are careless or negligent,
you cannot feel safe from their collapse and ruin. This being so,
how can you propose to alienate the person from whom you hope
to derive all good and with whom you expect to share both good
and bad fortune? Moreover, the harm in the first case affects one
of your benefits only. But in the case of your friend, the varieties
of harm which you will suffer as a result of alienating him and
breaking the ties of his affection are many and serious. For he will
turn into an enemy and his benefits to you will become harms.
[163] Thus, you will not be safe from his mischief / and his enmity, while,
at the same time, you will have been deprived of whatever is
desirable and beneficial in him. You will lose all hope of securing
something for which you can never find any substitute, alternative,

or equivalent. But if you observe the conditions of his friendship
and respect his rights and do so constantly, you will avoid all
of these [dangers].

5   Moreover, although it is necessary to avoid bickering with
anybody, you should be especially careful not to bicker with your
friend, for bickering with one's friend eradicates affection, it
being the cause of disagreement, and disagreement the cause of
discord. It is precisely this discord which we have tried to avoid
in favor of its opposite, and whose effects we have condemned.
Instead of it, we have chosen concord, sought and praised it,
and said that God (mighty and exalted is He!) has summoned
[us] to it by [the prescriptions of] the upright Law. I know the
10   type of man who likes bickering and pretends that it kindles his
thought, sharpens his mind, and stirs up his doubts. In the gath-
erings of men of learning and those who deal with the sciences,
he seeks deliberately to bicker with his friend and goes so far as
to use the words of the ignorant and lowly masses in order to add
to his friend's embarrassment and to make evident his inadequacy
and pretense. Yet, he does not act in this way when he is alone
15   with him or during their private discussions, but only [in gath-
erings] where he would be regarded as more penetrating, readier
in argument, ampler in knowledge, and sharper in wit. I cannot
but liken him to the wrongdoers and the despotic possessors of
fortunes and the spendthrifts who follow their example. For such
types of people hold one another in contempt, and each one of
them goes on disparaging the other, deriding his manliness,
looking for his defects, pursuing his faults, and doing his utmost
[164]   /to hurt him. The result is a state of complete enmity accompanied
by slander and the withdrawal of favors and going even as far
as the shedding of blood and all sorts of evils. How, then, can
any love subsist with bickering or how can any concord be
expected through it?

5   Furthermore, if you are learned in a subject or are distinguished by a certain culture, be careful lest you withhold this ac-
complishment from your friend or lest he suspect that you desire
to appropriate it exclusively and to keep it to yourself and away
from him. The men of learning do not look upon one another as
do the men of the world. For the goods of the world are few in
number; thus, when people compete for them, some hurt others

10 and each one diminishes the other's lot. But in knowledge the reverse is true, for one's lot is not diminished by what another takes from him; instead, it grows with spending, thrives on beneficence, and increases by being given and freely imparted. If the possessor of a certain knowledge is stingy with it, it is because of some conditions which characterize him, all of which are bad. His capital of knowledge may be small and he may thus be afraid lest it be exhausted or lest he come across something which he does not
15 know and thus lose his distinction in the eyes of the ignorant; or he may derive some material gain from it and therefore be afraid lest this gain be reduced and his share of it diminished; or he may be envious, and whoever is envious is far from all virtue, loving no one and loved by no one. Indeed, I am acquainted with persons who are not satisfied with being stingy with their own knowledge only, but who extend their stinginess to the knowledge of others. They are extremely displeased and angry with any one who helps
20 students that deserve the benefit of knowledge. How often do they go so far as to take books away from their owners and withhold these books from them! This is a trait of character with which no affection can last; rather, it brings to its possessor enmities that
[165] he cannot foresee and dispels / the hopes of his friends in his friendship.

Moreover, you should not allow your comrades, or your followers who sit in your intimate company, to be too free, nor let any of them say anything which relates to your friend, except in praise, especially if it is about him personally. Do not allow
5 any criticism of anything which pertains to him, let alone any criticism of himself. Let no one who is related to you or associated with you dare to utter such criticism either in earnest or in jest. For how would you allow this regarding your friend when you are his eye, his heart, and his representative among all the people— indeed, when you are his very self? If he hears of [the occurrence of] any of these things I have warned you about, he will not doubt that it has emanated from your own view and desire and he will consequently turn into an enemy and become as averse to you as
10 an opponent. If you yourself discover a defect in him, show him that you go along with it, in a gentle manner rather than rudely, because the tactful doctor may accomplish with a delicate treatment what others do by cutting, amputation, and cautery, or

may even restore the health of his patient by the use of diet without recourse to treatment by medicine. But I do not wish that you overlook what you know about your friend and fail to show that you went along with it, in the manner I have just described.

15 For you will then be disloyal to him and unmindful of what will cause him harm. It is not fair to [leave] a friend to be deceived and abused in the eyes of his antagonists so that they may censure and defame him.

Again, beware of slander and of listening to it. For evil people mix with those who are good under the cloak of counselers and, while pretending to give them good advice, transmit to them in the course of interesting conversations stories about their friends in distorted and falsified form. When [such evil people] become

20 bold enough to tell invented stories, they convey openly [to the good people] what will corrupt their affections and disfigure

[166] their friendships until they come to hate one / another. The ancients composed books on this subject, in which they warned against slander. They likened the slanderer to one who scratches with his nails the solid foundation of a structure until he makes a dent on it, and who then keeps on going further and deeper until he is able to insert a pickax and to destroy the structure at

5 its foundation. They illustrate this with many parables, similar to that of the ox and the lion in the book *Kalīlah wa-Dimnah*.[25]

We must be satisfied with these hints lest we go beyond the design of our work and disregard our principle, namely, brevity combined with [adequacy of] explanation. But even with conciseness and brevity, I do not want to fail to emphasize the importance of this subject and to repeat it to you so that you may know that the ancients would not have written books, related

10 parables, and cited numerous advices in this regard, had they not realized the great benefit which the virtuous who listen to them reap and had they not feared the grave damage to which the ignorant who disregard this matter are exposed. [This subject should be emphasized] also in order that you may understand the parable told about the powerful lions which are killed and destroyed by the weak but cunning fox that gets into their midst; or about the slanderers who find their way to the prudent king

15 and who, in the guise of counselors, succeed in destroying his confidence in his ministers, while these latter are doing their

utmost to give him good advice and striving to consolidate
his power. The slanderers succeed in causing him to become furious
against these ministers, to turn his eyes away from them, and,
instead of loving them and giving them preference even over
his own children, to be unable to endure their sight any more,
and [finally] to inflict upon them torture and death—although
they are neither guilty, nor wrongdoers, nor deserving of anything
but honor and beneficence. If [these parables show] so much
20 damage and mischief that slander can cause those [persons],
how much more damage and mischief will slander cause us
if we are not on our guard against it in the case of our
[167] friends whom / we have chosen [to aid us] against the vicissitudes
of time, whom we have reserved [to help us] in misfortunes, and
whom we have regarded as our very souls and have raised in
esteem and honor?

Virtues are realized only in association

From all that we have already said, the following should be
evident: Friendship and the kinds of love, by which the happiness
of man as a civic being by nature, is achieved, have been subject
5 to differences and to all kinds of corruption, have lost the character
of unity, and have met with dispersion. It has, therefore, become
necessary for us to [try to] preserve friendship and loves and to
toil hard to organize them because of the many imperfections
of our natures and our need to redress them, as well as because of
the accidents of change and corruption which occur to us. For
moral virtues have been ordained only for the dealings and the
10 associations without which human existence is incomplete. Thus,
justice is needed in order to set dealings aright and to remove
the character of injustice, which is a vice, from those who undertake them. Temperance is prescribed as a virtue because of the
evil pleasures which perpetrate great harms to the soul and the
body. Similarly, courage is considered a virtue because of the
15 terrible things which a person should at times risk rather than
avoid. The same is also true of all the good traits of character
which we have described and whose acquisition we have urged.
Furthermore, all these virtues need external causes and
greatly varying actions. I mean that the liberal man needs external

causes, such as money and its acquisition in proper ways, so that
20 he may thereby act as liberal men do. The just man needs something of the kind in order that he may reward with favor those
with whom he associates and recompense with beneficence
those with whom he deals. Also, all of these [virtues] cannot
[168] exist / without the bodies and the souls and what is external to
them, in accordance with the classification of the kinds of happiness which we have given previously. And, the more numerous
the needs, the greater is the demand for things which are external
to us.

This is the nature of human happiness which cannot be
5 achieved without bodily actions, civic conditions, good assistants,
and sincere friends. These [necessities] are, as you see, many in
number and require hard toil. He who is negligent in them fails
to attain the happiness proper to him. Thus, laziness and the love
of ease are among the greatest vices because they stand between
man and all the goods and virtues and deprive him of his
humanity.

10 It is for this reason that we have censored those who lead
an ascetic life when they seek solitude away from other men,
live in mountains and caves, and choose the state of savagery
which is the opposite of civilization, for they become deprived
of all the moral virtues which we have enumerated. How is it
possible for a person to be temperate, just, generous, or courageous,
if he forsakes other men, keeps away from them, and loses moral
virtues? Would he not be then in the rank of the inanimate or
15 the dead?

Human virtues and divine virtue[26]

On the other hand, the love of wisdom, the devotion to
intellectual conception, and the use of divine ideas are proper to
the divine part of man. They are free from any of the evils which
occur to the other kinds of love, and they are untarnished by
[169] any sort of corruption. For this reason, we have said / that they
are not affected by slander, or by any kind of evil, since they are
the first pure good and their cause is the first good which is free
from matter and not subject to the evils inherent in material
things. So long as man applies his human character and virtues

5 [exclusively], he is hindered by them from this first good and this
divine happiness, although he cannot achieve the latter without
them. But he who has acquired those virtues for himself and then
ceased to seek them because of his concern for the divine virtue
is, indeed, concerned with his own essence and has been delivered
from the struggles of nature and its pains and from the struggles
of the soul and its faculties. He joins the good spirits and mingles
10 with the favored angels. Thus, when he passes from his first to his
second existence, he gains eternal bliss and everlasting divine
pleasure.

Aristotle expressed himself in all of these terms. He said:
Complete and pure happiness belongs to God (mighty and
exalted is He!) and after Him to the angels and those who seek
to be like Him.[27] And he added: We should not attribute to the
15 angels those virtues which we have enumerated in our discussion
of the various kinds of human happiness, for angels do not have
transactions among themselves, nor does anyone of them have
in his possession a trust which he is obliged to return. No one
among them deals in business so as to need justice, or is afraid
of anything so as to need bravery. None has any expenses so as
to need gold and silver, or is subject to desires so as to need self-
control and the virtue of temperance, or is composed of the four
20 elements which are dissolved by their opposites so as to need
nutrition. These righteous and pure creatures of God (mighty
and exalted is He!) are not, therefore, in need of human virtues.
[170]   / God Himself (sanctified and exalted is He!) is more sublime
and loftier than His angels. Consequently, we should deem Him
above all the human virtues which we have mentioned. We
should only speak of Him in terms of the pure good which resembles Him and ascribe to him the intellectual concerns which are
worthy of Him. It is the necessary truth which admits of no
5 doubt that He is loved only by the good and happy man who
knows real happiness and the real good. That is why he endeavors to seek His favor through both [happiness and the good],
strives to the utmost of his ability to please Him, and imitates His
acts to the extent of his capacity. And he who shows such love of
God (exalted is He!), such interest in seeking His favor, and
such obedience to Him, will be loved, favored, and gratified by
God and will become worthy of His friendship—that friendship

10 which is ascribed to some men by the Law wherein Abraham is called "the friend of God" and Muḥammad "the beloved of God" (may peace be upon both of them!).

Aristotle went on to speak in terms which may not be common in our language, for he said: Whoever loves God is cared for by Him, as friends care one for another, and he becomes the object of His beneficence. That is why wonderful pleasures and extraordinary kinds of joy are attributed to the wise man, and why 15 anyone who cultivates wisdom thoroughly finds it so extremely delightful that he will not turn or pay attention to anything else. Such being the case, God (mighty and exalted is He!) is the Wise, the Happy, and the Perfect in wisdom and happiness, and He is loved only by the truly happy and wise man, for a being finds pleasure only in his like. Consequently, this happiness is 20 loftier and higher than the one we have described above. It is not to be attributed to man, for it is cleansed from the physical [171] life, / freed from the faculties of the soul, and completely unlike the latter. It is rather a divine gift which [God] bestows upon those of His servants whom He chooses and then upon those who beg Him for it, strive after it as one should, long for it, hold fast to it during all their lives, and endure toil and fatigue [in its 5 pursuit]. For he who does not endure constant toil longs for play, since play is like ease, and ease is not an attribute of complete happiness nor a cause of it. Only those are inclined to bodily ease whose constitution is physical and whose nature is beastly such as slaves, children, and beasts. No one ascribes happiness to the irrational animal, or to children, or to slaves, except those who are analogous to them. But the intelligent and good man 10 directs his aspirations to the highest ranks.

Aristotle said: Man's aspirations should not be human, though he be a man; nor should he be satisfied with the aspirations of the animal which is destined to die, though he himself also may be so destined. He should rather aim with all his capacities to live a divine life. For though man is small in body, he is great 15 by his wisdom and noble by his intellect. The intellect supersedes all created things because it is the chief essence which has predominance over all by the command of its Creator (exalted is His greatness!). We stated previously[28] that as long as man lives in this world, he needs a good external condition, but he must not

devote himself with all his power to the quest of this condition,
20 nor must he seek an excess of it. For one may attain virtue even
though he neither possesses much money nor is manifestly affluent,
and he who is wanting in wealth and property may perform noble
[172] actions. / That is why the philosophers have said that the happy
are those who are provided with a moderate amount of external
goods and who perform the deeds required by virtue even though
their possessions may be meager.

People's ranks in virtue and in happiness

This is what the philosopher [Aristotle] said about this rank
[of happiness] which we promised you we would discuss. He said
5 further: It is not sufficient to know the virtues; one must also apply
and practice them. Some people take up the practice of virtues,
are amenable to good counsel, and desire what is good. These
are few in number, and it is they who abstain from all that is evil
and wicked because of their good instincts and their superior
nature. Other people are led to what is good and abstain from
10 what is evil and wicked only by being threatened, frightened,
and warned of torture. They try to escape from Hell and the
Abyss and all the suffering that the Abyss has in store. For this
reason, we have concluded that some people are good by nature
and others by [following] the Law and by learning. The Law
serves the latter as water serves one who is choking with food:
15 it clears his throat. But he who is not amenable to it is like the
one who is choked with water: there is nothing with which his
throat can be cleared. He is the one who will perish, for whom
nothing can be done, and for whose reform and recovery there
is no hope. This is why we have said that whoever is by nature
good and virtuous is so because of God's love of him. His condition
is not due to us, nor are we the cause of [his virtue]. God (mighty
and exalted is He!) is the cause. It is of such a man that Aristotle
spoke [when he said] that God has favored him with greater
care.
20   From what we have already said, it follows that there are
[173] four kinds of happy people / which we can determine by examina-
tion and perception. Thus, we find the kind of man who is good
and virtuous from the beginning of his life. We observe his intelli-

gence in his childhood, and in his youth we perceive in him the
aptitude for success by his modesty and noble disposition, his preference for the company of the good and for the friendship of the virtuous, and his aversion to their opposites. But, as we have said before,
5   he cannot reach this condition without receiving attention from
the time of his birth. We also find the man who does not possess
this quality at the beginning of his life. He is like all other children,
but he strives, works hard, and seeks the truth whenever he sees
people disagreeing about it. He continues in this way until he
attains the rank of the philosophers, that is to say, until his knowledge becomes true and his action right. But he cannot get to
10   this stage except by the pursuit of philosophy and by casting away
prejudices and all the other things against which we have warned.
Finally, we find the men who are forced to achieve such a conduct
either by religious education or by philosophical instruction.
        It is evident that the rank which should be sought is the
second, since the other ranks are due to outside causes and cannot
15   be sought, that is to say that the one who happens to be born
happy and the ones who are forced into happiness do not belong
to the class of the diligent seeker. We have also seen clearly the
rank of the diligent seeker and the grade he attains in [the scale
of] complete and genuine happiness, and that, of all the classes of
men, he alone is the happy, the perfect, the seeker of proximity
to God (mighty and exalted is He!), the loving, the obedient,
and the one worthy of God's friendship and love—as we have
previously described.
20   This is the end of the fifth discourse.

SIXTH DISCOURSE

THE HEALTH OF THE SOUL:
ITS PRESERVATION AND ITS RESTORATION

/ SIXTH DISCOURSE¹

THE HEALTH OF THE SOUL: ITS PRESERVATION AND ITS RESTORATION

The diseases of the soul

    With God's aid and support, we will discuss in this discourse the cure of the diseases which affect the soul of man and their remedies as well as the factors and causes which produce them and from which they originate. For skilled physicians do not attempt to treat a bodily disease until they diagnose it and know

5 its origin and cause. Then they seek to counteract it by remedies which oppose it, beginning with dieting and light medicines and ending in some cases with the use of distasteful foods and unpleasant medicines and in others with amputation and cauterization.²

    Now, as the soul is a divine, incorporeal faculty, and as it

10 is, at the same time, used for a particular constitution and tied to it physically and divinely in such a way that neither of them can be separated from the other except by the will of the Creator (mighty and exalted is He!), you must realize that each one of them [i.e., the soul and the constitution] is dependent upon the other, changing when it changes, becoming healthy when it is healthy, and ill when it is ill. This we can observe directly and clearly from their activities which appear to us, for just as we can

[176] see the man who is ill in his body—especially when / the origin of his illness is in one of the two noble parts [of the body], namely, the brain or the heart—undergoing a change of intellect and an illness of soul whereby he repudiates his mind, thought, and imagination, and other noble faculties of his soul (he himself being aware of all of this), so also we can observe the man who is ill

5 in his soul, whether with anger, grief, passionate love, or agitated desires, undergoing a change in the form of his body whereby

157

he shakes, trembles, turns pale or red, becomes emaciated or
fat, and the form of his body is affected by the various [other]
changes which can be perceived by the senses.

Thus, we must inquire into the origin of the diseases of our
souls. If it lies in the soul itself—as is the case when we think of
10   evil things and ponder over them, or have a sense of fear, or are
frightened by accidental or expected occurences or by agitated
passions — we should try to remedy these diseases in the way
which is appropriate to them. But if, on the other hand, their
origin lies in the [physical] constitution or in the senses—as in the
case of the lassitude which results from a feebleness of the heat
of the heart combined with laziness and luxurious living, or of
passionate love which starts with gazing [at the object of one's
love] together with idleness and leisure—then we should attempt
to remedy it in the way which is appropriate to these diseases.

The preservation of the health of the soul

15   Moreover, as the medicine of bodies is divided primarily
into two parts, the first to preserve health if it is present and the
second to restore it if it is absent, so also we should divide the
medicine of souls in this same way, trying to restore their health
[177] if it is missing and proceeding to preserve it if it / is already there.
So we say: –

When the soul is good and virtuous, loving the acquisition
of virtues and desirous of attaining them and longing for the true
sciences and for sound knowledge, then its possessor should associate with those who are akin to him and seek those who resemble
5   him, and should not enjoy the presence of others or sit in their
company. He should be very careful lest he associate with the
wicked and the defective among the frivolous or among those who
display enjoyment of disgraceful pleasures and commitment of vile
deeds and boast of them and indulge in them. Let him not listen
to these people's tales with interest, nor recite their poetry with
approbation, nor sit in their company with delight; for sitting
10   once in their company, or listening to one of their tales, or reciting one verse of their poetry would attach to the soul such dirt
and filth as would not be washed away except with the passage
of a long time and with difficult treatments. It could be the

cause of the corruption of [even] the virtuous and experienced man and the seduction of the discerning knower and might lead to their infatuation—to say nothing of the youth who is growing
15 up and the student seeking guidance. The cause of all of this is that the love of physical pleasures and of bodily relaxations is inborn in man on account of his imperfections. We are inclined to them and we covet them by our primitive nature and our original disposition, and it is only by means of reason's restraint that we keep ourselves from them, stopping at the limits which reason prescribes to us and contenting ourselves with what is necessary.

20   The exceptions and stipulations which I noted at the beginning of this discussion were mentioned for the following reason: Association with one's friends, whose conditions I described in the preceding discourse and with whom, and through whom, I judged that complete happiness is attainable, cannot be
[178] successful / without friendliness and intimacy. This involves necessarily pleasant fun, agreeable conversation, the delightful exchange of jokes, and the pursuit of pleasures permitted by the Law and determined by reason without going beyond these pleasures to excessive indulgence, or, on the other hand, scorning
5 them and abstaining from them. For to be carried to one of the extremes would be called—if the extreme is excess—frivolity, depravity, dissoluteness, and other blameworthy qualities; if the extreme is deficiency, it would be stupidity, sternness, peevishness, and similar qualities which are also blameworthy. The mean between these two extremes is the graceful person who is distinguished by cheerfulness, pleasant disposition, and good companionship. However, it is as difficult to achieve the mean
10 in this case as it is with the other virtues.

Another obligation incumbent on the person who seeks to preserve the health of his soul is to apply himself to a duty relating to the theoretical part [of knowledge] as well as to the practical —a duty, which he should not, under any circumstances, be allowed to neglect, so that it may serve the soul as physical exercise is pursued to preserve the health of the body. Physicians ascribe great importance to exercise in the preservation
15 of the health of the body, and the physicians of the soul attribute even greater importance to it in the preservation of the health

of the soul. For when the soul ceases to speculate and loses the power of thought and of deep searching for meanings, it becomes dull, stupid, and devoid of the substance of all good. If it becomes accustomed to laziness, shuns reflection, and chooses to remain idle, it draws near to destruction, because, by this idleness, it casts
20   off its particular form and returns to the rank of beasts. This, indeed, is the relapse of character. May God protect us against it!
[179]   / If the youth who is growing up accustoms himself, from the start of his life, to intellectual exercise and pursues the four mathematical sciences,[3] he will become accustomed to truthfulness and will be able to bear the burdens of reflection and speculation. He will delight in the truth, his character will shun falsehood, and his ear will abhor lying. When he reaches his prime and proceeds to study philosophy, he will retain the same disposition as he goes
5   through it and will absorb from it what should be kept in store. Nothing in philosophy will seem strange to him, nor will he need to toil hard to understand its secrets or extract its hidden treasures. Thus, he will achieve rapidly the happiness which we have described. Further, should the one who is seeking to preserve this health [of the soul] become unique and eminent in knowledge, then let not his pride in what he has achieved cause him to cease to seek beyond, for knowledge has no limit, and above every man
10   of knowledge there is One who knows. Let him not be too lazy to review what he has learned and perfected by studying it [further], for forgetfulness is the bane of learning. Let him remember the words of al-Ḥasan al-Baṣri[4] (may God grant him mercy!): "Curb ye these souls, for they are inquisitive, and polish them, for they quickly become rusty." And let it be known to you that these words, though short, are full of meaning and, at the same time, they are eloquent and fulfill the condition stipulated by rhetoric.
15   Again, let the one who is seeking to preserve the health of his soul realize that, by so doing, he is indeed preserving noble blessings which are bestowed upon it, great treasures which are laid up in it, and splendid garments which are cast on it. Let him realize also that, if one possesses such sublime blessings within himself and is not obliged to seek them from outside, or to pay money to others for their sake, or to endure hardship and bur-
20   densome troubles in their pursuit—if such a person then shuns

and neglects them to the point of shedding them off and becoming
[180] devoid / of them, he, indeed, will deserve blame for his action, will
show poor judgment, and will prove to be neither wise nor successful. [The seeker of this health should realize this fact] all the more
as he observes how the seekers of external goods venture on far and
perilous journeys, travel frightful and rugged roads, and expose
themselves to all kinds of dangers and possibilities of destruction
5   by beasts of prey and wicked aggressors. In most cases, even after
undergoing all these horrors, such people fail and they may suffer
excessive repentance and crippling sorrows which stifle their breath
and sever the members of their body. And even if they attain one of
their desires, this is inevitably lost quickly or is exposed to loss
and holds no hope of endurance, since it is external. What is
10   external to us cannot be secure against the innumerable accidents
which affect it; and, at the same time, its owner is in a state of
intense fear, constant anxiety, and weariness of body and of soul,
trying to keep what can in no way be kept and to watch over
something where watchfulness is of no avail.

If the seeker of these external things is a ruler or the compan-
15   ion of a ruler, these dangers are multiplied many times for him
because of his great involvement and what he suffers from those
who oppose and envy him, both far and near, as well as because
of the vast provisions which he needs in order to win over his
associates and those next to them and to cajole both his
friends and his enemies. Yet in spite of all of this, he is blamed
and accused of being slow [to give]; he is reproached and charged
with falling short [of what is expected of him]. All his relatives
20   and connections are constantly asking more from him, but there
is no way to satisfy one of them—to say nothing of all. Reports
keep reaching him about those who are closest to him, such as
his children, his womenfolk, and others among his retinue and
[181] attendants—reports which fill him with anger and fury. / Their
mutual jealousies being what they are, he cannot feel himself
secure from their side against the enemies writing to them or the
envious conspiring with them. Moreover, the more helpers and
supporters he has, the more they add to his worries and bring
him troubles which he has not experienced before. People consider
5   him a rich man, and yet he is the poorest among them; they envy
him, and yet he is the one who envies most. For how could he not

be poor when poverty is, by definition, the excess of need? Those who have the greatest need are the poorest of people, while the richest are those whose need is least.

This is why we have concluded—and rightly so—that God (exalted is He!) is the richest of the rich, for He is in need of
10   nothing, and that the greatest of kings are the poorest of people, because of the many things they need. Abu-Bakr al-Ṣiddīq (may God be pleased with him!) was right when he said in one of his sermons: "Kings are the most wretched people in both this world and the next." Describing them further, he said: "When a king assumes kingship, God makes him indifferent to what he has and desirous of what others have. He shortens the term of his life and
15   fills his heart with anxiety. For the king begrudges the little and is embittered by plenty. He is bored by easy life, and splendor ceases to have attraction for him. He does not learn by example, nor has he confidence in [anybody's] trustworthiness. Like the counterfeit coin or the illusory mirage, he is gay on the surface but unhappy inside. And after his soul has passed away, and the years of his life have been exhausted, and his shadow has been effaced, then God (exalted is He!) will call him to account and will be severe in reckoning and sparing in pardon. Indeed, kings are the ones who deserve mercy!"[5]

[182]   / This, then, is the condition of the king if he gets a firm hold on his rule and does not neglect any part of it. I have heard the greatest among the kings whom I have known asking to have these words [of abu-Bakr] repeated to him and then weeping in grief because of their agreement with what was in his heart and their true reflection of his state and condition. He who sees the outside [of the life] of kings: their thrones, their beds, their
5   ornaments, and their furniture; and who beholds kings in processions surrounded by, and standing in the midst of, throngs [of retinue], with horses, carriages, slaves, attendants, chamberlains, and servants ready at their disposal—he who sees this is possibly struck with awe and imagines that kings are happy with what he takes to be theirs. No! By Him who has created them and saved us from their preoccupations! In such circumstances, kings forget indeed what the stranger sees to be theirs and are lost in thoughts which occur and recur to them regarding the needs which we
10   have described. We ourselves have experienced this condition in

the little that we possess, and it has led us to an understanding of
[the condition of] plenty which we have described. It may
be that some of those who attain to [a position of] kingship
or rule are happy for a very short time in the beginning,
until they become established in [this position] and look [at it]
with open eyes, but after this stage, all that they possess becomes
as a matter of course to them and they are neither delighted in
it nor mindful of it. They then look beyond to what they do not
15   possess, and, even if they come to own the [whole] world with all
that it includes, they still long for another world, or their aspiration
rises towards gaining the eternal life and the true kingship, with
the result that they become weary of all that they have achieved
and have been able to attain. For [the king] to maintain the things
of this world is extremely difficult on account of the [predisposition
to] dissolution and annihilation in the nature of those things
and because of what the king is obliged to do, as described above,
and the large sums of money which he needs in order to pay the
soldiers attached to him and the attendants in his service, as well
20   as the reserves and treasures which he must lay in store against
misfortunes and accidents from which one cannot be safe. This,
then, is the state of those who seek blessings which are external to
us.

As for those blessings which are in ourselves, they exist with
us and in us. They do not quit us, because they are the gift of God
[183]   the Creator (mighty and exalted is He!). / He has commanded
us to put them to use and to rise higher in their scale. If we follow
His commandment, these blessings will yield us [other] blessings in
succession and we will rise from one grade to another until they
lead us to the eternal bliss which we have described previously.
Here is that true kingship, which does not pass away, and that
5   eternal and pure happiness, which does not change. Who is it,
then, who suffers a worse deal or a more obvious fall than he who
loses precious and lasting gems which are with him and at his
disposal and seeks base and perishable unessentials which are
neither with him nor at his disposal? Even if he happens to obtain
the latter, they will not remain in his possession or be left with
him, for it is inevitable that either they will be separated from him
or he from them.

This is why we have said that the person who has been

sufficiently provided for and who has gained a moderate share
10   of external happiness should not be engaged in the superfluities
of life because they are endless and lead their seeker to endless
perils. We have explained to you previously what sufficiency
and moderation are. We have also explained that the true purpose sought through them is the treatment of one's pains and
the avoidance of falling victim to them, and not enjoyment and
the pursuit of pleasure. For when one treats hunger and thirst—
15   both of which are incidental diseases and pains—one should not
seek the body's pleasure but, rather, he should seek its health, and
he will get the pleasure eventually. But he who, through treatment,
seeks pleasure and not health, will neither obtain health nor keep
such pleasure.

As for the man who is not sufficiently provided [with external
goods] and who has to toil and worry to obtain sufficiency, he
should not go beyond moderation and the extent of his need
20   so as to be obliged to exert constant toil and relentless care and
risk the danger of being exposed to dishonorable gains and the
[184]   various kinds of perils and calamities. Rather, / he should conduct
himsel gracefully in their pursuit, as does the one who realizes their
worthlessness and the fact that they are necessary for him [only]
because of his deficiency, and who thus seeks them just as the other
animals seek their necessities. For when the intelligent man
considers the conditions of animals, he finds that some of them
feed upon dead carcasses or upon dung and excrement and yet
5   are happy and delighted in the food they get and do not feel any
aversion to it. They do not turn away from it as do the other
animals of opposite nature; instead, they turn away from the food
of the latter which is quite the opposite of their food in cleanliness.
Take, for instance, the scarab and the black beetle and contrast
them with the bee. They run away from fragant odors and clean
10   food, whereas the bee seeks them and is delighted in them. It
follows, then, that to each animal there is a food appropriate
to it; and each is satisfied with what sustains its existence and life,
desires it, and is delighted in it.

It is in this light that we should look upon our food. We should
put it in the same class as the toilet which we are forced to
visit in order to excrete what we were so anxious to get. We
should not set the two far apart because both of them are necessi-

15 ties. We should have recourse to them only as such and not worry
our heads in choosing and enjoying them, nor waste our lives
preparing for them and endeavoring to secure them, nor, on the
other hand, fail to provide for our needs of them. If we prefer the
one to the other and deem it appropriate to seek what goes into
our bodies and inappropriate to seek what they excrete, the reason
20 is that the first is a nourishment which agrees with us and takes
the place of the decomposed parts of our bodies. And as we do
[185] do not / feel alienation from, or aversion to, our bodies and do not
find them filthy, so also we are not averse to what we take to meet
their loss and to replace it. The second [the excrement], on the
other hand, is the residue of that food and the part which nature
ejects after taking its need of it, i.e., [after assimilating] what it
reduces into pure blood and distributes to the different organs
5 through the veins, and discarding the dregs which it does not
need and which are extremely different and distant from our own
constitution. Because of this difference and opposition we feel
alienated from [this residue] and averse to it, but we are forced
to eject, remove, and discharge it by means of the organs with
which we are endowed and which we use for this purpose, so
that its place may be taken by what will come after it and go
through the same process.

10   Another requirement which should be observed by whoever
is anxious to preserve the health of his soul is to refrain from
stirring his concupiscent and irascible faculties by reminding
himself of what he obtained from them and of the pleasure which
he has thus experienced through them. He should rather leave
them alone until they are stirred by themselves. I mean by this
that a person may remember the pleasures he has had from the
satisfaction of his passions and their delighfulness or the grades
he has achieved of the honor and glory of authority, and may
consequently desire these things. But once he desires them he
15 moves towards them; and when he does so he comes to regard them
as ends, and thus finds himself drawn to use his [power of] reflection and to employ his rational faculty to help him attain those
ends. This is like the one who arouses beasts of prey and excites
wild, rapacious animals and then seeks to appease them and
to be delivered from them. The intelligent man does not choose
to be in such a condition. This is rather the conduct of fools who

20   do not distinguish between good and evil, or between right and
     wrong. This is why he[who is anxious to preserve the health of his
     soul] should not remind himself of the actions of these concupiscent
[186] and irascible faculties, lest he desire them and seek them. / Let
     him, instead, leave them alone, for they will be aroused by them-
     selves, they will be excited when necessary, and they will seek
     what the body needs. You [the reader of this book] will find
     in the stimulus of nature what will save you the trouble of stim-
     ulating these two faculties by your thought, reflection, and
     discernment. Your thought and discernement will then be used
     in satisfying their need and in assessing the freedom that you
 5   should give them to ensure what is necessary and requisite for
     our bodies to preserve their health. This is the way to execute
     the will of God (exalted is He!) and to carry out His plan, for
     He (exalted and sanctified is He!) has endowed us with these
     two faculties, only in order that we use them when we need them
     and not to become their servants and slaves. Thus, anyone who
     puts the rational faculty in the service of its own slaves violates
     God's commandment, transgresses the limits which He has set,
10   and reverses His guidance and design. For our Creator (mighty
     and exalted is He!) has provided us with these faculties by His
     plan and design, and no justice could be nobler or superior to
     that of His provision and design. Anyone who opposes it [His
     justice] or deviates from it commits the greatest wrong and
     injustice towards his own self.
         Furthermore, he who wishes to preserve the health of his
15   soul should pay minute attention to of all his acts and plans in the
     execution of which he uses the organs of his body and soul, lest
     he use them by force of a previous habit which diverges from his
     judgment and reflection. How often it happens that a person sets
     out to do something which varies from his previous resolution
     and decision! Whoever finds himself in this position should fix
     for himself penalties to counteract such misdeeds. If [for instance]
20   he suspects himself of seeking some kind of harmful food, or failing
     to adhere to a self-imposed diet, or eating unwholesome fruits
     or pastries, he should penalize himself by fasting and should only
     break his fast by taking the lightest and the smallest amount of
[187] food. / If he is able to suffer hunger, let him do so and be more
     strict in his diet even though he may not need such strictness. In re-

proaching his soul, he may address it as follows: "You intended to take what is useful to you but you took, instead, what is harmful. Such is the conduct of whoever is devoid of reason. One would think that many animals are better than you, because none of them seeks what is pleasureable and then takes what is painful.

5 Hold now yourself, therefore, [ready] for the penalty."

Likewise, if he [who wishes to preserve the health of his soul] suspects himself of being aroused to an anger for which there is no reason, or which is directed against an innocent person, or which exceeds what is proper for himself, then let him react by exposing himself to a person who is insolent and whom he knows to be obscene and let him suffer to endure that person ['s abuse]; or let him humble himself before someone whom he knows to be good but towards whom he had not acted humbly before; or let

10 him impose upon himself a certain amount of money to give away as alms and make this a vow which he should never fail to execute.

Also, if he suspects in himself a certain laziness or neglect of any of his interests, let him punish himself by engaging in some hard labor, or a long prayer, or certain good works which entail toil and fatigue. In brief, let him impose upon himself certain definite prescriptions which he should consider as duties and punishments that admit of no infringement or compromise, when-

15 ever he suspects himself of violating his reason or transgressing its command. Let him be wary at all times of involving himself in any vice, or of helping a friend in it, or of violating what is right. Let him not consider as slight any of the small faults which he commits, nor try to excuse himself for them, because this would lead him to serious ones. Whoever is accustomed in his childhood and youth to controlling himself instead of surrendering to his

20 passions, to being magnanimous when his anger is aroused, to
[188] checking his tongue, and to enduring his companions / will bear lightly what others, who have not gone through this training, find burdensome. As evidence of this, we find that slaves and their like, whenever they have the misfortune of living under masters who revile them and insult their honor, become used to enduring easily what they hear until it ceases to affect them. Even when they hear a gross unpleasantness, they laugh among themselves

5 without affectation and proceed with their work meekly, cheer-fully, and without being perturbed, whereas previously [before

living under such masters] they used to be ill-natured, irritable, and unwilling to endure [insult], or to refrain from reacting and from avenging themselves with words and seeking to quench their anger by fighting. The same is true of us if we accustom ourselves to virtue, avoid vice, and refrain from repaying and retaliating [the injuries of] vicious people and from inflicting revenge on them.

10   Furthermore, he who is anxious to preserve the health of his soul should follow the example of those kings who are known for their prudence, for they prepare themselves for enemies with equipment, war material, and means of defense while they can still do so in ample time and with the possibility of looking ahead. If they were to neglect this until they fell prey to dangers and were overtaken by adversities, they would be overwhelmed and unable

15   to use their craftiness or good judgment. It is on this basis that we should establish our means in preparing for such enemies as greed, anger, and all that removes us from the virtues which we pursue. This preparation consists in accustoming ourselves to being patient where patience is necessary, to forgiving those whom we should forgive, to abstaining from wicked desires, and to mastering these vices before they rage, for then the task would

20   be very difficult if not utterly impossible.

       Moreover, he who desires to preserve the health of his soul

[189] should search / very diligently for his own defects. He should not be satisfied with what Galen said on the subject. In his work known as *Man's Understanding of His Own Defects*,[6] he said: Inasmuch as every man loves himself, he is not able to discover his faults, or to see them though they may be apparent. In this same book, Galen advised the person who wishes to become free

5   from defects to look for a perfect and virtuous friend. After a long period of intimacy, he should tell that friend that he will trust the sincerity of his affection only if he tells him the truth about his defects so that he may avoid them. He should take his pledge in this regard and should not be satisfied if this friend tells him that he does not discern in him any defect whatsoever. Rather, he should reproach his friend and contest what he says, telling him that he accuses him of betrayal. Let him ask his friend again and urge him. If this friend still declines to tell him of any of his

10   defects, let him show his resentment gently and his reproach

openly and pursue further his request from him with insistence.
If the friend still refrains, he should persist a little more. When this
friend [finally] tells him of some of the defects which he has found
in him, let him not show on his face or in his words any antip-
athy or distress. On the contrary, let him look at his friend with
a cheerful face and show pleasure in what he has brought forth
to him and called to his attention, and let him thank him as the
days go by and in times of intimacy, so as to make it easy for the
15 friend to tell him of similar defects. Then let him remedy that
defect until its trace is removed and its shadow is effaced. [If
you do this,] then he who guides you to your defect will be convinced that you are proceeding to improve your soul and endeavoring to remedy your disease and, consequently, he will not
refrain from coming back to you and giving you advice.

But this, which Galen prescribed, is wanting and non-existent,
20 and there is no hope of securing it. In this situation, an enemy
might be more useful than a friend, for he would not be diffident
of us in showing our defects; he might even go beyond the defects
which he knows to tell falsehoods and lies in their regard. In this
way, not only our attention would be called from the enemies'
side to many of our defects, but we would even go further to
impute to our souls that of which they are innocent.

[190]   /Galen has another treatise in which he states that good people
derive benefit from their enemies.[7] This is true, and nobody
disagrees with him on it because of what we have mentioned.

As for the view of abu-Yūsuf ibn-Isḥāq al-Kindi[8] on this
subject, it is expressed in the following [passage] which I relate
5 in his own words: "The seeker of virtue should look at the images
of all his acquaintances as if these images were to him mirrors
in which he can see the image of each one of these acquaintances as each of them undergoes the pains which produce misdeeds. In this way, he will not fail to notice any of his own misdeeds, for he will be looking for the misdeeds of others. Whenever
he sees a misdeed in some one, he will blame himself for it as
if he had committed it and will reproach himself exceedingly on its
10 account. At the end of every day and night, he will review all his
actions so that none of them will escape his attention. For it is disgraceful for us to strive to preserve those things which we have [in
fact] expended, such as base stones and extinct ashes[9] which are

alien to us and whose loss will not hurt us a bit on any day, while [on the other hand] we fail to preserve what we expend of our essences, whose abundance assures our existence and whose diminution brings our annihilation. Let us, therefore, whenever

15   we come upon a defect in our deeds, reprove our souls severely for it and impose upon them a punishment which we should prescribe and never lose sight of. If we review the acts of others and find a misdeed among them, let us reproach ourselves also for it, for the soul will then be loath to commit misdeeds and will get accustomed to deeds which are good. Misdeeds will thus remain constantly in our minds and we will not forget them; their memory will not be effaced [even] by the passage of a long

20   time. We should follow the same behavior in regard to good deeds in order that we may hasten to [perform] them and not miss [performing] any of them."

Al-Kindi said [further]: "We should not be content to become like notebooks and books, which convey to others the meanings of wisdom while remaining themselves devoid of such

[191]   meanings, or like the whetstone / which sharpens [other instruments] but does not itself cut. Rather, let us be like the sun which benefits the moon. Whenever the sun shines on the moon, it causes it to shine out of the emanation of its light and exerts its effect on it exactly in that way which makes it resemble itself, though not so radiant. The same should be true of us if we transmit

5   virtues to others." This, which al-Kindi said on the subject, is more meaningful than what was said by his predecessors.[10]

Discussion of the restoration of health to the soul when health is missing [11]

This discussion deals with the treatment of the diseases of the soul. We begin—with the aid of God (exalted is He!)—by mentioning the superior genera of these diseases, then by treating the most serious and harmful among them, one after another. So we say: The superior genera of these diseases are the opposites

10   of the four virtues which we have enumerated in the beginning of this work. Now, since the virtues are definite means [between extremes] and existing essences, they may be sought, pursued, and attained by activity, effort, and diligence. On the other hand, the other points which are not means are indefinite, do not have

existing essences, and exist *qua* accident rather than *qua* essence. For instance, the circle has only one center. This center is a single
15 point which has an existence of its own that can be sought and pointed out. If we do not locate it through our senses, or cannot point it out, we are yet able to deduce it and to demonstrate that it is the center to the exclusion of any other point. On the
[192] other hand, the points which / are not centers are infinite in number and do not exist in essence. Their existence is merely a matter of assumption, and they do not possess any concrete individual essence of their own. Thus, they are not sought, nor can they be deduced, for they are unknown and are diffused throughout the whole area of the circle. As for the two extremes
5 which we call opposites, they are definite existents because they are the two ends of a definite straight line and each is at the furthest distance from the other. For instance, if we draw a straight line from the center of a circle to the circumference, its two ends will thus be definite: the one is the center, the other the extremity of the line at the circumference. Here again, the two ends are at the furthest distance each from the other. A similar example from the domain of the senses is that of white and black. The one
10 is the opposite of the other, both are definite and existent, and they stand at the furthest distance each from the other, but the means that lie between them are infinite in number, and so also are the colors. The extremes of virtue, however, being more than one, cannot be called opposites, for a thing has only one opposite. We cannot find anything that has several opposites, for only two
15 opposites can lie at the furthest distance each from the other.
      A single virtue may have more than one extreme. If we imagine, for instance, the virtue as a center, and draw from this center a straight line ending at a certain point, we can also draw in the other opposite side another line as a straight continuation of the first and ending at another point. These two points will be
20 opposites to the center which we have assumed to be a virtue, but one of them will represent immoderation and excess, the other want and deficiency. Having understood this, let us note that every virtue has two definite extremes which can be indicated
[193] /and innumerable means between them which cannot be indicated. However, there is only one real mean, and it is this which we have called virtue.

Furthermore, let us note that, in accordance with this expo-
5   sition, we consider the genera of vices to be eight, because they are
twice the number of the four virtues which we discussed before.
They are: recklessness and cowardice, the two extremes of the
mean which is courage; profligacy and frigidity, the two extremes
of the mean which is temperance; ignorance and stupidity, the
two extremes of the mean which is wisdom; and [finally] tyranny
and servility—in other words, inflicting injustice and suffering
injustice—the two extremes of the mean which is justice. These,
10 then, are the superior genera of diseases, which stand in opposition
to the virtues that represent the health of the soul. Under these
genera, there are species beyond limit.

Anger: Its causes and treatment[12]

We begin by discussing recklessness and cowardice which
are the two extremes of courage—itself a virtue of the soul and
[a constituent of] its health. So we say: Their cause and origin is
the irascible soul. Thus, all three of them [recklessness, courage,
15 and cowardice] are related to anger. Anger is, in reality, an
agitation of the soul as a result of which the blood of the heart
boils in a passion for vengeance. If this agitation is violent, it
kindles and inflames the fire of anger, the heart's blood boils
more intensely, and the arteries and the brain become filled with
a dark and turbulent smoke which impairs the state of the mind
and weakens its activity. In this condition, a man becomes, as the
20 philosophers have said, like a cave ablaze and completely full
[194] of fire, and thus chocked with / flames and smoke, with the blaze
rising from it as well as the sound called "the voice of fire"
[*wahi al-nār*]. Such a fire is hard to control and impossible to
extinguish, and anything which one brings near to it for the
purpose of extinguishing it becomes a cause of its extension and
material for its intensification. For this reason, the [angry] man
becomes blind to reason and deaf to advice; on the contrary,
5   advice becomes, in such a condition, a cause for the stimulation
of anger and fuel for inflammation and flaring up, and there is
no hope for such a person.

People differ in this respect according to their temperaments.
If one's temperament is hot-dry, his condition is almost like that

of sulphur which bursts into flame when even a weak spark is brought near to it. The contrary is true of those whose tempera-
10 ment is opposed to this one. But this difference is only at the beginning and when anger is growing. When it blazes, however, the condition of the one becomes almost akin to that of the other. You can conceive this by comparing the degree of inflammability of the dry firewood with that of the moist. Imagine also the rapid and intense inflammability of sulphur and naphta and come down therefrom to the intermediate greases until you end with
15 friction. For although friction is usually a weak producer of fire, yet it may become so effective as to set on fire a huge jungle or a closely entangled thicket. Another example is that of the clouds which are composed of the two vapors and yet, through friction, they produce between them blazing fires and shoot down thunderbolts whose flame no material can withstand. Such thunderbolts leave anything they touch reduced to ashes, even though it be a bare mountain or a hard rock.

[195] / Socrates said: "I have more hope for a ship in the midst of raging winds, with waves slashing at its sides and hurling it into the deep troughs wherein there are big rocks, than for a man inflamed with anger. For in the case of a ship in this condi-
5 tion, its sailors take care of it and save it by various devices, while an enraged soul is beyond saving by any device whatsoever. This is because any attempt to calm anger, whether by supplication, advice, or submission, ends by becoming so much more firewood to inflame it and increase its intensity."

The causes that produce anger are: vanity, boastfulness,
10 bickering, importunity, jesting, self-conceit, derision, perfidy, wrongfulness, and the seeking of things which bring fame and for which people compete and envy one another. The culmination of all these causes of anger is the desire for revenge; all of them lead to it. Among the consequences of anger are: repentance, expectation of retaliatory punishment sooner or later, change in temperament, and quickening of pain. For anger is temporary
15 madness and may even lead to death by stifling the heat of the heart or to serious diseases which cause death. It results also in one becoming the object of dislike to his friends, of malicious joy to his enemies, and of ridicule to those who are envious or vicious.

Now, each one of these causes has a remedy which one may attempt [and then pursue] until it is completely uprooted. [196] When we proceed to sever and remove these causes, / we weaken the power of anger, cut off its substance, and protect ourselves against its consequences so that, should it befall us in some form, we would be amenable to reason and would abide by its rules. The virtue associated with anger—namely, courage—would appear, and any venture which we may then undertake would be 5 in the right way and place, in the right measure, and against the right person.

As for vanity, when we come to define it, [we find that] it is, in fact, a false belief in one's self whereby that self is held to belong to a rank which it does not deserve. But he who knows his own self should be aware of the many vices and defects which blemish it, and [should realize] that virtuousness is divided among men and that no one can attain perfection without the virtues of 10 others. Consequently, when one's virtues depend upon others, it is one's duty not to be vain.

The same is true of boastfulness, for it consists in taking pride in things which are external to us. But he who takes pride in that which is external to him is doing so in regard to things which he does not possess. For how can one possess what is subject at every hour and every moment to evils and to destruction, and of which we are not sure at any time whatsoever. The most 15 correct and the truest of parables is that told by God (mighty and exalted is He!) when He said: "And set forth to them as a similitude: two men, on one of whom We bestowed two gardens of vines," up to the words: "Then began he to wring his hands for what he had spent on it, as it was falling down upon its trellises." Said He further (exalted is He!) : "And set forth to them the similitude of the present life: It is as water which We send down 20 from Heaven; the earth's vegetation mingles with it, and it then becometh chaff which the winds scatter. Verily, God hath power over everything." [13] The Qur'ān is full of such parables, and so also are the traditions reported from the Prophet (may peace [197] be upon him!)./ If one boasts of his descent, the most that he can claim—assuming that he is truthful—is that his father was virtuous. But suppose that that virtuous [father] comes and says: "This virtuousness which you claim is my own. I lay claim to

it all, leaving nothing to you. What then do you possess of it, which is not found in others?" The son would be unable to answer and would be reduced to silence. Many genuine traditions in this sense are reported from the Apostle of God (may the
5 prayer and peace of God be upon Him!). One such tradition is the one in which he said (may peace be upon Him!): "Do not come to me with your pedigrees, but with your deeds," or words with the same purport.[14] It is related of a slave, who belonged to a certain philosopher, that, when one of the chiefs of his time boasted of his superiority to him, he said: "If you boast of your superiority to me because of your horse, the beauty and liveliness are the horse's and not your own; if you take pride in your clothes
10 and your outfit, the beauty is theirs and not yours; and if you brag of your ancestors, they were the meritorious people and not you. Thus, if the merits and the virtues are outside of yourself and you are divested of them, and [if] we have returned them to their owners (in fact, they have not been really taken away from them, so they do not have to be returned to them)—then who would you be?" It is also related that a certain philosopher called on a man of affluence and wealth, who had amassed ornaments
15 and boasted of his abundant money and means. Feeling the need to spit, this philosopher cleared his throat, turned in the house right and left, and then spat right in the face of the owner of the house. When he was rebuked for his action, he said: "I looked around the house and all that was in it, and I could not find there anything uglier than the man himself, so I spat at him." This is the lot of those who are devoid of virtues of their own and boast of things which are outside of themselves.

20   As for bickering and importunity, we have shown in the preceding discourse[15] how disgraceful they are and how much dissension, discord, and mutual hate they cause among friends.

[198]   / Jesting is laudable so long as it is moderate. The Apostle of God (may the prayer and peace of God be upon him!) used to jest, but never said anything that was not true. The Prince of Believers[16] talked often jestingly, so that some one criticized him, saying: "If only he were not given to jesting!" But it is hard to
5 keep jesting within a moderate measure, and most people begin but do not know where to stop, so they overstep the limit and endeavor to outdo their friends until their jesting becomes a cause

of estrangement, rousing a latent anger and sowing a lasting hate. It is for this reason that we have recknoned it among the causes [of anger]. Thus, whoever does not know its right limit should avoid it. Let him remind himself of what has been said: "Many a difficult situation is brought about by play." And again:
10 "Sometimes a war begins as jesting." Jesting may also create dissension which it is then unable to remedy.

Self-conceit is similar to vanity. The difference between the two is that the vain man deceives himself in what he thinks of himself, while the self-conceited is haughty towards other people but does not deceive himself. However, the remedy of the latter is exactly the same as that of the former, namely, by making him realize that intelligent men consider what he boasts of to
15 be petty, and they attach no importance to it. This is so because of its low value and its trivial share of happiness, because it is changing, ephemeral, and of doubtful permanence, and because wealth, furniture, and other worldly goods may be found among the depraved and the foolish, while wisdom is found only among the wise.

[199]   / Derision is practiced by buffoons and clowns and those who do not care what they suffer in return since they have accepted to endure such suffering and even many times as much. Thus, the one who is in this category laughs and feels satisfied in the face of the different forms of scorn which befall him. Indeed, he earns his living by subjecting himself to humiliation and abasement. By beginning to ridicule others slightly, he exposes
5 himself to greater ridicule in order to arouse the laughter of others and to receive a little of their favor. The free and virtuous man is in a far different position, for he regards himself and his honor too highly to expose them to insolent people; nor would he sell them for all the treasures of kings, much less for what is petty and trivial.

Perfidy has many aspects. I mean that it may be employed
10 in respect to wealth, reputation, womenfolk, or affection. Whichever of these many aspects it takes, it is decried by every tongue and considered disgraceful by everyone. The listener loathes to have it mentioned before him and no man, no matter how small is his share of humanity, will admit to it. It is present only among a single race of slaves who are avoided by people and disliked by

the other types of slaves. For loyalty—which is the opposite of
15 perfidy—is found among the Greek, the Ethiopian, and the
Nubian races. In fact, we have seen more good loyalty displayed
by slaves than by many of those who call themselves free. Whoever
knows the meanness which the word "perfidy" implies, and the
aversion which intelligent people feel to it, and whoever understands its true meaning, will not practice it, especially if he is
endowed with a good nature or has read what we have presented
earlier in this work and cultivated it, and reached in his reading the present point.

20   Wrongfulness is causing others to suffer injustice. Anger arises
in defiance of it and in a passion for revenge. We have already
discussed both the inflicting of injustice and the suffering of
injustice and have described the condition of each of them. Let
us not, therefore, when we are wronged, hasten to take our
[200] revenge / before we have considered the wrong carefully, and
let us beware lest the harm that the revenge would bring us be
more serious than the bearing of that wrong. To consider and to
take heed in this way is to follow the counsel of reason. It is the
essence of magnanimity.

As for the seeking of those things which bring fame and for
5 which people compete with one another, it is an error which is
committed by kings and great men as well as by ordinary people.
For when a king has in his treasury a highly valuable object or a
precious jewel, he is thereby exposing himself to the grief which
he would suffer if he lost it. Such things cannot escape evils
because of the nature of the world—I mean the world of generation
and corruption—in which things are subject to change and transformation, and what is acquired and treasured up is liable to
10 corruption. If the king lost a rare treasure, he would look like
a bereaved person who had suffered the loss of a dear one. His
need of something comparable to it, but which he would be
unable to find, would become evident, and both friend and foe
would know of his grief and distress. It is told of a certain king
that he received a dome-shaped piece of crystal of amazing
clarity and purity and which was also extremely well cut. Its
maker had carved out from its surface columns and figures and
15 had repeatedly risked [breaking] it in his attempt to refine the
engravings, letters, and concaves that ran among the figures and

the foliage. When it came into the king's possession, his amazement
and his admiration of it were immense. He ordered it to be kept
in his private treasury. But before long it suffered the kind of
damage which usually affects such objects. When the news reached
the king, he showed such sorrow and distress that he was unable
20 to conduct his business, or to attend to his tasks, or to hold court
for his soldiers and retinue. People exerted themselves to find
something similar to it, but were unsuccessful. As for the king
himself, the incapacity which he thus revealed and his inability
to attain his object served to double his distress and sorrow.
[201]   / Turning now to ordinary people, we find that, whenever
one of them treasures up a costly object or a precious jewel or
acquires a sprightly mount or anything of the kind, he may be
asked by someone, whose request he cannot refuse, to hand it over
to him. Should he keep it from him and hold on to it, he would
expose himself and his prosperity to ruin, and, on the other hand,
5 should he give it up, he would cause himself unnecessary grief
and anguish.
Precious stones, such as rubies and the like for which people
vie with one another, while they may be free from internal corruption, cannot be secure against external evils such as theft
and various forms of cheating. When a king amasses them, he
derives little benefit from them when he needs them, and they
10 may become useless to him all at once. For if he should need
them, they would prove to be of no help to him in the immediate
situation and the pressing necessity. Indeed, we have ourselves
observed how the greatest of the kings of our time, when he needed
his precious stones after all his money had been expended and his
treasures and castles exhausted, he could not find any person
who was able to pay their price, or anything approaching it. All
that he got from them was the disgrace [which resulted from the
revelation] that he was in need of his subjects for part of their
value and that he was unable to obtain a small or a large fraction
15 of their price. In the meantime, these gems were being offered
cheaply and circulated among brokers, merchants, and the common people, who admired them but could not afford what they
were worth. Furthermore, even if someone could afford the
price of some of them, he would not dare to offer it for fear
that he would later be pursued, discovered, and dispossessed of

them. This, then, is the fate of such treasures when possessed
by kings and others. When it comes to merchants who are in
20   this trade, they may live in a favorable time, with peace among
the chiefs and security in the land, but their goods would still be
[202] in little demand since they are saleable / only to those kings who
are secure, who are not troubled by any misfortune, who have
long enjoyed affluence, and who have accumulated more wealth
than can be hoarded in treasures and castles. Those kings are
deceived by good fortune, and thus fall prey to such illusions
[as we have mentioned] and end in that state against which we
have given warnings.

5   These, then, are the causes of anger and the diseases which
result from it. We have mentioned their remedies and warned
against their causes and against being affected by them. He who
has known justice and cultivated it as we have written in the
preceding parts will find it easy to remedy this disease, because
it is a form of injustice and immoderation. Thus, we should not
call it by names which imply praise. I mean by this that some
10   people call this form of injustice—that is unjustified anger—
manliness and firmness and treat it as if it were courage, a name
which implies praise in the true sense of the word. But what a
great difference there is between the two forms of conduct! For
the possessor of the trait which we have condemned commits
many bad acts in which he wrongs first himself, then his friends,
and, one after another, the nearest of those with whom he deals,
15   and finally his slaves, servants, and womenfolk. He is to them as a
whip of torture, neither forgiving any of their faults, nor showing
mercy at any tear they shed, even though they may be innocent
of any offense and may have committed no crime or evil. On
the contrary, he accuses them unjustly and is aroused at the least
cause that may give him a chance at them. He goes so far as
to attack them with his tongue and hands, while they, on their
part, offer no resistance and dare not repulse him, but rather
20   submit to him and confess offenses which they did not commit
in order to escape his mischief and appease his anger. Yet he
keeps on in his own course, restraining neither his hands nor his
tongue. He may even proceed to apply the same treatment to
irrational animals and to inanimate utensils. A man of this evil
[203] character may fall upon / a donkey or a pack animal, a pigeon

or a bird, and beat and injure it, or he may bite a lock which proves too difficult [to open], or he may break vessels which do not conform to his wishes. This sort of bad character is known among many ill-bred people who vent their anger against clothing, 5 glassware, ironware, and other objects.

Kings that belong to this category become enraged against rains and winds, and the air if it blows contrary to their whims, or the pen if it does not comply with their desires; they curse the former and break the latter. One of the early kings used to 10 be furious at the sea if a ship was delayed because of the sea's agitation and the tossing of its waves, even going so far as to threaten to cast the mountains into it and fill it up with them. And in our times, one insolent person used to get angry at the moon and curse it, and he satirized it in a famous poem because he was annoyed by it whenever it shone during his sleep. All such deeds are disgraceful, and some of them are, in addition, funny and expose one to ridicule. How can these, therefore, be 15 praised as indicating manliness, strength, and the soul's nobility and might, when they are deserving of blame and exposure rather than of praise? And how much might and strength do they embody when we find them more prevalent among women than among men and more among the sick and weak than among the healthy and sturdy, and when we observe that boys are more quick to anger and irritation than men and the old more so than the young?

20 We also find the vice of anger accompanying that of greed, for the greedy man who does not obtain what he desires becomes [204] angry and irritated against those / of his women, servants, or other intimates who prepare his food and drink. The same is also true of the miser, who, when he loses any of his possessions, is immediately roused to anger against his friends and companions and accuses his trustworthy servants and subordinates. The only results that this class of people derive from their [bad] 5 character are loss of friends and good counselors, speedy regret, and painful rebuke. Such traits cannot lead to any happiness or joy. Their possessor is always sad and depressed, troubled in his life, and discontented with his situation. This places him in the condition of the unhappy man who evokes compassion.

The courageous and self-respecting man, on the other hand,

is he who overcomes his anger by magnanimity, who is able to discern and consider what comes suddenly upon him, and who
10   is not roused by any of the causes which provoke anger until he has reflected and considered how, upon whom, and in what measure to take his revenge, or how and whom to pardon and condone, and for which offense. It is related of King Alexander that he was informed of a friend who was criticizing and disparaging him. "Why not impose upon him, O king!," said one of his counselors, "a punishment that will ruin him?" His answer
15   was: "But, after punishing him, how deeply engaged he will be in slandering me and looking for my defects! For then he will talk more freely and will find more sympathy among people." On another occasion, one of his enemies, who had gained power, rebelled against him and caused much havoc in his territories. This person was brought into his presence and was pardoned by him. "If I were you," said one of those in his company, "I would have killed him." "Since I am not you," retorted Alexander, " I will not kill him."

[205]   / We have now mentioned most of the causes of anger and indicated the ways of treating them and putting an end to them. Anger is the most serious of the diseases of the soul. If one proceeds early to put an end to its cause, he will then have no fear that it will take hold of him. Whatever anger will then arise in him will be easy to remedy and quick to vanish, as it will have no
5   material to allow it to flare and continue to burn and no cause to inflame and kindle it. [The faculty of] reflection will have a chance to ponder and to deliberate on the virtue of magnanimity, as well as to reward, in case that is right, or to ignore, in case that is the way of prudence.

Fear: Its causes and remedy

The treatment of this disease of the soul [anger] is followed by the treatment of cowardice which is the other extreme of the
10   health of the soul. Now, since each of two opposites can be known from the other, and since we have come to know one of the extremes—which we have defined as a strong and violent agitation of the soul the result of which is the boiling of the blood of the heart in a passion for revenge—it follows that we thereby

know its opposite. I mean [by this] the other extreme which is a quiescence of the soul when it should be agitated and an absence of the passion for revenge. This is the cause of cowardice and

15 faintness. It results in humiliation and an unfortunate life, in being at the mercy of the low classes as well as of one's relatives, children, and those with whom one has dealings, and in a lack of steadiness and patience in situations where steadiness is required. It is also the cause of laziness and of the love of ease which are the causes of all vice. Among its consequences are: subservience

20 to everyone, acceptance of every humiliation or wrong, enduring all sorts of scandal affecting one's self, one's relatives, or one's

[206] possessions, hearing every form of vile and offensive / insult and calumny, enduring every type of injustice from all those with whom one deals, and an inability to disdain what is disdained by free men.

The remedy of these causes and consequences can be effected through their opposites, that is through the awakening of the soul which suffers from such a disease, by shaking and agitating

5 it. For the irascible faculty cannot be so completely lacking in a person that it has to be brought to him from another place. The fact is, rather, that in such a case this faculty is weaker than it should be and resembles a fire which has nearly gone out but which has still enough left to be affected by fanning and blowing. If it is stirred in a suitable way, it will inevitably be animated and will revive the burning and the blazing which are in its nature. It is said of one of those who

10 were engaged in philosophy that he used to look deliberately for dangerous places and put himself in them, and to induce himself to take grave risks by trying to confront them. He used to go out on the sea when it was disturbed and agitated so that he could train his soul to be steadfast in dangerous situations, to rouse its quiescent [irascible] faculty whenever such rousing was needed, and to deliver it from the vice of laziness and its consequences. It would not hurt a person who is affected with

15 such a disease to engage in some quarrels, and to expose himself to abuse and to the antagonism of those from whose danger he is safe. In this way, he could approach the virtue which is a mean between the two vices, namely, courage, which is the desired health of the soul. When he achieves it and comes to feel

it in himself, he should cease and stop without going any further lest he pass to the other side [that of anger] whose remedy we have taught you.

20   Now, since excessive and unjustified fear is one of the diseases of the soul, and since it is related to the same [irascible] faculty, it is necessary for us to mention it and to note its causes and remedy. So we say: Fear is caused by either the anticipation [207] of an evil or the expectation / of a danger.[17] Anticipation and expectation relate only to those events which will take place in the future. And those events may be either serious or trivial, and either necessary or contingent. Contingent events may be caused either by us or by other people. None of these [above—

5   mentioned] categories should be feared by the intelligent man. Concerning contingent events, they generally may or may not take place. One should not, therefore, count on their taking place, become apprehensive about them, or anticipate the evil of the suffering which they might cause, since they have not yet occurred and they may [very well] not occur. The poet was right when he said:

10   "When seized by fear, say to thy heart:
             Be comforted; most fears are false."

Such, then, is the condition of those [fearful things] which are due to external causes. We have told you that such things do not belong to the category of the necessary which must definitely take place. Consequently, fear of the evil which such things bring should be relative to the possibility of their occurrence.

15   And, indeed, life is agreeable and happy only with good trust and strong hope and the abandonment of worry about any evil which may not occur. As for those fearful things which are caused by our own bad choice and by what we inflict on ourselves, we should guard against them by avoiding offenses and crimes whose consequences we dread and by refraining from venturing on any action from whose danger we cannot be safe. For a person

20   who acts in this way forgets that the contingent either may or may not take place. When he perpetrates an offense or commits a crime, he presumes that it will either remain hidden and undisclosed or, if the contrary is the case, that it will be disregarded, or that no harm will ensue from it. It seems, then, that such a person, like the former one whose fear is of the first kind

[208] [i.e., from outside causes], considers / the contingent as necessary. But while this one feels safe particularly from what is dangerous, the former [on the contrary] is afraid particularly of what is safe. I mean by this that, since the contingent is half-way between the necessary and the impossible, it is, as it were, like an object which has two sides, the one adjoining the necessary, the other

5   adjoining the impossible. For instance, in the [straight] line ACB: A represents the necessary, B the impossible, and C the contingent. The contingent is at an equal distance from both A and B, one side of it extending towards A, the other towards B. When its future has become past, we should cease calling it the contingent and it will have moved either to the side of the necessary or to

10   that of the impossible. However, so long as it is the contingent, one should not reckon it either on this side or on that, but should rather attribute to it its own appropriate nature, that is, that it may move either here or there. This is why the philosopher said: "The aspects of contingent things are [revealed] in their consequences."

Concerning the fear of things that are necessary, such as

15   old age and its concomitants, [we say that] the remedy is to realize that if a man desires a long life he also certainly desires [to reach] old age and anticipates it as something inevitable. Old age is accompanied by a diminution of the innate heat and of the original moistness which accompanies it, by the predomi- nance of their opposites: coldness and dryness, and by the weaken- ing of all the principal organs. This is followed by reduction of movement, fading of energy, enfeeblement of the organs of

20   digestion, falling off of the grinding organs, and abatement of the faculties that regulate life, i.e., those of attraction, discharge, withholding, and nutrition, as well as the other accompanying constituents of life. Diseases and pains are nothing other than

[209] these / things. To them should be added the death of one's be- loved and the loss of those who are dear to him. He who, in the beginning of his life, anticipates these things and observes their requirements will not fear them, but will rather expect them and look forward to them. Others will wish that they be granted to him and he himself will solicit them from God (exalted is He!) in prayers and when he is in mosques and shrines.

Fear of death: Its causes and remedy[18]

5   So much for a summary discussion of fear in general. Now, as the most serious fear which affects man is the fear of death, and as this fear is not only prevalent but also more intense and far-reaching than any other kind of fear, it is necessary that we discuss it fully. So we say: Fear of death befalls only the person who does not know what death really is; or who is not aware of the ultimate destiny of his soul; or who believes that when his body

10   dissolves and decomposes his essence thereby dissolves and his soul decomposes to the point of annihilation and effacement, and that— as is believed by those who are ignorant of the immortality of the soul and of the life to come—the world will continue to exist after him and he himself will not exist in it; or who thinks that death involves a great pain other than the pain of these diseases which may precede it, or lead to it, or be the cause of its occur-

15   rence; or who believes that a punishment will befall him after death; or who is puzzled, not knowing what he will face after he dies; or [finally] who is grieved because of the money and possessions which he will leave behind.

    All of these are false beliefs and devoid of truth. To the one who is ignorant about death and does not know what it really is, we explain that death is nothing more than the soul's abandon-

[210]   ment / of the use of one's tools, namely, the organs which, when taken as a whole, are called a body, just as an artisan abandons the use of his own tools. [We explain also] that the soul is an incorporeal substance, and not an accident, and that it is not subject to corruption. To understand this explanation, one needs to have gone through certain sciences which precede it; it is demonstrated and thoroughly explained [elsewhere] in its proper

5   place. Whoever looks for it and strives to grasp it will not find his goal hard to attain. And he who is content with my statement in the beginning of this work and is satisfied with it will know that this substance [the soul] is unlike the substance of the body and that it differs from it completely in its essence, properties, actions, and effects. When it leaves the body, in the manner we have described and according to the condition we have laid down, it achieves the eternal life which is proper to it, becomes cleansed

10   from the impurity of nature, and experiences complete happiness.

There is absolutely no way for it to perish or to be annihilated.
For a substance does not perish *qua* substance, nor can its essence
be nullified. Only accidents, properties, and the proportions and
relations which exist between the substance and bodies are nullified by their opposites. But the substance itself has no opposite;
and when anything is corrupted, its corruption is due to its
15   opposite. You may understand this easily from the first principles
of logic even before you reach its proofs. And if you observe a
bodily substance—which is base as compared with that noble
substance [the soul]—and examine its condition, you will find
that it does not perish nor pass away *qua* substance, but that some
parts of it are transformed into others and, in this way, its
properties and accidents disappear gradually. The substance itself,
20   however, remains and cannot, in any way, be annihilated or
nullified. Take, for instance, water; when it is transformed into
vapor or air, or, similarly, when air is transformed into water
or fire, the accidents and properties of the substance disappear,
but the substance *qua* substance remains and cannot, in any
way, be annihilated. If this is the case with the bodily substance
which is subject to transformation and change, how can we imagine
that the spiritual substance will perish and be annihilated, when
[211] it is not subject to transformation or / change in itself, but
receives rather its own perfections and the completions of its
forms?

Proceeding to the person who fears death because he does
not know the ultimate destiny of his soul, or because he believes
that, when his body dissolves and decomposes, his essence is there-
5   by dissolved and his soul nullified, or because he is ignorant
of the immortality of the soul and the nature of the life to come—
such a person does not, in reality, fear death but is only ignorant
of what he should know. Ignorance, then, is what makes him
afraid. And it is this ignorance which impelled the philosophers to
seek knowledge, to work hard for it, to give up bodily pleasures
and comforts for its sake, to choose toil and night work in its
stead, and to hold that the comfort by which one is relieved
10   from ignorance is real comfort while real hardship is that which
is caused by ignorance—because ignorance is a chronic disease
of the soul and recovery from it brings to the soul salvation,
eternal rest, and everlasting pleasure. When the philosophers

became certain of that, reflected on it, grasped its truth, and attained the spirit and the comfort embodied in it, nothing in the world was too hard for them. They came to despise all that the
15 mass of the people honors: property, wealth, sensual pleasures, and all the other desires which lead to them. For such things are unstable and transient; they soon vanish and pass away; they cause great worries when they are achieved and great pains when lost. Thus, the philosophers sought only as much of such things as is necessary to life and did not care for the superfluities which have all the defects that I have mentioned as well as those that I have not. Such things are at the same time endless, for,
20 in seeking them, if one attains a certain end, his soul still yearns for another end without stopping at any limit or terminating at any time. Death is indeed this condition itself, and not what he [the type of person who fears death out of ignorance] fears. To covet this condition is to covet the ephemeral, and to be preoccupied with it is to be preoccupied with what is false. For
[212] this reason, the philosophers affirmed / that death is of two kinds: the voluntary and the natural, and that life also is of the same two kinds. By voluntary death, they meant the suppression of desires and their abandonment, and by natural death the separation of the soul from the body. Voluntary life was to them what man
5 seeks in this world of such things as food, drinks, and desires, while natural life was to them the eternal existence of the soul in everlasting bliss through one's acquisition of the true sciences and his purification from ignorance. Thus Plato advised the student of philosophy by telling him: "Die by will, and you will live by nature."[19]

But he who fears man's natural death fears what he should
10 really wish for, because this death is the realization of what is implied in the definition of man, namely, that he is a living being, rational, and mortal. By death, he becomes complete and perfect and attains his highest plane. He who knows that every thing is composed of its definition, that its definition is composed of its genus and its differentia, and that the genus of man is the living being and his two differentia are the rational and the mortal—such a person will realize that man will be resolved into
15 his genus and his differentia, since every composite must inevitably be resolved into that of which it is composed. Who, then, is

more ignorant than the one who is afraid of his own completion, and who is more miserable than the one who supposes that he is annihilated by living and that he becomes incomplete by being complete? For when one who is incomplete is afraid of becoming complete, he thereby proves himself to be extremely ignorant. The intelligent man should, therefore, shrink from incompletion and find comfort in being complete. He should seek everything

20   that could make him complete and perfect, that could ennoble him and raise his rank, and that could free him in such a way as to make him safe from falling into captivity rather than tighten his fetters and add to his complexity and entanglement. He should also trust in the fact that when the noble and divine substance is delivered from the thick and corporeal one, in purity and

[213]   clarity / rather than in mixture and turbidity, that substance attains happiness, returns to its heavenly abode, becomes near to its Creator, wins the proximity of the Lord of the universe, associates with its kindred and fellows among the good spirits, and escapes from what is contrary and foreign to it. It follows, then, that the soul, which at the time of its separation from the body still yearns and cares for it and is afraid to leave it, is ex-

5   tremely miserable and at the utmost distance from its own essence and substance, following a course which is furthest removed from its own abode, and seeking security for that which can never be secure.

As for the one who believes that death involves a great pain other than the pain of the diseases which may have preceded and caused it, the remedy is to demonstrate to him that this is a false belief since pain belongs to the living being only, and a living being is one that is subject to the effect of the soul. A body

10   which is not subject to this effect does not suffer or feel. Consequently, death, which is the separation of the soul from the body, does not involve any pain because the body suffers and feels only by virtue of the effect of the soul on it, but, when it becomes merely a body and devoid of this effect, it neither feels nor suffers pain. It is evident, therefore, that death is a condition of the body which it does not feel or suffer because this condition

15   involves the loss of that by which the body felt and suffered.

To the one who is afraid of death because of the punishment with which he feels threatened after it, we must explain that he

is not, in fact, afraid of death but of the punishment. Now, such punishment is suffered only by something that will still be living after the body has perished. And whoever acknowledges that something survives the body, acknowledges also necessarily

20 that he has committed offenses and bad deeds for which he deserves punishment. At the same time, he acknowledges that there is a Ruler who is just and who punishes for bad deeds and does not punish for good ones. [It can be seen, then, that] such a person is, in fact, afraid of his own offenses and not of death. If one fears punishments for an offense, his duty is to guard against it and to avoid it. Earlier, we have clearly shown that

[214] /the bad deeds which are called offenses originate from bad dispositions. Bad dispositions belong to the soul, and are the vices which we have enumerated and whose opposite virtues we have made known to you. Consequently, he who fears death in this way and for this reason is ignorant of what he should fear and

5 afraid of what has no effect and should not be feared. The remedy for ignorance is knowledge. It is, therefore, wisdom that releases us from these pains and these false suppositions, which are the consequences of ignorance. And, indeed, God will lead to what is good!

In the same way, we address the person who is afraid of

10 death because he does not know what he will face after he dies, for this is again the case of an ignorant person who is afraid because of his ignorance. The remedy is for him to learn so he will know and have faith. For whoever believes in a certain state for his soul after death, and yet does not know what that state is, is confessing his ignorance. And the remedy for ignorance is knowledge. He who has knowledge is confident; he who is confident knows the way to happiness and thus follows it; and he

15 who follows a straight path to a worthy goal attains it inevitably. Such confidence, which is born of knowledge, is certitude. It is the state of the man who reflects deeply on his religion and holds fast to his philosophy, and whose rank and dignity we have already described to you in the course of this work.

[Finally,] he who claims that he does not fear death but is grieved because of the relatives, descendants, wealth, and property which he will leave behind, and who regrets the delights

20 and desires of this world which he will miss—such a person must

be told clearly by us that grief is the anticipation of a pain or an
evil and that such grief brings no benefit whatsoever. We shall
[215] discuss the remedy of grief in / a special section reserved for it,
since in this section we are dealing only with the pain of fear and
its remedy. We have treated this subject in an adequate and
convincing manner, but in order to explain and clarify it further
we say: Man is one of the generables. Philosophical views have
made it clear that every generable is inevitably corruptible.
5 Thus, he who wishes not to suffer corruption also necessarily
wishes not to be, and he who wishes not to be also necessarily
wishes for his own corruption. It is as if he wishes [both] to suffer
corruption and not to suffer corruption, to exist and not to exist.
This is impossible and would not occur to the mind of an intelligent person.

Furthermore, had our predecessors and ancestors not passed
10 away, we could not have come into existence. If it were possible
for man to live forever, our predecessors would have continued
to live. But if this had happened and our predecessors, given
their reproductiveness, had not died, the earth would not be
large enough to contain them. You will see the truth of this
statement from the following: Let us suppose that a person who
was alive four hundred years ago were still alive at this time.
Let him be one of the famous personalities so that his descendants
can be found and recognized. Take, for instance, 'Ali ibn-abi-
15 Ṭālib (may peace be upon him!) and suppose that he had had
children and children's children and that they had continued to
reproduce in this fashion without any one of them passing away;
how many of them would there have been at the present time?
You would be able to find more than ten million of them. Indeed,
in spite of the deaths and the devastating massacres which these
descendants have suffered, more than two hundred thousand
of them have survived. Now, if you were to make the same calcu-
20 lation for everyone who lived in that age on the surface of
the earth, east and west, [you would find that] you would not be
[216] able to determine their/multiplicity or to reckon their number.
If then you surveyed the surface of the earth, [you would find also
that] it is limited and its area defined, and you would realize
that, in that event, the earth would not be spacious enough to
hold all of these people even if they were standing and crowded

together, much less if they were seated or engaged in activities. There would be left no more place for construction, nor ground for cultivation, nor the possibility for one to walk or move about—to say nothing of other activities. And this is only in a short period of time. What would happen then if the time were extended and people kept reproducing at the same rate? Such, then, is the state of ignorance and stupidity of those who desire the eternity of this life and abhor death, and who imagine that eternity is possible or desirable! It is, therefore, evident that consummate wisdom as well as the justice established by divine planning are the right course which we should not shun and from which we should not deviate, and that this also represents the very extreme of generosity, beyond which there is no further end for the persistent seeker or the one who covets benefit. To fear it is to fear the justice of the Creator and His wisdom—or, indeed, His generosity and munificence.

It has become now quite evident that death is not an evil, as the mass of the people supposes, but that the evil, indeed, is the fear of death and that whoever is afraid of death is ignorant of it and of his own self. It has also become evident from our preceding discussion that the reality of death is the separation of the soul from the body and that this separation is not a corruption of the soul but only the corruption of the composite. As for the substance of the soul, which forms the essence, core, and quintessence of man, it is immortal and, being incorporeal, it is not subject to the attributes of bodies which we mentioned a little earlier. Nor is this substance subject to any of the accidents of bodies: it is not crowded in space, for it has no need of space, nor does it seek any permanence in time, for it can dispense with time. The senses and the bodies have imparted to this substance a certain perfection./ But having achieved this perfection through them, if it was then liberated from them, it would pass to its noble world which is near to its Creator and Maker (exalted and sanctified is He!). We have already, in our preceding discussion of this subject, explained this perfection which it acquires in the sensible world and shown you the way to it. We have noted that it is the extreme happiness which man can attain, and we have also informed you of its opposite which is man's extreme misery. But, along with this, we have explained the different grades of happiness, as well as the ranks of the righteous and their share of the favor of God (mighty and exalted is He!) and of His Paradise, this being the lasting abode. Similarly, we have described to you the ranks of the opposites of the righteous [and their share of] God's wrath and their downward stages in Hell, this being the abyss where there is no rest. We solicit God's good help in what will bring us nigh unto Him. Generous is He indeed, munificent, compassionate, and merciful!

The remedy of grief [20]

10   Grief is a suffering of the soul occasioned by the loss of a dear one or the failure to fulfill a desire. Its cause is concern for material acquisitions, covetousness of bodily desires, and sorrow for what one loses or misses of these things. But a person is grieved and distressed at the loss of what is dear to him or at his failure to attain his desires, only if he believes that the coveted worldly things which he acquires can endure and remain stable for him,
15   and that all that he seeks of the worldly things which he misses will inevitably be achieved and possessed by him. If, however, he is fair to himself and realizes that everything in the world of generation and corruption is neither enduring nor stable and that the only stable and enduring things are those which belong to the world of the intellect, then he will not crave the impossible or endeavor to get it. And when he ceases to crave it, he will also cease to be grieved if he loses what he desires or if he fails
20   to secure what he wishes in this world. He will direct his efforts to ends that are pure and limit his attention to the seeking of permanent goods only. He will discard all that is not by nature
[218] stable and enduring. When he obtains / any one of these goods, he will immediately put it in its proper place and take only as much of it as is necessary to remove the pains which we have enumerated, such as hunger, nakedness, and similar exigencies. He will not try to treasure up these things, or to seek to accumulate them or to show them off and boast of them. He will not entertain
5   the hope of amassing them, nor will he long for them. If he loses them, he will not regret them, nor care about them. Whoever accepts this advice will feel confident rather than distressed, joyous rather than grieved, and happy rather than miserable.

But he who does not accept it and who does not treat himself
in this way will continue to be in constant distress and unabating
grief. For such a person cannot at all times be immune from the
failure to fulfill a desire or from the loss of something that is dear
to him. Such failure and loss are bound to take place in this world
10 of ours, it being a world of generation and corruption. And
whoever expects what is subject to generation and corruption not
to be generated and not to be corrupted is expecting the impossible; and he who expects the impossible is always disappointed,
and the disappointed man is always grieved, and he who is grieved
is miserable.

On the other hand, he who acquires by good practice the
feeling of being satisfied with all that he finds and of not being
grieved at anything he loses will always be joyful and happy.
15 Should one doubt that such a feeling could be possible or helpful,
let him consider the feelings of people in regard to the aims which
they seek and the lives which they lead, and observe how people
differ in such matters according to the intensity of these feelings.
This consideration will reveal to him clearly and openly the
joy of people in their own lives—no matter how different those
lives may be—and the contentment of those who practice different
crafts in their various occupations. Let him note this carefully
in one class after another among the common people: he will
20 not fail to observe the joy of the merchant in his trade, of the
soldier in his courage, of the gambler in his gambling, of the
swindler in his swindling, and of the effeminate in his effeminacy.
[219] / Each one of these people comes to think that anyone who is
not in the same condition as he and who thus misses its joy is
certainly duped, and that anyone who is ignorant of that condition and thus deprived of its pleasures is a fool indeed. This is only
because each group feels strongly that its own course is the right
one and because it becomes attached to that course by long
practice. Now, if the seeker of virtue stays attached to his particular course, if his feeling [that it is the right course] becomes
5 strong, and if his judgment remains sound and his practice is
prolonged, he will be more entitled to joy than all those classes
of men who stray in the darkness of their ignorance. Indeed,
his share of the lasting bliss will be greater because he is right and
they are wrong, he is certain and they are uncertain, he is sane and

they are ill, he is happy and they are miserable, he is God's friend
and they are His enemies. And God (exalted is He!) has said:
"Verily, God's friends—no fear shall be on them, nor shall they
10   be put to grief."[21]

Al-Kindi's remarks on grief

In his work called *The Repelling of Griefs* [*Daf' al-Aḥzān*],[22]
al-Kindi made the following remarks which show you clearly
that grief is brought forth by man and imposed on himself and
is not a natural thing:

"If a person who has lost a property or who seeks an object
15   without finding it, and is grieved in consequence, considers his
grief philosophically; if he realizes that the causes of this grief
are not necessary; and if he realizes also that many people who
do not possess such property instead of being grieved are, on the
contrary, joyful and happy—if such a person does this, he will
undoubtedly come to know that grief is neither necessary nor
natural and that he who is grieved and brings this accident
upon himself will inevitably be comforted and will return to his
20   natural state. Indeed, we have observed people who were strongly
afflicted by the loss of children, friends, or some who were dear
to them or loved by them, and who after a while returned to the
[220]   state of joy, / laughter, and happiness and regained the condition
of those who have never been distressed. The same is true of the
one who is deprived of his money, his estate, and all the desirable
possessions which man may acquire and whose loss would bring
him disappointment and grief. Such a person is finally consoled,
his grief fades away, and he inevitably regains his cheerfulness
and happiness. Therefore, if the intelligent man reflects on the
conditions of people when they are in grief and on the causes
5   of grief, he will know that he is not the particular victim of a
strange misfortune, that he is not distinguished from others by
a singular distress, that the ultimate end of his misfortune is
consolation, and that grief is an accidental disease which
resembles the other evils. He will thus not subject himself to an
evil accident, nor get an acquired disease—I mean a disease
which man brings upon himself and which is not natural."
10   "Such a person should remember what we have mentioned

previously about the man who is presented with a rare [and fragrant] object on condition that he smell and enjoy it and then return it for others to smell and enjoy as well, but who covets it and thinks that it is bestowed upon him permanently, so that when it is taken away from him, he is grieved, disappointed, and angered. This is the condition of the man who has lost his reason and who craves the impossible. It is the condition of the
15 envious man, because he desires to monopolize the goods without sharing them with others; and envy is the worst of diseases and the most horrid of evils. That is why the philosophers said: Whoever desires evil to befall his enemies is a lover of evil, and the lover of evil is a wicked man. More wicked is he who desires evil to befall those who are not his enemies, and still worse is he who wishes no good to come to his friends. He who wishes
20 to deprive his friends of the goods is wishing them evil."
[221]   /"The consequence of these evils is that one becomes grieved at the goods which people obtain and envies them on account of what they attain of them. It matters not whether these goods are, or are not, among our acquisitions and possessions, for all of them are common to mankind as a whole. God has entrusted them to
5   His creatures, and it is His right to withdraw these entrusted goods at any time and through whatever person He wishes. It is not a disgrace for us nor a shame to return these goods. On the contrary, it is both a shame and a disgrace to be grieved when they are withdrawn from us. It also represents ingratitude, because the least appreciation that we owe to anyone who lends us something is to return it to him willingly and to respond to him with alacrity when he wants it back. Especially should this be the case when the lender leaves with us the best of what
10 he has lent us and takes back the meanest."
       Al-Kindi said [further]: "By the best and noblest, I mean that part which no hand can reach, and which no one else can share with us, that is, the soul, the intellect, and the virtues which are granted to us as a gift which will never be taken back or withdrawn." He said also: "If as justice demands, God withdraws the smaller and meaner part, He leaves with us the greater and
15 better part, and if we were to grieve for everything we lose, we would be in permanent sorrow. The intelligent man should not, therefore, think of harmful and painful things, and, since

the loss of property is a cause of grief, he should acquire as little of it as possible. It is said of Socrates that when he was asked about the cause of his liveliness and lack of sorrow, he said: 'I do not acquire the things whose loss would put me to grief.' "

20   We have discussed the genera of the diseases which affect
[222] the soul, / indicated their treatments, and pointed out their remedies. Now, the intelligent man, who cares for his soul and who endeavors to rid it of its pains and to save it from its perils, should not find it hard to examine the diseases which fall under these genera as species and individuals, to cure his soul of them, and to treat them with their opposite remedies. Then the help of God
5   (mighty and exalted is He!) should be solicited to ensure success. For success is coupled with diligence: neither can be achieved without the other.

This is the end of *The Book of Purification Concerning the Refinement of the Sonl.* Praise be unto God, at the beginning and at the end. May His blessings be upon His Prophet Muḥammad and his family, and may His salutations of peace be abundant!

NOTES

PREAMBLE

1- p. 1, l. 26   Sūrah XCI (al-Shams: The Sun), 7–10.

FIRST DISCOURSE

1- p. 5, title   Title in the original.

2- p. 12, l. 9   See *infra*, Third Discourse, p. 70, l. 18 – p. 71, l. 33.

3- p. 13, l. 25   Sūrah XXXII (al-Sajdah: Adoration), 17.

4- p. 14, l. 27   Miskawayh refers to this work elsewhere in the *Tahdhīb* under different titles. (See p. 45, l. 13, *The Order of the 'Happinesses' and the Grades of the Sciences* [*Tartīb al-Saʿādāt wa-Manāzil al-ʿUlūm*]; p. 81, ll. 23–24, *The Order of the 'Happinesses'* [*Tartīb al-Saʿādāt*]). It is probably the same work mentioned by Yāqūt in his list of Miskawayh's works in *Irshād al-Arīb* (ed. D.S. Margoliouth, Gibb Memorial Series VI, 7 vols., Cairo, 1907–26), II, 91, where a copyist's error makes the title: *Tartīb al-ʿĀdāt* [*The Order of the Habits*]. It is probably also the same work which has been published in Cairo (1917, 1928) under the title *al-Saʿādah* [*On Happiness*], but which has not yet been critically edited. It is not mentioned by Brockelmann (*GAL*, Vol. I, pp. 342–43, *Supp.*, pp. 582–84).

5- p. 14, l. 33   Miskawayh derives his views of the three faculties of the soul (the rational, the irascible, and the concupiscent) and of the resulting four cardinal virtues (wisdom, courage, temperance, and justice) from the well-known Platonic doctrine (*The Republic*, Book IV; and commentators thereon). On the Platonic elements in Miskawayh and in Islamic philosophy in general, see:

    Franz Rosenthal, "On the Knowledge of Plato's Philosophy in the Islamic World," *Islamic Culture*, XIV (1940), pp. 387–422; and Richard Walzer, "Platonism in Islamic Philosophy," in *Greek into Arabic* (Oxford, 1962), pp. 236–52.

6- p. 15, l. 27   " *ʿIlm*," which is rendered in this translation as "knowledge," or "science," depending upon the context. "Knowledge" is also used for "*maʿrifah*." (Plural: "*maʿārif*" also "knowledge"; sometimes "forms of knowledge.")

7- p. 16, l. 2   "*Ḥukamā'* " is rendered as "philosophers" in most instances, but also as "wise men" (p. 85, l. 2). "*Ḥikmah*," as a virtue, is "wisdom"; otherwise, it is either "philosophy" (ex.: p. 55, l. 30), or "wisdom" (ex.: p. 76, ll. 5–6, 39), according to the context.

197

8- p. 16, l. 31   See *infra*, Sixth Discourse.

9- p. 17, l. 23   Schemes of the divisions of virtues are not given by Plato or Aristotle, but they occur in later writings such as the pseudo–Aristotelian *De Vertutibus et Vitiis* and among the Stoics. See W.D. Ross, ed., *The Works of Aristotle* (11 vols., Oxford, 1912–31), X, Introduction, p. xxii; and R. Walzer, *Greek into Arabic* (Oxford, 1962), pp. 222–23. See also, on the Greek influences on Miskawayh's enumeration and division of the virtues, M.C. Lyons, "A Greek Ethical Treatise," *Oriens*, XIII – XIV (1960–61), pp. 35–57.

10- p. 18, l. 18   Title in the original.

11- p. 18, ll. 19,   This is a rendering of *"al-ḥurrīyah,"* which is elsewhere (p. 112, ll. 17,
      33   20, 27, 37) translated: "liberality." This virtue which, like *al-sakhā'*, is here considered as a division of temperance, is akin to *al-sakhā'*, and the term "liberality" which is used for the latter virtue seems to be equally appropriate for it in the above-mentioned parts of the text. *"Al-ḥurr"* and its plural: *"al-aḥrār"* are rendered as "liberal" (p. 99, ll. 31–33; p. 112, ll. 25, 31, 38; p. 113, l. 1), but also as "free" (p. 176, l. 28; p. 177, l. 4).

12- p. 19, l. 12   Title in the original.

13- p. 19, l. 31   *"Al-Sharī'ah"* rendered throughout as "the Law," by which is meant the Islamic Divine Law.

14- p. 20, l. 1   Title in the original. Of the divisions of the virtues, *al-sakhā'* (liberality) is here singled out and itself subdivided. Elsewhere *al-sakhā'* is also given prominence along with the four cardinal virtues (p. 26, l. 5; pp. 95–99). This may be due to Aristotelian influence, as liberality is given an important place in Book IV of the *Nicomachean Ethics*.

15- p. 20, l. 19   Title in the original.

16- p. 21, note   See Muḥammad Arkoun, "A propos d'une édition récente du *Kitāb Tahḏīb Al-'Akhlāq,*" *Arabica*, IX (1962), pp. 63–65.

17- p. 22, l. 4   Miskawayh bases his discussion here on the Aristotelian principle that virtue is a mean (*Nicomachean Ethics*, Book II, 1107a ff.), which was adopted generally by Islamic philosophical ethics and formed one of its main constituent elements.

18- p. 22, l. 30   *Nicomachean Ethics* 1106b 32–33.

19- p. 25, l. 9   See *infra*, Fourth Discourse, p. 101, l. 13–16.

SECOND DISCOURSE

1. p. 29, title   Title in the original.

2. p. 30, l. 18   Ibn-al-Nadīm cites three ethical works by Galen (*al-Fihrist*, ed. Flügel, 2 vols., Leipzig, 1871–72, I, 291): *Kitāb Ta'rīf al-Mar' 'Uyūb Nafsihi*, translated by Tūmā and revised by Ḥunayn; *Kitāb al-Akhlāq*, translated by Ḥubaysh; and *Kitāb Intifā' al-Akhyār bi-A'dā'ihim*, translated also by Ḥubaysh. The same three works, with variations

in the titles of the first and the third, are also mentioned by Ibn-abi-Uṣaybi'ah, *Ṭabaqāt al-Aṭṭibbā'* (2 vols., Cairo, 1300. A.H.), I, 100–101. See Max Meyerhof, "New Light on Ḥunain Ibn Isḥâq and his Period," *Isis*, VIII (1926), pp. 685–724, which analyses Ḥunayn's *Risālah* on Galen's works that were, and those that were not, translated into Arabic.

P. Kraus published the text of an Arabic summary of the translation of Galen's *Kitāb al-Akhlāq* in *Bulletin of the Faculty of Arts of the University of Egypt*, Vol. V, Pt. 1 (May, 1937, published 1939), pp. 25–51 (Arabic section). On Galen's ethical works and their influence on Islamic ethical philosophy, see Kraus's introduction to this text (pp. 1–24), and the two studies by R. Walzer, "New Light on Galen's Moral Philosophy" and "A Diatribe of Galen" in *Greek into Arabic* (Oxford, 1962), pp. 142–74.

3- p. 31, l. 6   The *Ethics* of Aristotle, most probably the *Nicomachean*, as well as the commentaries of Porphyry and Themistius, were translated into Arabic by Isḥāq ibn-Ḥunayn (or according to al-Qifṭi, in the case of the text with Porphyry's commentary, by Ḥunayn ibn-Isḥāq) and were known to Arab philosophers. See Ibn-al-Nadim, *al-Fihrist* (ed. Flügel, 2 vols., Leipzig, 1871–72), I, 252; and al-Qifṭi, *Ta'rīkh al-Ḥukamā'* (ed. Lippert, Leipzig, 1903), p. 42. See the discussion of Miskawayh's sources, and particularly of the way(s) the *Ethics* reached him in R. Walzer, "Some Aspects of Miskawaih's Tahdhīb al-Akhlāq," *Greek into Arabic* (Oxford, 1962), pp. 220–35.

An Arabic translation of the *Nicomachean Ethics* was recently discovered among the manuscripts of the Qarawīyīn Library in Fās. See:

A. J. Arberry, "The Nicomachean Ethics in Arabic," *Bulletin of the School of Oriental and African Studies*, XVII (1955), pp. 1–9.

D.M. Dunlop, "The Nicomachean Ethics in Arabic, Books I–VI," *Oriens*, XV (1962), pp. 18–34.

L.V. Berman, "A Note on the Added Seventh Book of the Nicomachean Ethics in Arabic," *Journal of the American Oriental Society*, LXXXII (1962), pp. 555–56.

The *Ethics* is referred to in the title of the Fās manuscript as نيقوماخيا (Dunlop, *ibid.*, p. 18). It is also mentioned in this form (without the *fatḥah*) by al-Fārabi in his *al-Jam' bayn Ra'yay al-Ḥakīmayn* (ed. Dieterici in *al-Thamarah al-Marḍiyah fi Ba'ḍ al-Risālāt al-Fārābiyah*, Leiden, 1890), p. 16, l. 21. In this work (p. 17, l. 9), al-Fārabi mentions that he wrote a commentary on it. نيقوماخيا is also cited in this form in the *Tahdhīb*, p. 116, l. 3 of my edition (*infra*, p. 103, l. 28).

4- p. 31, l. 32   *N.E.* 1103a 18–24.

5- p. 34, l. 4   Cf., *N.E.* 1094a 26 – 1094b 11 where politics is considered the master art. ". . . It would seem to belong to the most authoritative art and that which is most truly the master art. And politics appears to be of

this nature; for it is this that ordains which of the sciences should be
studied in a state, and which each class of citizens should learn and
up to what point they should learn them;... now, since politics uses
the rest of the sciences, and since, again, it legislates as what we are
to do and what we are to abstain from, the end of this science must
include those of the others, so that this end must be the good for man."

6- p. 34, l. 10   The variant *"wa-al-'ilāj"* in Ms. ﻭ, and *"wa-al-'ilājah"* (?) in the
related Ms. ﺍ, meaning "treatment," may fit the sense better than the
reading *"wa-al-filāḥah"*: "agriculture" adopted in my text (p. 37, l.
9 and n. 5) from the other and generally more reliable Mss.

7- p. 35, l. 4   This tradition is not reported in the authoritative collections.

8- p. 35, l. 7   A kind of sword which does not bend.

9- p. 35, l. 8   A weak, worthless kind of sword.

10- p. 35, l. 30   This is probably the same work as the *Tartīb al-Sa'ādāt* referred to by
Miskawayh under different titles. See *supra*, First Discourse, n. 4.

11- p. 38, l. 1   *"yakhluf,"* also p. 74, l. 20; p. 105, l. 3. The same rendering: "deputy"
for *"khalīfah"* (p. 109, l. 34; p. 117, l. 24), but p. 147, l. 30: "representative").

12- p. 40, l. 17   See *supra*, Second Discourse, n. 2. Other authors (al-Bīrūni, Ibn-abi-
Uṣaybi'ah, and Ibn Jabīrūl) call this work, as does Miskawayh here,
Akhlāq al-Nafs. See P. Kraus's introduction to his publication of a
summary of Galen's *"Kitāb al-Akhlāq," Bulletin of the Faculty of Arts
of the University of Egypt*, Vol. V, Pt. 1 (May, 1937), pp. 15, 18, 19. On
this particular reference by Miskawayh to Galen's work, see the text
of the summary, p. 36.

13- p. 41, l. 33   Miskawayh often uses *"quwwah"* (faculty) and *"nafs"* (soul) inter-
changeably, as in the present sentence. See also *supra*, p. 15, ll. 10–11,
and *infra*, p. 46, ll. 33–35.

14- p. 46, l. 7   This is an interesting allusion to Miskawayh's own personal experience, which was no doubt affected by his ethical study and reflection.
Cf., the equally interesting *"waṣiyah"* (testament) cited by Yāqūt in
the *Irshād* (ed. Margoliouth, II, 95–96), which Miskawayh took upon
himself as an engagement: *"mu'āhadah"* and a reminder: *"tadhkirah."*
The same *"waṣiyah"* is quoted by al-Tawḥīdi, *al-Muqābasāt* (ed. Ḥasan
al-Sandūbi, Cairo, 1929, pp. 323–26), where Miskawayh's name does
not appear, and the author is given merely as *"ba'ḍ aṣḥābina"* (one of
our friends), and in the text *"fulān ibn fulān"* (so-and-so). Cf., another
"waṣiyah" published by Mohammed Arkoun from *Ṣiwān al-Ḥikmah*,
"Textes inédits de Miskawayh," *Annales Islamologiques*, Publications
de l'Institut Français d'Archéologie Orientale du Caire, V (1963),
pp. 191–94 and the preceding introduction by Arkoun.

15- p. 46, l. 14   In the original: *"ḥayawānāt"* (animals), which raises a question about
"malik" translated as "king". Cf., the designation of the three faculties
of the soul as *"malikīyah"* (kingly), *"sab'īyah"* (leonine), and *"bahī-
mīyah"* (beastly), *supra*, p. 15, ll. 16–20.

16- p. 50, l. 2   A Greek author, probably of the Neo-Pythagorean School and of the 1st century A.D. See, regarding his name, identity, work, and influence, Martin Plessner, *Der OIKONOMIKOC des Neupythagoreers 'Bryson' und sein Einfluss auf die islamische Wissenschaft* (Heidelberg, 1928). Regarding the relation of this work to the *Tahdhīb*: pp. 49–52, 139–141, *et passim*. The text of this work had been published by Louis Cheikho, but with no definite identification of the author, *Al-Machreq*, XIX (1921), pp. 161–81; and *Majmūʿat Arbaʿat Rasāʾil* ... (Beirut, 1920–23), pp. 13–33.

17- p. 54, l. 7   The Arabic original of this word is not clear in the Mss., or in the texts used by Plessner (p. 192, l. 12; p. 194, l. 3; and p. 196, l. 11) or by Cheikho (p. 178, l. 2). See my edition of the *Tahdhīb*, p. 60, n. 1. The reading adopted here: "*yufattiḥuhu*," (and p. 54, ll. 10, 35; p. 57, l. 4: "*al-tafattuḥ*") agrees with Plessner's reading in the first two references in his text. Plessner renders this word as "ihn öffnet (d.h. schlaff macht)" (*Ibid.*, p. 250, l. 24; p. 251, l. 19), and mentions (p. 285 § 133) Bergsträsser's derivation of this word from the root *ftḥ* 'im Sinne von فتح المسام "die Poren des Körpers öffnen", d.h. "verweichlichen." '

18- p. 59, l. 13   A weak tradition not included in the authoritative collections, but reported by al-Suyūṭi in *al-Jāmiʿ al-Ṣaghīr* with slight variation and as part of a longer tradition. See ʿAbd-al-Raʾūf al-Munāwi, *Fayḍ al-Qadīr Sharḥ al-Jāmiʿ al-Ṣaghīr* (6 vols., Cairo, 1256–57 A.H.), II, 94–95.

19- p. 63, l. 4   Sūrah XXXII (*al-Sajdah*: Adoration), 17.

20- p. 63, l. 8   This tradition is quoted directly, or its words used, elsewhere in the *Tahdhīb* following, as here, the above-mentioned Qurʾānic verse. (See *supra*, p. 13, ll. 26–28, and *infra*, p. 82, l. 39 – p. 83, l. 2). It is a well-known tradition and included with variations in the two *Ṣaḥīḥs* of al-Bukhāri and Muslim and in other authoritative collections. (See al-Bukhāri, *Ṣaḥīḥ* (9 vols., Cairo, 1314–15 A.H.), IV, Badʾ al-Khalq, p. 118, and Muslim, *Ṣaḥīḥ* (8 vols., Cairo, 1334 A.H.), I, Īmān, p. 121. See, for other references in the two *Ṣaḥīḥs* as well as in other authoritative collections, A. Wensinck, *Concordance et indices de la tradition musulmane* (Leiden 1936 –   ), under عين and أذن . Cf., I Corinthians 2, 9.

21- p. 65, l. 8   *Nicomachean Ethics*

THIRD DISCOURSE

1- p. 69, title   Title in the original.

2- p. 69, l. 8   *Nicomachean Ethics* 1094a 2–3.

3- p. 70, l. 7   Cf., the opening sentence of *N.E.* 1094a 1–2.

4- p. 70, l. 20   See *supra*, Second Discourse, n. 3 for the relevant references to Porphyry and Themistius as commentators on the *Ethics* in the works of

Ibn-al-Nadīm, al-Qifṭi, and al-Fārābi (*op. cit.*, p. 17, l. 10). It is interesting to note that this section of the *Tahdhīb* dealing with the divisions of the good seems to be nearer to the *Magna Moralia* than to the *Nicomachean Ethics*.

5- p. 70, l. 29   *M.M.* 1183b 20–37.

6- p. 70, l. 37   *M.M.* 1184a 3–14. See also, on the origin of this text dealing with the divisions of the good, S. Pines, "Un texte inconnu d'Aristote en version Arabe," *Archives d'Histoire Doctrinale et Littéraire du Moyen Age,* 1956 (Paris, 1957), pp. 5–43, particulary pp. 5–7.

7- p. 71, l. 12   *M.M.* 1183b 37 – 1184a 3.

8- p. 71, l. 31   *N.E.* 1096a 20–29; *M.M.* 1183a 9–11.

9- p. 72, l. 3   *N.E.* 1099a 31 – 1099b 7.

10- p. 72, l. 9   *N.E.* 1099b 11–14. This text, like many similar borrowings from the Greek philosophers, is put in Islamic terms. Aristotle speaks of "the gods." (*theōn*).

11- p. 72, l. 11   *N.E.* 1100a 1–3.

12- p. 72, l. 37   In two of the Mss. which seem to belong to one group, the reading is: "وبقراط" (Hippocrates). My reading "وسقراط," adopted on textual grounds agrees with Walzer's view, *Greek into Arabic*, p. 224, n. 3.

13- p. 77, l. 34   *Faḍā'il al-Nafs.* The Arabic sources do not cite a work by Aristotle with this title. Nor is such a work mentioned in the Arabic data on abu-'Uthmān al-Dimashqi to whom Miskawayh attributes its translation into Arabic (*supra*, p. 81, ll. 9–18.) According to S. Pines who discussed the origin of this text in the *Tahdhīb*, and of the above-mentioned work attributed to Aristotle, this work is probably Neoplatonic, but preserves an authentic Aristotelian core. See Pine's article referred to in n. 6, *supra*.

14- p. 81, l. 11   Abu-'Uthmān Sa'īd ibn-Ya'qūb al-Dimashqi, a celebrated translator, physician, and mathematician who flourished in Baghdād in the first part of the 4th c. A.H. (10th c. A. D.) under the patronage of the vizier 'Ali ibn-'Isā. In 302 A.H. (915 A.D.), this vizier entrusted to him the supervision of the hospitals of Baghdād, Makkah, and al-Madīnah. Ibn-al-Nadīm, *al-Fihrist* (ed. Flügel), I, 298, speaks of him as one of the proficient translators ("*aḥad al-naqalah al-mujīdīn*") in a text which is copied by Ibn-abi-Uṣaybi'ah, *Ṭabaqāt al-Aṭṭibbā* (Cairo 1300 A.H.), I, 205. The latter author mentions (I, 234) two works by abu-'Uthmān both derived from Galen, the first being a collection of topics (*masā'il*) from Galen's *Ethics* (*fi al-Akhlāq*). See also George Sarton, *Introduction to the History of Science* (3 vols., Baltimore, 1927–48), I, 631.

15- p. 81, l. 33   *Al-'āmilah al-nāṣibah.* This form may be due to the conception of this group as a "*madīnah*" (city), like the various "*mudun*" (cities), which are described by al-Fārābi as opposed (*muḍāddāt*) to the virtuous city "*al-madīnah al-fāḍilah.*" See *Ārā' Ahl al-Madīnah al-Fāḍilah* (ed.

	Dieterici, Leiden, 1895), pp. 61–63.
16- p. 82, l. 8	*N.E.* 1095a 2–8.
17- p. 82, l. 37	Sūrah XXXII (*al-Sajdah*: Adoration), 17. On the tradition following this verse, see *supra*, Second Discourse, n. 20.
18- p. 83, l. 22	*N.E.* 1098a 18–19.
19- p. 83, l. 39	*N.E.* 1099a 20–25.
20- p. 86, l. 23	*N.E.* 1102b 20–22.
21- p. 86, l. 32	In the original, here and *supra*, p. 88, l. 9, برنامس (Prnāms), with no vocalization (only one of the six Mss. is not clear). In his versified translation of the *Iliad, Ilyādhat Hūmīrūs* (Cairo, 1904), see index, Sulaymān al-Bustāni refers to him as فريام (Firyām).
22- p. 87, l. 2	*N.E.* 1100a 4–14.
23- p. 87, l. 16	*N.E.* 1100a 14–31.
24- p. 88, l. 5	*N.E.* 1100b 18–33.
25- p. 88, l. 14	*N.E.* 1100b 33 – 1101a 14.
26- p. 88, l. 35	*N.E.* 1101a 21 – 1101b 9.
27- p. 88, l. 36	On Miskawayh's views on pleasure, see also his epistle *Fi al-Ladhdhāt wa-al-Ālām (On Pleasures and Pains)* edited and discussed by Mohammed Arkoun in "Deux épîtres de Miskawayh," *Bulletin d'Etudes Orientales*, Institut Français de Damas, XVII (1961–62), pp. 7–74.
28- p. 91, l. 28	*N.E.* 1101b 10 – 1102a 4.

FOURTH DISCOURSE

1- p. 95, title	Title in the original.
2- p. 95, title	Concerning Miskawayh's views on justice, to which this discourse, is devoted, see also his epistle on the subject, *Risālah fi Māhīyat al-'Adl* which has recently been edited and translated into English: M.S. Khan, *An Unpublished Treatise of Miskawaih on Justice*, Leiden, 1964.
3- p. 95, l. 26	*M.M.* 1191b 10–22.
4- p. 97, l. 25	*M.M.* 1190b 9 – 1191a 36. It is interesting to remark here again that Miskawayh's discussion of the false virtues seems to be nearer to this section of the *M.M.*, and the one referred to in the previous note, than to the relevant sections of the *N.E.* (on courage 1115a 6 – 1117b 21; on temperance 1117b 22 – 1119b 20).
5- p. 97, l. 26	'Ali ibn-abi-Ṭālib the first *Imām* of the Shī'ites and the fourth Orthodox Caliph. This qualification of 'Ali, and the following invocation (also *supra*, p. 190, l. 25) which is used for the Prophet only, are an indication of Miskawayh's shī'ism. It is taken as such by al-Sayyid Muḥsin al-Amīn al-'Āmili in his biography of Miskawayh in *A'yān al-Shī'ah* (48 vols., Damascus and Beirut, 1936–60), X, 144.
6- p. 97, l. 31	See *Nahj al-Balāghah* (ed. Muḥammad Muḥyi-al-Dīn 'Abd al-Ḥamīd with Muḥammad 'Abdūh's commentary (3 pts., Cairo, n.d.), II, p. 4.

7- p. 100, l. 17   *N.E.* 1119b 20 – 1122a 17; *M.M.* 1191b 39 – 1192a 20.

8- p, 101, l. 16   See Aristotle's derivation of the Greek word *dikaion* (just) from *dicha* (2 equal parts), *N.E.* 1132a 30–32.

9- p. 101, l. 33   I have not been able to trace any reference to this work in the Arabic sources in the accounts of Miskawayh's life and writings.

10- p. 102, l. 7   *N.N.* 1130a 30 – 1131a 9. Aristotle here divides what he calls particular justice into two kinds: one which is manifested in distributions of honor or money or other divisible assets, and one which plays a rectifying part in transactions. He then divides the latter into two subdivisions depending upon whether transactions are voluntary or involuntary.

11- p. 102, l. 13   *N.E.* 1131a 10 – 1131b 24.

12- p. 103, l. 7   For justice in the second and third divisions, see Aristotle's discussion of the corrective or rectificatory kind of justice, *N.E.* 1131b 25 – 1132b 20.

13- p. 103, l. 18   *N.E.* 1133a 19–21.

14- p. 103, l. 24   *Nāṭiq*, which means also "rational" as used elsewhere in the *Tahdhīb*.

15- p. 103, l. 27   *N.E.* 1133a 30–31 where Aristotle derives the Greek *nomisma* (money) from *nomos* (law). The Arabic word *nāmūs* goes back to the latter.

16- p. 103, l. 28   This is the only reference in the *Tahdhīb* to the *Nicomachean Ethics* by name. But the quotation which follows has no exact counterpart in that work. It is one more indication of the fact that Miskawayh knew the *Ethics* through later commentaries, and that he also adapted ⸴ many of Aristotle's ideas and expressions to Islamic beliefs. See *supra,* Second Discourse, n. 3.

17- p. 104, l. 4   *N.E.* 1132b 33–34.

18- p. 104, l. 32   *N.E.* 1129b 11–25.

19- p. 104, l. 35   *N.E.* 1132a 8–10.

20- p. 105, l. 1   The reading and meaning of this word are not very clear. Neither the adopted reading: *al-firyah, al-faryah,* or *al-farīyah,* nor the variant: *al-gharīyah* has a meaning which fits in with the context, namely, an instrument of torture. Could it be *al-qarīyah* meaning stick? (See *Lisān al-'Arab* and *al-Qāmūs*). Other alternatives may be *al-firyah*: slander, calumny; or from *fara, yafri*: to split leather, meaning possibly a lash made of split leather.

21- p. 105, l. 4   *Ṣāḥib al-Sharī'ah.* See also p. 110, l. 30; p. 127, l. 34; p. 129, l. 10; p. 132, l. 34. It means prophet, whereas *Musharī' al-Sharī'ah* (p. 132, ll. 35-36), the Prescriber of the Law, refers to God.

22- p. 105, l. 6   I have not been able to trace this tradition. It is not reported in the authoritative collections.

23- p. 106, l. 7   *N.E.,* Book V **8**, 1135a 15 – 1136a 9.

24- p. 108, l. 1   Galen. See Ibn-al-Nadim, *al-Fihrist* (ed. Flügel), I, 290 and Ibn-abi-Uṣaybi'ah, *Ṭabaqāt al-Aṭṭibbā'* (Cairo, 1300 A.H.), I, 94–96. See also, on Galen's works translated into Arabic, Max Meyerhof, "New Light on Ḥunain Ibn Isḥāq and his Period," *Isis*, VIII (1926), pp. 685–724.

25- p. 110, l. 26 These terms have their origin in the Qur'ān (*zaygh*, Sūrah III, 7; *rāna*, Sūrah LXXXIII, 14; *ghishāwah*, Sūrah II, 7; *khatama*, Sūrah XLV, 23).

26- p. 111, l. 4 *N.E.* 1133b 33–35. The attribution by Miskawayh of this and of the following quotation to Plato shows the influence of the later Neoplatonic works through which he knew Aristotle's *Ethics*.

27- p. 111, l. 11 *N.E.* 1134a 6–13.

28- p. 112, l. 16 *N.E.* 1129a 6–17.

29- p. 113, l. 24 Cf., Aristotle's treatment of this question, *N.E.* 1138a 4 – 1138b 16.

30- p. 116, l. 18. The Prophet Muḥammad. I have not been able to trace this tradition. It is not reported in the authoritative collections.

31- p. 119, l. 2 *Wajh wāḥid*. Miskawayh may also have meant *One Face* following *wajh Allah* (the Face of God) in the preceding sentence.

FIFTH DISCOURSE

1- p. 123, title Title in the original. For all this discourse, devoted to the discussion of love and friendship, see *N.E.*, Books VIII and IX. Some particular references are given in the following notes.

2- p. 123, l. 24 *N.E.* 1155b 17–21; also 1104b 30–35.

3- p. 125, l. 14 *N.E.* 1158a 10–14; 1171a 10–13. On the distinction between *ṣadāqah*, *maḥabbah*, and '*ishq*, see R. Walzer, *Greek into Arabic*, pp. 227–28 and 241.

4- p. 125, l. 22 *N.E.* 1156a 31 – 1156b 6.

5- p. 125, l. 29 *N.E.* 1156a 21–30.

6- p. 126, l. 13 The name appears in different forms in the Mss. through the errors of copyists. See my edition, p. 138, l. 17, n. 5, and Mājid Fakhri, "Qudamā' Falāsifat al-Yūnān 'ind al-'Arab," *Al-Abḥāth*, X (1957), pp. 391-404.

7- p. 126, l. 17 *N.E.* 1155a 32 – 1155b 8. Miskawayh attributes here mistakenly to Heraclitus the view of Empedocles ("Like seeks after like") which is opposite to what Heraclitus is reported here by Aristotle to have said ("Opposition unites"; "The fairest harmony springs from difference"; "It is strife that makes the world go on."

8- p. 127, l. 3 This is the translation of my adopted reading "*wa-lā ya'tariḍ 'alayha al-malik*," but there are in the Mss. variants of the last word which would make it read: "*al-malal*". Thus the original phrase could have been: "*wa-lā ya'riḍ 'alyaha (or laha) al-malal*," meaning: "is not subject to boredom."

9- p. 127, l. 5 It is interesting to note Miskawayh's emphasis on the social values

THE REFINEMENT OF CHARACTER

in asserting *"uns"* ("fellowship," "sociability") as basic in man's humanity, and in bringing out the social implications of the Islamic religious requirements in worship. This social emphasis appears also in other parts of the *Tahdhīb* (*supra*, pp. 25–26, and *infra*, pp. 149–50).

10- p. 127, l. 8   *N.E.* 1157a 16–20.

11- p. 127, l. 10   *N.E.* 1156a 13–21; 1157b 1–4.

12- p. 128, l. 33   Founder of the Sassanid dynasty of Persia (+ 240 A.D.). His '*Ahd* (Testament) written for the guidance of his successors was translated into Arabic and was well known in Arab ruling and intellectual circles. See Iḥsān 'Abbās, ed., '*Ahd Ardashīr*, Beirut, 1967. (For the above quotation on religion and kingship, para. 4, pp. 53–54). It is interesting to note that Miskawayh preserved a complete text of this '*ahd* in his historical work, *Tajārib al-Umam* (Gibb Memorial Series VII, London, 1909–17), I, 99–127. It was one of three texts on which Iḥsān 'Abbās based his recent edition.

13- p. 130, l. 9   *N.E.* 1164a 6–22; and, on the lover and the beloved mentioned in the following sentence, *N.E.* 1157a 2–15.

14- p. 131, l. 8   *N.E.* 1166a 31–32; 1169b 5–7; 1170b 5–7 (a friend is "another self" or "a second self"). On this definition of the friend as the "*alter ego*," see abu-Ḥayyān al-Tawḥīdi, *al-Muqābasāt* (ed. Ḥasan al-Sandūbi, Cairo, 1929), pp. 359–62, and *Risālat al-Ṣadāqah wa-al-Ṣadīq* (ed. Ibrāhīm al-Kaylāni, Damascus, 1964), pp. 55–57.

15- p. 133, l. 3   On these kinds of friendship and love (king and subjects, parents and children, man and wife), see *N.E.*, Book VII **10–13**, 1159b 31–1163a 23.

16- p. 133, l. 34   Sūrah XII (*Yūsuf*: Joseph), 106.

17- p. 134, l. 39   On this discussion of the disciple's love of the philosopher, and on the concept of the master as "*wālid rūḥāni*" ("spiritual father"), l. 29, see R. Walzer, *Greek into Arabic* (Oxford, 1962), pp. 228–32 and 241–42. See also the forty-fifth epistle of Ikhwān al-Ṣafa, *Rasā'il Ikhwān al-Ṣafa* (4 vols., ed. Khayr al-Dīn al-Zirikli, Cairo, 1928), IV, p. 113 where the teacher is referred to as "*Ab li-nafsika*" ("a father of your soul").

18- p. 137, l. 1   *N.E.* 1166b 12–30.

19- p. 137, l. 8   On beneficence and love see *N.E.*, Book IX **7**, 1167b 17 – 1168a 28.

20- p. 140, l. 12   *N.E.*, Book IX **11**, 1171a 20 – 1171b 28.

21- p. 140, l. 23   Frank Rosenthal has analyzed this quotation and the one following it, as well as the subsequent borrowing from Socrates (p. 142, l. 7 ff.), and shown that they are wrongly attributed to Socrates and are derived from the work of the celebrated commentator Themistius, *On Friendship*. See Franz Rosenthal, "On the knowledge of Plato's Philosophy in the Islamic World," *Islamic Culture* XIV (1940), pp. 387–422, particularly pp. 402–405.

22- p. 141, l. 19   Cf., the discussion, in this section and the following one, of the choice of friends and duties towards them, with the material on the same subject in the forty-fifth epistle of Ikhwān al-Ṣafa, *Rasā'il Ikhwān al-Ṣafa* (4 vols., ed. Khayr al-Dīn al-Zirikli, Cairo, 1928) IV, pp. 107–112.

23- p. 143, l. 29   On the desirable number of friends, see *N.E.*, Book IX, **10**, 1170a 20 – 1171a 20; particularly, in regard to this paragraph of the *Tahdhīb*, 1171a 5–11.

24- p. 144, l. 3   From a poem by Ibn-al-Rūmi (+ *ca.*, 896 A.D.). See *Dīwān ibn-al-Rūmi* (2 vols., ed. Muḥammad Sharīf Salīm, Cairo, 1917), I, p. 313, and 'Abbās Maḥmūd al-'Aqqād, *Ibn-al-Rūmi: Ḥayātuhu min Shi'rihi* (Cairo, 1963), p. 406.

25- p. 148, l. 22   *Kitāb Kalīlah wa-Dimnah* (ed. Ṭ. Ḥusayn and 'A. 'Azzām, Cairo, 1941), pp. 43–97; *Le livre de Kalila et Dimna* (tr. André Miquel, Paris, 1957), pp. 49–104.

26- p. 150, l. 27   From here to the end of this discourse we see many of Aristotle's ideas on the rational and contemplative activities and happiness in *N.E.*, Book X **7–9**, 1177a 11 – 1180a 5, but, as they appear in the *Tahdhīb*, they bear Neoplatonic influences, derived from the Neoplatonic commentator or commentators through whom Miskawayh knew the *Ethics*, and they are naturally also adapted to Islamic beliefs.

27- p. 151, l. 13   "*Al-muta'llihūn*"; according to R. Walzer, *Greek into Arabic* (Oxford, 1962), p. 228: "the divine men".

28- p. 152, l. 37   *Supra*, p. 71, l. 36 – p. 72, l. 35.

SIXTH DISCOURSE

1- p. 157, title   Title in the original.

2- p. 157, l. 10   The view that vices are diseases of the soul, that these diseases should be subject to treatment as are the diseases of the body, and that their treatment and remedy are by appropriate means of moral education — this view is common in Muslim ethical writings and among Muslim mystics. See al-Ghazzāli, *Iḥyā' 'Ulūm al-Dīn* (4 vols., Cairo, 1352 A.H.), III, 52 ff. The influence of Miskawayh's *Tahdhīb* is evident in this part of the *Iḥyā'* (Third Quarter: "Rub' al-Muhlikāt," "The Quarter on the Destructive [Vices]"), and particularly in the Second Book containing the above-mentioned reference: "Kitāb Riyāḍat al-Nafs wa-Tahdhīb al-Akhlāq wa-Mu'alajat Amrāḍ al Qalb" ("The Book on the Training of the Soul, the Refinement of Character, and the Treatment of the Diseases of the Heart"), III, 42 ff.

3- p. 160, l. 10   "*Al-ta'ālīm al-arba'ah.*" See al-Tahānawi, *Kashshāf Iṣṭilāhāt al-Funūn* (2 parts, Calcutta, 1862), p. 1066. The four mathematical sciences are: geometry, arithmetic, music, and astronomy. See Ibn Khaldūn, *al-Muqaddimah* (Beirut, 1900), pp. 478–79.

4- p. 160, l. 26   One of the greatest intellectual and religious figures of the first century of Islām (+ 110 A.H., 728 A.D.). An authoritative transmitter of tradition, jurist, scholar, and teacher, he was known and revered for his ascetic piety and exerted a deep influence on the rise of Muslim theology, mysticism, and other intellectual and religious movements in Islam. Numerous pious sayings, such as the one quoted by Miskawayh, are ascribed to him and are often reported in Muslim writings.

5- p. 162, l. 22   See the texts of this sermon in al-Jāḥiz, *al-Bayān wa-al-Tabyīn* (ed. 'Abd-al-Salām Muḥammad Hārūn, 4 vols., Cairo, 1948–50), II, 43–44; Ibn Qutaybah, *'Uyūn al-Akhbār* (ed. Dār al-Kutub al-Miṣrīyah, 4 vols., Cairo, 1925–30), II, 233; and Ibn-'Abd-Rabbihi, *al-'Iqd al-Farīd* (ed. A. Amīn, A. al-Zayn, and I. al-Ibyāri, 7 vols., Cairo, 1940–53), IV, 59–60. There are slight variants among these texts and the text in the *Tahdhīb*. The only noteworthy one is in the last sentence, where the three above-mentioned texts have: "*al-fuqarā'* " ("the poor"), instead of "*al-mulūk*" ("the kings").

6- p. 168, l. 26   See *supra*, Second Discourse, n. 2. There are slight variants in the title. Both Miskawayh and Ibn-abi-Uṣaybi'ah have "*Ta'arruf*" ("Understanding," "Acquainting oneself"), whereas Ibn-al-Nadīm has : "*Ta'rīf*" ("Causing to understand," "Acquainting").

7- p. 169, l. 24   See also *supra*, Second Discourse, n. 2. There are here also variants in this title: In *Ṭabaqāt al-Aṭṭibbā'*, it includes "*qad*" ("may" benefit). Max Meyerhof, p. 700 : *That the Best People take Advantage of their Enemies.*

8- p. 169, l. 26   On the ethical treatises ascribed to al-Kindi, the first Arab philosopher (+ *ca.*, 260 A.H., 873 A.D.), see Richard J. McCarthy, *al-Taṣānīf al-Mansūbah ila Faylasūf al-'Arab* (Baghdād, 1962), Index.

9- p. 169, l. 39   This passage is not very clear. I presume that by "stones and ashes" al-Kindi means the remnants that are left from the destruction of buildings. The use of the word: "expended" ("*anfaqnāhu*," paralleling "*nunfiquhu*" further on in the sentence) adds to the obscurity of the passage.

10- p. 170, l. 26   Cf., on this subject: man's understanding of his defects, al-Ghazzāli, *Iḥyā' 'Ulūm al-Dīn* (4 vols., Cairo, 1352 A.H.), III, 55–56.

11- p. 170, l. 27   Title in the original.

12- p. 172, l. 13   Of these eight superior genera of vices, Miskawayh proposes to limit himself to two only: recklessness and cowardice, which are the two extremes of the virtue of courage, and which, like courage, originate in the irascible faculty. In fact, Miskawayh does not deal with these two vices, as with the dispositions and the "diseases" of the irascible faculty which produce these vices: anger on the one hand, and fear on the other. The discussion of fear leads to that of grief. Cf., on anger, al-Ghazzāli, *op. cit.*, III, 143–52.

13- p. 174, l. 34   Sūrah XVIII (*al-Kahf*: The Cave) 32, 42, 45.

14- p. 175, l. 8   I have not been able to trace this tradition in the authoritative collections.

15- p. 175, l. 30 *Supra*, Fifth Discourse, pp. 146.

16- p. 175, l. 35 'Ali ibn-abi-Ṭālib. See *supra*, Fourth Discourse, n.5.

17- p. 183, l. 8 *N.E.* 1115a 9.

18- p. 185, l. 1 Cf., *Risālah fī Dafʿ al-Ghamm min al-Mawt* in M.A.F. Mehren, ed. and tr., *Traités mystiques d'Aboû Alî al-Hosain b. Abdallah b. Sîna ou d'Avicenne*, IIIième Fasc. (Leiden, 1894), pp. 49–57 (tr., pp. 28–33). Mehren edited this treatise from two Mss., one in London and the other in Leningrad, both of which ascribe it to Ibn-Sīna. This treatise is identical (with some variations) with this section of the *Tahdhīb*, pp. 185-92. Mehren noted this identity, but considered that this section of the *Tahdhīb* is copied from Ibn-Sīna's treatise, without any mention of the original author (*Ibid.*, p. 49, n.a; p. 28, n. 1).

In 1908, Louis Cheikho published the same text, *Al-Machreq*, XI (1908), pp. 839–44, from a Ms. in the Bibliothèque Nationale, which did not give the author's name. Aḥmad Tīmūr Pasha called Cheikho's attention to the identity between this text and that published by Mehren. See *Al-Machreq*, XI (1908), pp. 958–61, where Cheikho concluded that the author was probably Miskawayh. He republished it with indications of the variants between the Mehren edition and the *Tahdhīb* (Cairo, 1298 A.H.) in *Maqālāt Falsafīyah Qadīmah li-Baʿḍ Mashāhīr Falāsifat al-ʿArab* (Beirut, 1911), pp. 103–114. It is evident that this text was taken out of the *Tahdhīb* and wrongly ascribed to Ibn-Sīna, and not the other way around, as Mehren thought.

19- p. 187, l. 28 See Franz Rosenthal, "On the Knowledge of Plato's Philosophy in the Islamic World," *Islamic Culture*, XIV (1940), p. 409.

20- p. 192, l. 9 Title in the original.

21- p. 194, l. 4 Sūrah X (*Yūnus*: Jonah), 62.

22- p. 194, l. 6 See Ibn-al-Nadīm, *al-Fihrist* (ed. Flügel, Leipzig, 1871–72), I, 260. This treatise is mentioned, under varying titles, by Ṣāʿid al-Andalusi, al-Qifṭi, and Ibn-abi-Uṣaybiʿah. See Richard J. McCarthy, *al-Taṣānīf al-Mansūbah ila Faylasūf al-ʿArab* (Baghdād, 1962), p. 31, no. 171, and p. 65, no. 17. It was published with an introduction by H. Ritter and R. Walzer, "Studi su al-Kindi II, Uno scritto morale inedito di al-Kindi," *Memorie della Reale Academia Nazionale dei Lincei*, Ser. VI, Vol. VIII, Fasc. 1 (1938), pp. 1–38. See also Franz Rosenthal's review in *Orientalia*, IX (1940), pp. 182–91.

GLOSSARY *

<table>
<tr><td>Altruism</td><td>إيثار</td></tr>
<tr><td>Charity</td><td>مؤاساة</td></tr>
<tr><td>Evil</td><td>آفة</td></tr>
<tr><td></td><td>تأكُّد . راجع : توحُّد</td></tr>
<tr><td>Good manners (traits), morality</td><td>أدب ، آداب</td></tr>
<tr><td>Moral</td><td>ادبية (نفس)</td></tr>
<tr><td>Discipline, education</td><td>تأديب</td></tr>
<tr><td>Original, principal</td><td>أصلي</td></tr>
<tr><td>Realm, plane</td><td>أفق</td></tr>
<tr><td>Affinity</td><td>إلف</td></tr>
<tr><td>Concord</td><td>ألفة</td></tr>
<tr><td>Harmony, composition</td><td>تأليف</td></tr>
<tr><td>Art of harmony</td><td>التأليف ، صناعة</td></tr>
<tr><td>Proportion of harmony</td><td>التأليفية ، النسبة</td></tr>
<tr><td>Harmonize</td><td>تألّف</td></tr>
<tr><td>Harmony</td><td>ائتلاف</td></tr>
<tr><td>Those who seek to be like God</td><td>المتألهون</td></tr>
<tr><td>Contemplate, observe</td><td>تأمل</td></tr>
<tr><td>Fellowship</td><td>أنس</td></tr>
<tr><td>Humanity</td><td>إنسانية</td></tr>
<tr><td>Defiance, arrogance</td><td>أنفة</td></tr>
<tr><td>First</td><td>أوّل</td></tr>
<tr><td>Organ</td><td>آلة</td></tr>
</table>

ب

<table>
<tr><td>Luck, good fortune</td><td>بخت</td></tr>
<tr><td>Principle, origin</td><td>مبدأ</td></tr>
<tr><td>Prodigality, dissipation</td><td>تبذير</td></tr>
<tr><td>Righteous</td><td>ابرار</td></tr>
<tr><td>Demonstration, demonstrated proof</td><td>برهان</td></tr>
<tr><td>Demonstrative knowledge</td><td>العلم البرهاني</td></tr>
<tr><td>Simple</td><td>بسيط</td></tr>
<tr><td>Simple elements</td><td>بسائط</td></tr>
<tr><td>To be nullified, to disappear</td><td>بطل</td></tr>
<tr><td>Hatred</td><td>بغض</td></tr>
<tr><td>Wrongdoers</td><td>البغي ، اهل</td></tr>
<tr><td>Dullness</td><td>بلادة</td></tr>
<tr><td>Consummate wisdom</td><td>البالغة ، الحكمة</td></tr>
<tr><td>Stupidity</td><td>بله</td></tr>
<tr><td>The beastly (faculty, soul)</td><td>البهيمية ، القوة ، النفس</td></tr>
<tr><td>Difference, discord</td><td>مباينة ، تباين</td></tr>
</table>

ت

<table>
<tr><td>Completion, realization</td><td>تام</td></tr>
<tr><td>Self-conceit</td><td>تيه</td></tr>
</table>

ث

<table>
<tr><td>Fortitude</td><td>ثبات</td></tr>
</table>

---

* It is hoped that this glossary will be useful to the reader, although in many cases the rendering given has to be taken within the context of the original Arabic text.

211

ج

Cowardice	جبن
Slyness	جربزة
Particular	جزئي
Repayment, reward	جزاء
Affirm	جزم
Good, fine	جميل
Genus, type	جنس

الاجناس . راجع : العالية

Ignorance	جهل
Ignorant, ill-bred	جاهل
Generosity	جود
Injustice, wrongdoing	جور
Substance	جوهر

ح

Love	محبة
Youths, young	احداث
Definition	حدّ
Liberal, free	حر ، أحرار
Integrity, liberality	حرية
Heritage	حسب
Sensible	محسوس
Fair play	حسن الشركة
Honest dealing	حسن القضاء
Good disposition	حسن الهدي
Beneficence	احسان
Beneficient	محسن
Beneficiary	محسَن اليه
Men of good deeds	محسنون
Merits	محاسن
Circumspection	احتياط
To substantiate	حقق

Thorough investigators	محققون
Judge, conclude	حكم
Philosophy, wisdom	حكمة

الحكمة . راجع : البالغة

Ruler	حاكم
Philosopher, wise man	حكيم
Magnanimity	حلم
To have as attribute, to support	حمل
Endurance	احتمال الكد
Condition, state	حال
Transform, change	استحال
Modesty	حياء
Qua	حيث ، من حيث هو
Anxiety	حيرة

خ

Slyness	خبث
Seal	ختم
Deceit	خدعة ، خديعة
Excessive bashfulness	خرق
Disgrace	خسار
Property, characteristic	خاصة
Error	خطأ
Sincere	مخلص
Dissoluteness	خلاعة
Deputy, representative	خليفة
Character, trait(s) of character, ethics	خلق ، اخلاق
Cultivate	تخلّق
Quality, attribute	خلّة
Frigidity	خمود الشهوة
Faintness	خور
Good	خير
Image	خيال

Arrogance	خيلاء

د

Manager	مدبّر
Management, planning	تدبير
Grade, degree	درجة
Perceive	أدرك (الحسّ)
Sedateness	دعة
Demonstrate	دلّ
Proof, demonstration	دليل
Benignity	دماثة
Craftiness	دهاء
Vicissitudes of fortune	دول
Low, lowest	دون ، أدون

ذ

Retention	ذكر
Intelligence	ذكاء
Offense	ذنب
Self, essence	ذات

ر

Head, chief	رئيس
Authority	رئاسة
Judgment, opinion	رأي
Lord	ربّ
Learned in the knowledge of the divine	عالم ربّاني
Rank, grade	رتبة ، مرتبة
Arrange, set in order	رتّب ، ترتيب
Baseness	رداءة
Vicious	رذل ، رذيل
Composite	متركب

Center	مركز
Ease, comfort, relaxation	راحة
The Stoics	الرواقيون
Deliberation, reflection	رويّة
Discipline	رياضة
Submission (to passion)	دين

ز

Excess	زيادة
Deviation	زيغ

س

The leonine (faculty, soul)	السبعية ، القوة ، النفس
Liberality	سخاء
Quickness of understanding	سرعة الفهم
Extravagance	سرف
Happiness	سعادة
Impudence	سفه
Fall	سقوط ، مساقط
Power, dominion, sultan, ruler	سلطان
Mildness	مسالمة
Open-handedness	سماحة
Remission	مسامحة
Glimpse, blessing	سنح
Capacity for learning easily	سهولة التعلم
Equality	مساواة
Guide, direct	ساس
Guidance, direction, government, administration	سياسة

ش

Courage	شجاعة

Individual, person	شخص
Wickedness	شرارة
The Law	الشريعة
Custodian of the Law	الشريعة ، صاحب
Prescriber of the Law	الشريعة ، مشرّع
Profligacy, intemperance, greed	شره
Turbulent	شغب
Peevishness	شكاسة
Shape	شكل
Figure	شكل (القياس)
Similar	أشكال
Similarity	مشاكلة
Firmness	شكيمة ، شدة
Improper	شنع
Manliness	شهامة
Desire, passion, lust	شهوة
The concupiscent (faculty, soul)	الشهوية ، القوة ، النفس

ص

Self-control, patience	صبر
Verify	صحّح
Friendship	صداقة
Clarity of mind	صفاء الذهن
Righteous, good	صالح
Reformers	مصلحون
Art	صناعة
Form, image	صورة
Conception	تصوُّر

ض

To be opposite	ضادَّ
Opposition	مضادّة

Mood	ضرب (القياس)
Disturbance	اضطراب
Wrongfulness	ضيم

ط

Natural disposition, temperament	طبع
Nature, natural disposition	طبيعة
Natural, physical, inborn	طبيعي
The Naturalists	الطبيعيون
Extreme, extremity	طرف
Harbinger	مطلع (سعد ، نحس)
In the absolute, in general	الاطلاق ، على

ظ

Injustice, doing (inflicting) injustice	ظلم
Suffering injustice	انظلام

ع

Piety	عبادة
Sternness	عبوس
Vanity	عجب
Numerical (proportion)	العددية ، النسبة
Aptitude	استعداد
Justice	عدل ، عدالة
Counterbalance	عدل
Equilibrium	اعتدال
Non-existence	عدم
Self-possession	عدم الطيش
Accident, unessential	عرض
Avoidance	إعراض
Knowledge, forms of knowledge	معرفة ، معارف
Fame, might	عزّة

Kinsmen, relatives	عِشيرة
Passionate love	عشق
Composure	عظم الهمة
Veneration	تعظيم
Temperance	عفة
Alternation	معاقبة
Reason, intelligence	عقل
Rational, intelligent	عاقل
Intelligible	معقول
Rationality	تعقّل
Remedy, treatment	علاج
Treatment	معالجة
Knowledge, science, learning	علم
Instruction	تعليم
The cognitive (faculty)	العالمة ، القوة
The practical (faculty)	العاملة ، القوة
Superior genera	العالية ، الاجناس
Deal with	عامل
Dealing, transaction	معاملة
Meaning, entity, character, attribute	معنى
Cooperation	تعاون

غ

Bliss	غبطة
Perfidy	غدر
Innate	غريزي
Purpose, object, motive	غرض
Oppressive	غشمي
Veil	غشاوة
Anger	غضب
The irascible (faculty, soul)	الغضبية ، القوة ، النفس
Domination	غلبة
Usurper	متغلب

Change	تغيُّر
Otherness	غيرية
Zealous	غيور
End, limit	غاية

ف

Abominable	فاحش
Boast, take pride in	افتخر
Boastfulness	افتخار
Stupidity	فدامة
Excess of praise	تفريط
Corruption	فساد
Depravity	فسق
Discrete (proportion)	المنفصلة ، النسبة
Superiority, excellence, virtuousness	فضل
Virtue, value	فضيلة
Virtuous	فاضل
Benevolence	تفضّل
Act, action, activity	فعل
Active	فاعل
Passive	منفعل
Agitations	انفعالات
Reflection, thought	فكر
Understanding	فهم
Discrepancy	تفاوت
Victors	فائزون
Emanate, pour forth	فاض
Emanation	فيض

ق

Disgraceful, detestable, mean, vile	قبيح
Distress	انقباض
Receive, assume, take on	قبل

Dispositions	قابلات	Assume	تكيّف بـ
Antecedent	مقدم		
Mental altertness	قريحة	**ل**	
Division, category	قسم	Importunity	لجاج
Separation	انقطاع	Pleasure	لذة
Paucity	قلّة	Follow necessarily	لزم من
Sobriety	قناعة	Curse	لعينة ، لعائن
Community	قوم	Criticize, reproach, blame	لام
Subsistence	قوام	Reproachful (love)	اللوامة ، المحبة
Station, rank, grade	مقام		
Upright	قويم	**م**	
Training, rectification, correction, reform	تقويم	Parable	مثـل
Faculty, capacity, force	قوّة	Frivolity	مجون
راجع : البهيمية ، السبعية ، الشهوية ، العالمة ، العاملة ، الغضبية ، الملكية ، الناطقة ، الوهمية		Matter, material, substance	مادة
		Civic	مدني
		Bickering, quarrel	مراء
In potency, potential	بالقوة	Manliness	مروءة
Deduction, syllogism	قياس	Constitution, temperament	مزاج
		Jesting	مزاح
ك		Measure	مساحة
		Geometrical (proportion)	المساحية ، النسبة
Greatness of spirit	كبر النفس	Loathing	مقت
Multiplicity, collectivity	كثرة	Aptitutde	ملكة
Turbidity	كدورة	The kingly (faculty, soul)	الملكية ، القوة ، النفس
Generosity	كرم		
Antipathy	كراهية	Money, property	مال
Misfortune, trouble, danger, evil	مكروه	Discernment, judgment	تمييز
Recompense	مكافأة	Predisposition	ميل
Universal	كليّ		
Universals, totalities	كليات	**ن**	
Perfection	كال		
Generation, coming into being	كون	Nobility	نبل
Generable	كائن	The conclusion of the syllogism follows	منتج (القياس)
Nature, quality	كيفية		

Intrepidity	نجدة
Regret	ندامة
Rank, stage, grade, position	منزلة
Relation, proportion	نسبة
	النسبة . راجع :
	التأليفية ، العددية ، المساحية ، المنفصلة ، المتصلة
Proportionate relation, similarity	مناسبة
Toiling	ناصبة
Regulate	نظّم
Self-discipline	انتظام
Rational, articulate	ناطق
The rational (faculty, soul)	الناطقة ، القوة ، النفس
Favor	نعمة
Bliss	نعيم
Discordance	منافرة
Soul, self	نفس
	راجع : البهيمية ، السبعية ، الشهوية ، الغضبية ، الملكية ، الناطقة
Prodigal	منفاق
Deficiency	نقصان
Law	ناموس
End	نهاية
Repentance	انابة
Species, kind	نوع

هـ

Refinement, improvement, education	تهذيب
Anarchy	هرج
Derision, ridicule	استهزاء
Abandon	انهاك
Aspiration	همة

Recklessness	تهوّر
Servility	مهانة
Contempt	استهانة
Disposition	هيئة
Ecstasy	هيمان
Matter	هيولى

و

Rebuke	توبيخ
Existent	موجود
Face, form	وجه
Unity	وحدة
Unification	توحُّد ، تأحُّد
Union	اتحاد
Affection	مودة
Amiability	تودُّد
Piety	ورع
Mean	وسط
Intermediateness	توسُّط
Family fellowship	صلة الرحم
Attachment	اتصال
Continuous (proportion)	المتصلة ، النسبة
(Divine) condition, ordinance, prescription	وضع (الهي)
Subject, object	موضوع
Harmony	اتفاق
Shamelessness, impudence	وقاحة
Staidness	وقار
Rapture	وله
Imagination	وهم
Imaginative faculty	الوهمية ، القوة
Ascertained	يقيني
Men of certitude	الموقنون

INDEX

219